Praise for

Meeting the Great Bliss

D0447237

"This book is a breakthrough in feminist cross-cultural reflection on self and subjectivity. An eminent scholar of Tibetan Buddhist studies, Anne Klein has distilled twenty-five years of her rich research and personal experience in this compelling study. She succeeds in showing the current relevance of Buddhism to Western feminists without minimizing any of its challenge to certain notions about selfhood. The conversation constructed around the Great Bliss Queen is artful, elegant, and of importance to anyone interested in feminist theory, Buddhist religious philosophy in America, and different meanings of the self."

—NANCY K. FRANKENBERRY, Dartmouth College

"A groundbreaking and important book. Klein is one of the few scholars in the Buddhist studies field who has devoted serious attention to the literature of Western feminism; likewise, her long experience in the field of Tibetan Buddhist study and practice provides her with the solid grounding necessary to speak for that tradition. The bringing together of these totally dissimilar worlds holds great promise for adding new insights to contemporary discussions of the nature of the self; indeed, it is difficult to imagine that the kind of conversation Klein proposes will not end by profoundly transforming the participants on both sides."

—Jan Nattier, Indiana University

"Anne Klein's *Meeting the Great Bliss Queen* presents us with a new and welcomed approach to the conversation between Buddhism and feminist thought. With 'the self' and 'subjectivity' as its central themes, the work is a lively yet rigorous discussion of Buddhist textual traditions in light of contemporary feminist theory. At the same time there is an element of personal reflection in Klein's work that makes the book immediately approachable, and that contextualizes the scholarly material in a way that is rare in contemporary writing in the field of Buddhist studies. A work of great erudition and sensitivity. A must read for anyone interested in the dialogue between Buddhism and feminism."

—José Ignacio Cabezón, Iliff School of Theology

"In this highly personal reflection about the construction of identity in Tibetan and Western cultures, Anne Klein weaves together various strands of Buddhist and Western philosophy, deconstructionism, and feminism and provides numerous insights into Tibetan Buddhist meditation, ritual, and doctrine. Through the symbol of the Great Bliss Queen, a mythical figure of Tibetan Buddhism, she explores the problems of a cross-cultural dialogue between women.

Anne Klein's well-wrought work challenges traditional understandings of Buddhist textual and interpretive traditions, as well as a number of feminist assumptions. The book will be welcomed by those of us who examine gender issues in the classroom as well as in our own work. Anne Klein's *Meeting the Great Bliss Queen* moves the debate forward, and opens it to new participants."

—BERNARD FAURE, Stanford University

"An astute and absorbing exploration of the interface between Buddhism and feminist perspectives."

—TSULTRIM ALLIONE, founder of Tara Mandala
and author of *Women of Wisdom*

"*Meeting the Great Bliss Queen* is a gift to everyone interested in illuminating contemporary Western thought with ancient Eastern wisdom. . . . [Klein's] book signals a new direction in feminist thought that is likely to lead us beyond formulae that have ceased to be productive."

—NAOMI R. GOLDENBERG, University of Ottawa,
and author of *Resurrecting the Body*

"Engaging a rich knowledge of Buddhist methods of meditation, argumentation, and value-orientations together with contemporary issues of women's lives and the historical trajectories of Western feminist theories, Klein makes a unique contribution to comparative religion, feminist studies, and anthropology. But above all, she brings into view an important new social and cultural formation of Buddhism in the West that is neither dabbling in exoticism nor mere New Age play, and one that may provide interesting challenges in the future for Old World Buddhist societies as well."

—MICHAEL M. J. FISCHER, Massachusetts Institute
of Technology, and coauthor of
Anthropology as Cultural Critique

MEETING THE GREAT BLISS QUEEN

Anne Carolyn Klein

Meeting the Great Bliss Queen

Buddhists, Feminists,
and the Art of the Self

Beacon Press • Boston

BEACON PRESS
25 BEACON STREET
BOSTON, MASSACHUSETTS 02108-2892

BEACON PRESS BOOKS
ARE PUBLISHED UNDER THE AUSPICES OF
THE UNITARIAN UNIVERSALIST ASSOCIATION OF CONGREGATIONS.

99 98 97 96 95 8 7 6 5 4 3 2

TEXT DESIGN BY WESLEY B. TANNER, ANN ARBOR
COMPOSITION BY WILSTED & TAYLOR

LIBRARY OF CONGRESS CATALOGING-IN-PUBLICATION DATA

KLEIN, ANNE C.
    MEETING THE GREAT BLISS QUEEN: BUDDHISTS, FEMINISTS, AND THE ART
OF THE SELF / ANNE CAROLYN KLEIN.
        P. CM.
    INCLUDES BIBLIOGRAPHICAL REFERENCES AND INDEX.
    ISBN 0-8070-7306-7 (CLOTH)
    ISBN 0-8070-7307-5 (PAPER)
        1. WOMAN (BUDDHISM) 2. YE-ŚES-MTSHO-RGYAL, 8TH CENT.
    3. FEMINISM—RELIGIOUS ASPECTS—BUDDHISM. 4. BUDDHISM—SOCIAL
    ASPECTS—CHINA—TIBET.
    BQ4570.W6Y435 1994
    294.3'378344—DC20   94-7678
                                                           CIP

This book honors the many contributions to women's public and private lives of

Constance H. Buchanan

Founding director and ongoing inspiration of the Women's Studies in Religion Program at Harvard Divinity School, where she is also Associate Dean for Program Development, she tirelessly and elegantly cultivates in others what she herself exemplifies: a passion for drawing on the best of theoretical insights to encourage a more ethical and equitable world for women, men, and their children.

CONTENTS

The old beliefs are wearing thin and there is a groping for new. It is not a matter, you see, of being a Christian or a Muslim or a Buddhist or a Jew. We do not yet have another answer to the old problems. We know only a little bit about the direction in which the changes are taking place, but nothing about where the changes will end up. We have to have in mind not an orthodoxy but a wide and compassionate recognition of the storm of ideas in which we all are living and in which we must make our nests—find spiritual rest—as best we can.

Gregory Bateson and Mary Catherine Bateson, *Angels Fear*

Acknowledgments

I am grateful to the friends and colleagues who gave me substantial commentary on much or all of various drafts of this book: Mitchell Aboulafia, Harvey Aronson, Constance Buchanan, Michael Fischer, Nancy Frankenberry, Janet Gyatso, Donald S. Lopez, Jr., Michele Martin, Helena Michie, Jan Nattier, and Meredith Skura. Very special thanks to my delightful and ingenious editor, Lauren Bryant.

Thanks too for the help given by Elizabeth Long, Kathryn Milun, and Sharon Traweek, long-term stalwarts of my Writing Group, which met under the auspices of the Rice Feminist Faculty Reading Group, and for the decisive help from group founder Livia Polanyi and members Gudrun Klein, Diana Strassmann, and Angela Valenzuela. I also happily acknowledge the important suggestions I received from Barbara Ellman, Werner Kelber, Susan Lurie, Philip Wood, and Edith Wyschogrod. Crucial moments of inspiration and encouragement also came, sometimes in a single conversation, from Sandy Boucher, L. Annette Jones, P. J. Ivanhoe, Marilyn Massey, Nancy and Steve Mayer, Phyllis Pay, Mary Rollins, George Quasha, and Frances Wilson. I am also grateful for the gallant proofing volunteered by Jim Casilio, L. Annette Jones, and Belita Leal.

I continue to draw inspiration from my fellow 1982–83 research associates in Women's Studies at Harvard Divinity School, in particular the early critiques and conversations of Sheila Briggs and most memorably the encouragement and friendship of Kitty Prelinger until her death in 1992. Their initial enthusiasm made possible the beginnings of this project, and therefore all that followed.

This book also could not have been written, or even imagined, without the extensive contact I have enjoyed with traditional teachers of Buddhism. I am grateful to all of them, and in this context especially to those whose example and scholarship I have drawn upon in this writing. In the chronological order of my meeting with them, they are Gyumay Kensur Ngawang Lekden, Geshe Wangyal, Śri Satya Narain Goenka, Geshe Ngawang Dhargyey, His Holiness the Dalai Lama, Lati Rinboche, Geshe Rabten, Khetsun Sangpo Rinboche, Loling Kensur Yeshey Tupden, Denma Lochö Rinboche, Lama Gompo Tsayden, Ven. Tulku Thondup, Namkhai Norbu Rinboche, Lama Tharchin, Gen Lam Rimba, Lobön Tenzin Namdak, Khenbo Palden Sharab, Tenzin Wangyal Rinboche, and Ani Mu Tso.

Portions of chapter 2 appeared in different form in "Primordial Purity and Everyday Life: Exalted Female Symbols and the Women of Tibet" in *Immaculate and Powerful: The Female in Sacred Image and Social Reality*, ed. Clarissa Atkinson, Constance Buchanan, and Margaret Miles (Boston: Beacon Press, 1985). Portions of chapters 3 and 5 appeared in different form in "Finding a Self: Buddhist and Feminist Perspectives" in *Shaping New Vision*, ed. Clarissa Atkinson, Constance Buchanan, and Margaret Miles (Ann Arbor: UMI Research Press, 1987). Portions of chapter 4 appeared in different form in "Gain or Drain: Buddhist and Feminist Views of Compassion" in *Women and Buddhism: A Special Issue of the Spring Wind Buddhist Cultural Forum, Spring Wind* 6 (1986): 1–3. Portions of chapters 6 and 7 appeared in different form in "Non-dualism and the Great Bliss Queen" in *Journal of Feminist Studies in Religion* 1, no. 1 (1985).

This book is a conversation between the profoundly different voices of Tibetan Buddhism and Western feminism. In some ways their worlds are incommensurable. Feminism is a modern, largely secular quest for political power and psychological well-being; Buddhism is an ancient religious quest for spiritual insight and inner discipline. Yet Buddhists and feminists share important common ground in that questions of selfhood are central to both. My engagement with the unexpectedly fruitful interaction of specific Buddhist and feminist perspectives on questions about the self gave rise to this book.

In the fall of 1969, I enrolled at the University of Wisconsin as an M.A. student in Buddhist Studies. Founded by Richard Robinson, this was the first academic program in the United States to focus on Buddhism. For someone interested in a living Buddhist tradition, the timing of the program was perfect. During its early years, some of the most highly regarded Tibetan scholars and practitioners of their generation, exiled in India since the Chinese takeover in 1959, had begun to receive invitations to visit the West, including Wisconsin. Thus, when I began my work in Madison, it was possible to meet and talk with persons who still carried the speech, world view, and textual training that had characterized Tibetan Buddhism for 600 years and more. Seven years later, after a year and a half among Tibetans in India and three years of informal study of Buddhist thought in the

United States, I entered the graduate program at the University of Virginia, where, much to my satisfaction at the time, the terms of discussion were set almost entirely by Indo-Tibetan philosophical agendas from the sixth through fourteenth centuries.[1] The modern West was a distant planet.

I spent the decade of the 1970s, as well as the early 1980s, between Asia and graduate school, studying a variety of texts and practices with refugee Tibetan lamas in India, Nepal, and the United States. During my time in India and Nepal, I studied in much the same way Tibetans themselves did, but always with the significant difference that I got special attention, time, and even food and lodging from the leading figures of the communities I visited, owing to my "importance" as a Westerner and the irrelevance in that context of my being a woman.[2] I eventually formed especially close ties with several Tibetan teachers from the newest (fourteenth century) and oldest (eighth century) orders of Tibetan Buddhism. These are the Geluk (rhymes with "hey look"), sometimes known as the "Yellow Hat," order and the Nyingma (rhymes with "sing Ma"), or "Ancient," order. For me this enterprise completely eclipsed the more contemporary forms of "consciousness-raising" then engaging Western women. I knew virtually nothing of feminism or the women's movement until I emerged from Charlottesville and entered an outstanding community of women scholars at Harvard Divinity School in 1982.

The Women's Studies in Religion Program at Harvard, where I was a research associate and then a visiting scholar, was a revelation to me: many of the issues that had initially drawn me toward the study of Buddhism—questions of personhood and identity, the epistemology of intellectual and personal development, as well as a certain metaphysical *joie de vivre*—were being addressed by women scholars informed by an entirely different context. Their camaraderie, interest, and intellectual expansiveness made possible my first ventures across the boundaries of feminist and Buddhist thought and practice.

My interest in continuing the dialogue stems from that initial recognition that such discussions were both possible and enriching. Subsequent encounters helped shape the way this conversation would develop.

In 1987 I was invited to speak on the topic of women and Buddhism at the Conference on World Buddhism in Ann Arbor, Michigan. Although I accepted, I felt a gnawing dissatisfaction at having been assigned this topic, a surprising reaction given that the proposed talk dovetailed so well with my interests. My antipathy passed only when I saw my unease as symptomatic of previously unacknowledged tensions between these two subjects. The detailed discussions in Buddhist texts about the nature of reality, or descriptions of exalted mental states, can make concern for women's special qualities, stories, or needs seem trivial. Since most of the attendees would be male Buddhist scholars or monks, did this mean my paper would not, in the conference's scheme of values, be "important"? At the same time, I recognized that a grounded interest in how real people, women and men, behave in the everyday world can make Buddhist philosophical nuance seem abstract and irrelevant. From that point on, the tensions between Buddhist and feminist orientations became for me a crucial element in the conversation between them. Each one, too narrowly understood, is in a position to trivialize the other.

But I do not mean to say that these tensions preclude meaningful connections. Buddhist theorizing is in principle aimed at practical benefits for real people, and feminist practicality is sometimes associated with a rhetoric whose abstractness matches that of the most rarefied Buddhist metaphysics. More to the point, Buddhist and feminist perspectives, however diverse, are dedicated to the fruitful interaction of theory and experience; they both focus on questions of self and identity and, equally significant, have appeared on the Western intellectual landscape at approximately the same time. They also share a radically critical view of the status quo in which they find

themselves. For feminists, everyday assumptions about gender and
identity are marred by age-old male-based models and agendas. For
Buddhists, ordinary (mis)understanding causes us to believe ourselves and others to be enduring in ways that Buddhist analyses find
absurd.

The usefulness of Buddhist material for feminist concerns requires a consideration of how Buddhist theories and practices reso-
nate with twentieth-century North American women, and this resonance has everything to do with the cultural context of their
encounter. In 1988 I was at an American Academy of Religion session
attended by Buddhist and Christian women from the United States,
Korea, and Japan. A Christian woman from Japan rose and addressed a Buddhist woman from the United States, saying, "From
our point of view, it is incredible that you should take up Buddhism,
because in our history, Buddhism's coming to Japan was the beginning of the end of powerful positions for women." Hearing this, I saw
that the Asian Christian and North American Buddhist women were
mirror images of one another. Each had chosen a religious path on
the margins of her culture at least partly because she found there the
greatest freedom and creativity. Indeed, women throughout the
United States are today playing formative leadership roles in developing Buddhist communities, both as scholars and as meditation
teachers.[3] These budding Buddhist centers do not carry, as do Christian institutions, a long and vexed history with respect to Western
women, and they are not in the same way beholden to a worldwide in-
frastructure dominated by male authority. Buddhist perspectives can
be a resource for Western feminist theory partly because they are for
feminists a completely fresh perspective. The benefits that Buddhism
and feminism bring to each other spring from this widening of perspectives, not from the intrinsic superiority of either side. As Buddhist
traditions come to North America from countries such as Burma,
Cambodia, China, Japan, Korea, Thailand, Tibet, and Vietnam, they

raise tantalizing questions about how their views and practices might relate to Western cultural experience. Fruitful responses to these questions require recognizing that Western feminists and Asian Buddhists are starting from very different cultural and philosophical understandings of personhood.

Western women are likely to experience themselves as individuals first and members of society second, despite the fact that they seek to undermine the hyperindividualism associated with male-centered ideas in Europe and North America.[4] Their sense of individuality is less than that of Western men, but far greater than that of their Asian counterparts. Far more than in the modern West, in Asian cultures one lives within a well-articulated social matrix intricately connected with one's own projects and sense of identity. Even the freest and most independent of Tibetan religious seekers is embedded in cultural and social certainties in ways virtually unknown in the West today. This is true of other Asian cultures as well. Japanese are said to see babies as overly individualistic and in need of training to become connected; in the United States babies are seen as too connected and in need of training to become individuals.[5] Analogously, the Korean-born therapist Kim Insoo Berg, who now works and teaches in the United States, observes that in the United States it is common to punish children by confining them to home. In Korea, the greatest punishment is to turn them out of the home, the place they most want to be.[6]

In tracing points of contact between Buddhist and feminist perspectives, this book describes the major cultural and philosophical pictures of the self associated with each of them. It thereby complements recent historical and anthropological studies of women and Buddhism, which have mainly focused on the real and mythical lives of Buddhist women.[7] It broadens the scope of those valuable inquiries and opens new ground by putting Buddhist reflections on selfhood in conversation with contemporary feminist thought.

The conversation between Buddhist and feminist voices necessarily takes place across several crucial divides, all of which are formidable. It moves not only between East and West, but between secular and religious, male and female, traditional and modern. Though difficult to negotiate, these divides are well worth exploring, for they reveal the diverse perspectives at play in the identities of many contemporary Western women. Conversation between Buddhist and feminist perspectives is one way to illuminate the internal dialogues produced by this diversity, helping to crystallize new understandings of ourselves and the selves we are becoming.

MEETING THE GREAT BLISS QUEEN

⚕ TERMS OF THE DISCUSSION

CHAPTER 1

Introduction: Opening the Conversation and Meeting the Great Bliss Queen

One is not born a woman, but, rather, becomes one.
                    Simone de Beauvoir, *The Second Sex*

> *"Virtuous one, what are you figuring to do, sitting there in meditation?"*
> *"I'm figuring to make [myself] a Buddha."*
> *The master thereupon took up a tile and began to rub it on a stone.*
> *"Master, what are you doing?"*
> *"I'm polishing the tile to make a mirror."*
> *"How can you make a mirror by polishing a tile?"*
> *"How can you make a Buddha by sitting in meditation?"*
>   Zen tale from the *Ching te ch'uan teng lu*

How can one become a woman if one wasn't a woman all along?
                    Judith Butler, *Gender Trouble*

> *Even flies, mosquitoes, bees and bugs*
> *Will achieve the unsurpassable and difficult to achieve enlightenment*
> *If they develop the power of effort.*
>   Shantideva, *Guide to the Bodhisattva's Way of Life*

The belief that "one is a woman" is almost as absurd and obscurantist as the belief that "one is a man."   Julia Kristeva, "Woman Can Never Be Defined"

> *The nature of our mind is . . . neither corrupted in samsara nor improved in nirvana, neither born, nor ceases to be.*
>   Dudjom Rinboche, *The Alchemy of Realization*[1]

How can I discover what I am? How can I become what I am not? Can I do one without the other? In either being or becoming, can I recognize what is particular to my experience and still find commonality with others whose experience is different? These questions, with very different implications, govern debates central to contemporary feminist reflection and traditional Buddhist thought.

3

Certain forms of Buddhism, like Zen, emphasize that unless one is already an enlightened Buddha, enlightenment is impossible. In this view, enlightenment can only be discovered, not developed. Other forms of Buddhism, including some of the major traditions of Tibet, focus on the process of becoming enlightened, emphasizing the effort involved and making a clear distinction between the path and the goal, between who one is and who one will become. Somewhat analogously, feminist theory moves between two important convictions: one, that essential commonalities among women exist and can be discovered, and two, that gender and all experiences associated with it are cultural constructions.

The opposition between these two positions is an important dimension of what Ann Snitow calls "the great divide" in the feminist movement, a divide she characterizes as a tension between celebrating the fact of womanhood and distancing oneself from it, or in Catharine Stimpson's terms, between maximizing womanhood as a category and minimizing its significance in one's construction of selfhood.[2] There is also an inevitable tension between recognizing the role played by culture and society in forming one's identity and the crucial need to express and experience identity as genuinely one's own, not simply the construction of other forces. Women, it has been observed, are continually being asked to behave as "women" and at the same time to accommodate themselves to male social roles and expectations. When the distinctions between the development and discovery of oneself go unrecognized, impossible and confusing demands are made.

These tensions are played out in what has become known as the essentialist-postmodern debate in feminism. They are not just intellectual or political tensions. They reveal an important discrepancy between how experience feels—intimate, utterly our own and at the core of our being—and what even a moment of reflection tells us, namely, that any given sensation is the product of innumerable internal and external conditions specific to our time and place. Yet experience still *feels* like ours, which may be all that it means for something to *be* ours. This sensation is not to be theorized away. As Jean Martin Charcot wryly puts it, "Theory is good, but it doesn't prevent things from existing."[3] Can a recognition of complex constitutive conditions be compatible with a coherent sense of one's own selfhood? To investigate this, we will discuss several of the major theories and meditation practices in which Buddhists engage and consider their relevance for feminist theory and Western cultural constructions of selfhood.[4] First, however, let us briefly review the terms of debate between feminists in the West today.

THE FEMINIST DEBATE

Much has been written about the essentialist-postmodern debate in feminism. In my usage of the terms, "essentialists" are those whose understanding of self assumes an intrinsic and universal womanhood. "Postmodern" feminists, in contrast, see all aspects of self, including gender, as constructed. To this constructionist position, they add skepticism about the classic Enlightenment categories of self, language, truth, and knowledge.[5]

Historically, claims that women possess an "essential nature" have been used to curtail their choices: if it is woman's nature to be mother, caretaker, and nurturer, conventions that enmesh her in these roles will prove highly resistant to change.[6] Most feminist essentialists today, however, do not passively accept cultural notions of womanhood; they themselves claim the power to define what women are. Insofar as they understand a womanly essence to be dynamic and open to multiple possibilities, their definitions belie older essentialist understandings premised on the "natural" functions of home and hearth. Mary Daly's discussion of "biophilic be-ing" and Luce Irigaray's descriptions of fluidity are prime examples of such open definitions.[7] But can they avoid too much generalizing about "women"?

Irigaray is certainly aware of the problem of overgeneralizing womanhood and explicitly writes against it: "Woman is not to be related to any simple designatable being, subject, or entity, nor is the whole group (called) women. One woman + one woman + one woman will never add up to some generic entity: woman."[8] But although she writes that "one must assume the feminine role deliberately," she shares with Daly the suggestion of an essential femininity. "Assuming the feminine role" for Irigaray involves discovering the nature of femininity as fluid: "Why is setting oneself up as a solid [as men do] more worthwhile than flowing as a liquid from between the two [lips]?" she asks.[9] Yet if the essence of woman is fluid, it is hardly capturable; indeed, it is barely nameable and displaces itself continually. It is thus perhaps a quintessentially "postmodern" essence, except that it does not really acknowledge individual particularity.

Essentialist theories draw on an empowering sense of being clearly located within one's own mind and body. Male influence, it is argued, must be offset by cultural expressions that stem from womankind. For this reason, essentialists are sometimes called cultural feminists (even though the latter category also includes feminists who recognize "womanhood" to be historically produced).[10] An essential nature offers a place to rest in oneself, as well as coherence and strength, but an emphasis on essence tends to overlook particularities of social, political, or psychological circumstances. Largely for this reason, many feminists in Europe and North America—what I refer to here as "the West," even though there is no such demarcation on the globe—today emphasize that all self-experience is a construction.[11]

The term "postmodernism," as has often been pointed out, is too broad to be very useful.[12] But it is also by now too common a term to eschew completely. Especially important for our discussion is the postmodern emphasis on the complex processes by which selves are constructed, and on the crucial role of language in that process.

When all identities are regarded as culturally constructed, the category "woman" can no longer be taken for granted. For postmodern feminists, a female body does not a woman make; it takes culture and history to produce gender identification, and that identity is constructed through variable and specific social and historical circumstances. Even one's most intimate thoughts are constructed from impersonal forces.

For Teresa de Lauretis, subjectivity arises from "a complex of habits resulting from the semiotic interaction of 'outer world' and 'inner world,' the continuous engagement of a self or subject in social reality." Judith Butler, equating the subject with the "I," finds that identity is something that cannot exist prior to language, and furthermore, that identity is above all a *practice*. What kind of practice? One that "inserts itself in the pervasive and mundane signifying acts of linguistic life."[13]

Language, that most elusive and culturally diverse phenomenon, is hardly a stable anchor for a sense of self, and thus both de Lauretis's and Butler's positions are in keeping with postmodern emphases on the formative role of language in self-experience. But from a Buddhist perspective, it is insufficient to conceive of subjectivity and selfhood only in relation to language; the insistence on doing so is particular to Western intellectual history. Indeed, the split between essentialist and postmodern positions is often a split between emphasizing the realm of mind, and language (as do Judith Butler, Chris Weedon, and Teresa de Lauretis) and emphasizing the body (as do Mary Daly, Luce Irigaray, and Adrienne Rich).[14] In this way, the feminist debate replicates a Western cultural tendency most feminists decry: the bifurcation of mind and body.

The lines along which essentialist-postmodernist debates are currently drawn often obscure the potentially fruitful balance between them. Through postmodern perspectives, for example, I understand the endless connections of which my life is comprised. To recognize this vast and endlessly supplemented nexus is to know that no one person, life, event, or word contains its own significance.[15] Their play of differences suggests an openness to others, knowing we can never be closed. With such insights, postmodernists unlock the narrow enclosure of essentialized constructions of the individual. Yet because postmodernists are at best uneasy about recognizing the depth and strength of selfhood or womanhood as a category, some balance is required.

We will revisit the issue of essentialism in hope of illuminating ways in which its strengths can be incorporated into constructionist and postmodern understandings of women's selves.[16] However overwhelmed by the theories that counter them, essentialist positions speak to a deeply rooted need to honor what to the individual seems most intimately part of her self, and they also address the need to have a spiritual or psychological place to call one's own. Thus even though postmodern perspectives seem by and large to have won the day, feminists still struggle to recognize and name the commonalities among women that justify concern for women's lives around the world and produce political and social alliances.[17]

Paul Ricoeur once said that although in the United States the postmodern strategy of deconstruction has become especially prominent among literary critics, it is a particularly useful way of addressing religious issues. In this context he described deconstruction as a way of unmasking the questions behind the answers of a text or tradition.[18] And many of the questions embedded in the essentialist-postmodern debate are, in my view, profoundly spiritual questions. Though issues of selfhood are closely associated with the political and social issues to which feminist theory has devoted much of its energy, they cannot be explored fully in these dimensions alone. I am interested in the implicit religious, spiritual, and existential questions raised by the essentialist-postmodern debate but rarely addressed by feminist theory.[19] To address them means bringing feminist theory into the religious sphere and reconsidering what that sphere consists of. It also means asking how Buddhist philosophies, which unlike the Western philosophies that underlie North American feminisms were never secularized, can emerge into the very different life and thought of Western women today.

BUDDHIST AND FEMINIST THEORIES IN CONVERSATION

It is clear that both essentialist and postmodern feminists threaten the "individual." In the essentialist view, no matter whether the essence is concrete or abstract, the individual woman is in danger of disappearing into it. Conversely, to focus only on the multiple particularities of any given life is to raise questions about personal coherence and agency. If essentialists seem to limit women's horizons by favoring the general over the particular, constructionist and postmodern feminisms threaten both women and men by doing the opposite: the very possibility of "having" a self is undermined, let alone a coherent one.[20] Although much feminist theory has been cast as a debate between the essentialist and postmodern views, the opposition between them is to some extent a false one, just as the dichotomy between Buddhist developmental and discovery models cannot be drawn cleanly. Each contains and requires something of the other. Hence the ongoing effort to find a place "between the two," in Merleau-Ponty's phrase.[21] After all, why bother to speak about female essence if not to reconstruct her own experience and society's characterization of it? Why protest current conditions unless the category "women" is in some way a meaningful one? Moreover, in Diana Fuss's words, "essence *as* irreducible has been *constructed* to be irreducible." This book's reframing of an already well-rehearsed debate is in the spirit of Teresa de Lauretis's inclination to "release its terms from the fixity of meaning into which polarization has locked them, and reintroduce them into a larger contextual and conceptual frame of reference."[22] The central dilemma is clear: how can we suggest a female sense of

self that is neither overly essentialized nor so contingently constructed that its existence is in question? It is in reframing this oppositional relationship that Buddhist perspectives seem most useful for
contemporary feminist debates and women's lives. Buddhist theories
also question the status of individual selves, but these questions
emerge from a cultural understanding of persons quite unlike the
contemporary Western one.

In 1975, an eminent Tibetan doctor of traditional medicine was
invited to speak at the University of Virginia. Dr. Losang Dolma had
succeeded in bringing a variety of Tibetan medicines into the United
States by a clever ruse. When questioned by suspicious customs
agents about the dark, aromatic balls of herbs that occupied half her
suitcase, she avoided confiscation by telling them it was Tibetan
chocolate. Her independence and ingenuity were well known. After
all, she had won a considerable reputation in a profession that required rigorous training and was dominated by men.[23] During her
U.S. visit, members of the Virginia Buddhist Studies program invited
her to lunch at the home several of them shared. She was asked what
she would like to eat, and this was served to her. As lunch progressed
she became visibly moody, even angry. It took a long time to find out
why, but we eventually learned that she had found it deeply offensive
for each person at the table to fix herself whatever she liked. In polite
company, everyone should be eating the same thing. It is easy to confuse the independence for which Tibetans are justly known with the
modern Western understanding of individuality. Though both are
forms of autonomy, Western individuality further emphasizes the
unique characteristics, choices, and creativity available to a particular person.

Buddhist notions of subjectivity and techniques for cultivating
certain subjective states provide a new way of looking at the tensions
of the essentialist-postmodern debate. Unlike either essentialist
or postmodern feminist reflections, Buddhist traditions value each

of the supposedly opposed categories of constructed and nonconstructed, or what they refer to as the conditioned and unconditioned. Buddhist traditions are therefore particularly interested in describing and cultivating a subject that participates in both conditioned and unconditioned categories. That subject, however, is not defined in terms of the unique expressiveness valued by Western individuals.

By and large Buddhist practice engenders, and Buddhist philosophy describes, a powerful sense of the present in all its particularity. This is especially so in the cultivation of "mindfulness," which is the ability to sustain a calm, intense, and steady focus when one chooses to do so. Mindfulness has the power and centeredness associated with essentialist orientations and also makes one keenly observant of causal processes in a manner analogous to constructivist or postmodern thought. Mindfulness suggests an alternative to the narrative coherence of self rendered impossible by feminist and other postmodern perspectives. It also suggests the possibility of a dimension of subjectivity not entirely governed by language. This is a category of mind that, once understood, can dissolve the antagonisms between the outlooks defined as essentialist and postmodern feminism.

I think of the interaction of Buddhist and feminist perspectives in this book as a conversation rather than a comparison because, even though I make comparative observations, I am not objectively juxtaposing Buddhist and feminist perspectives. I cannot, since I do not occupy some mythical Archimedean point from which to survey the conversational landscape. I am in the midst of it. This conversation, however rigorously constructed, is based on my particular interests and predilections. As one often does in the course of conversations, I appeal sometimes to the intellect and documentable data, sometimes to intuitive association and anecdote. Further, these reflections are explicitly on a human scale, asking questions that matter for individual persons, and not only for intellectual play or heuristic purposes. I am interested in the juxtaposition of theory as well as the practical implications for women and men who, like myself, are engaged in both feminist and Buddhist reflection.

The conversations in this book move within a matrix created by four basic positions: discovery, developmental, essentialist, and postmodern positions. Their interplay is structured by the analogy to which I have already alluded between Buddhist discovery and feminist essentialist positions, and between Buddhist developmental and feminist postmodern orientations.[24] Essentialists seem to say that we are either separate or connected through sameness. Postmodernists suggest that we are connected through difference. The Buddhist developmental orientation suggests we are separate from our own best possibilities and that we must therefore cultivate them carefully; the discovery model emphasizes instead that our highest potential only awaits discovery. The main question with which we move into this matrix is, How do we live with the powerful pulls between the experiences of relatedness and autonomy, connection and separateness, that "essentialism" and "postmodernism" entail? This is not a question about theory only, but speaks to deeply rooted sensibilities regarding what it means to exist as a human being, particularly as a woman. What it means to be a person, and to be a woman, is of course construed very differently in contemporary Western and traditional Buddhist culture. It is crucial, therefore, to pay attention to the cultural assumptions that underlie the theories discussed throughout this book. By understanding the different ways in which North American and Tibetan cultures construct persons as connected or separate, we can better understand what a Western woman can appropriate from Buddhist traditions, how she might change or contribute to them, and what the limitations are of using them as a resource.

In bringing forward these questions, I raise also the issue of how one facilitates fruitful cross-cultural conversation. Where do the meaningful questions lie? Talking across cultures and disciplines enables us, as Jonathan Z. Smith has observed, to "make the familiar strange."[25] But the same process can also make the foreign unduly exotic, a strangeness that comes not from seeing it afresh but from being ignorant of its context. For example, the apparent ferocity of some Tibetan deities may seem incompatible with a religion known to emphasize compassion, until one learns that these figures are not in any way malevolent, but only display the kind of powerful energy associated with enlightenment. It is also useful to consider that, for someone from another culture, the display in holy Western sanctuaries of a bleeding man, cruelly and unaccountably fastened to a wooden frame, is shocking. Context is crucial.

In my view, both essentialist-like discovery and constructionist-like developmental models are necessary to the art of expressing and understanding the wide range of experiences that make up what each of us calls her or his self. The act of conversation itself requires these two models. In finding something to say, one behaves, if only for a moment, as if there were something to be discovered. In listening to another, one develops a new configuration of self. The same is true in both interpersonal and cross-cultural conversations.

The conversation pursued in this book is stimulated by my wish to explore the connection that I, as a twentieth-century, white, middle-class North American woman, have with an ancient tradition whose ideas, in the form of books as well as persons and practices, have been an important focus for all my adult life. To a certain extent, I have followed in the traces of earlier Western students of Buddhism, whose work has focused on the study, translation, and editing of important texts.[26] Unlike these scholars, however, my engagement with Buddhist texts has been facilitated by both Western universities and Asian and Western Buddhist communities, sometimes in overlapping settings.[27] Moreover, "Oriental" studies of an earlier era were not concerned with feminist perspectives. Less obviously, but equally important, Buddhist Studies in the West has only recently begun to consider the cultural context that produced the texts it values so highly.[28]

This book benefits from the unique confluence of Western feminist reflection and scholarly interest in Buddhist culture. Its conversation centers on Buddhist and feminist reflections on selfhood and the cultural conceptions of self in which they are anchored. My description of "traditional Tibet" is what H. Stuart Hughes has called "retrospective cultural anthropology."[29] It is constructed from what I have gleaned while living in Tibetan communities in India and Nepal, and with individual Tibetan teachers in the United States, as well as from Tibetan texts, and the written record of first-hand Western observations about life in that geographical area prior to Chinese occupation, and also from two brief tours of Tibet in 1987 and 1988. Seeking to avoid "Orientalist" Western constructions, I have for many years listened closely to what Tibetans have to say about their tradition, though I cannot know the extent to which what I heard was altered by the fact that they said it to me, an outsider, when they too were outside their homeland.

As a result of all this, I am in the privileged yet awkward position of being far better educated in Buddhist than in Western religious and philosophical thought. Yet, however familiar, Tibetan culture and its multiple religious traditions are ultimately unknowable to me. Postmodern feminists express well the impossibility of capturing such richness. At the same time, recognizing the complexities of my position in relation to Tibetan traditions names something essential about me, and especially about the need to incorporate their insights into the milieu that is more my own, the late twentieth and early twenty-first century in the United States. I do so by featuring in this conversation a female figure of enlightenment in whose person and symbolism many of the themes discussed in this book coalesce. Part historical figure, part myth, she is a luminary in a tradition that uses both developmental and discovery strategies. And as a female exemplar of enlightenment, she raises questions about the status of actual women in Tibetan culture.

MEETING THE GREAT BLISS QUEEN

> From the mouth of a lotus was born
> The swift goddess, heroic liberator
> Who went forth in human form
> Amid the snowy mountains of Tibet.
> Jigmay Lingpa[30]

Yeshey Tsogyel (rhymes with "may say so well"), later known as the Great Bliss Queen, was reportedly born under miraculous circumstances. The sound of a Sanskrit mantra echoed in the air, and her mother gave birth painlessly, as had the Buddha's mother, who was in fact an early emanation of Yeshey Tsogyel. A nearby lake increased vastly in size, hence, perhaps, the name "Primordial (*ye*) Wisdom (*shes*) Queen (*rgyal mo*) of the Lake (*tso*)," which a contemporary writer has rendered as "Ocean Woman Who Already Knows."[31]

Tsogyel was sought after by such a multitude of suitors that, in order to prevent fighting among them, a specially convened council declared that only established monarchs would henceforth be considered worthy candidates. The suitors dispersed, whereupon two princes arrived with rich treasure to ask for her hand. Her parents left the choice to her but would not listen to her pleas to remain free of marriage altogether.

> Although I begged them earnestly, my parents were adamant. "There are no finer palaces in the known world than the residence of these two princes," my father told me. . . . "I will give you to one of these princes." . . .
>
> . . . I was involuntarily led out of the house. The instant I stepped outside, the rivals rushed towards me. [One] caught me by the breast and attempted to lead me away. However, I braced my legs against a boulder so that my feet sank into it like mud. To move me was like trying to move a mountain, and no one succeeded. Then

those fiendish officials took a lash of iron thorns, and stripping me
naked they began to whip me.[32]

Finally forced to join the prince's entourage, she petitioned the
Buddhas for protection. The men guarding her fell asleep, and she
escaped, becoming the object of a widespread search. To bypass
these riotous claims on her person, she was eventually given in marriage to the emperor himself, the famous religious king Tri-song-
day-tsen (740 to c. 798), who greatly encouraged the growth of
Buddhism in Tibet. It was he who invited Padmasambhava from
India in order to spread the new tradition. Yeshey Tsogyel is identified with this queen, although she is to a large extent a mythical
figure.

Padmasambhava became one of the most important figures in
the early transmission of Buddhism from India to Tibet. He possessed a potent magic able to overcome spirits inimical to the Buddhism encroaching on their territory. Both the king and Tsogyel revered him, and Tsogyel became his foremost student, as well as his
consort ("given" by her husband in accord with her own wishes) and
preserver of his teachings.

Both Tsogyel and Padmasambhava were allied against the non-
Buddhist religious traditions of Tibet, commonly known as Bön. Tsogyel's "autobiography" describes her debate with Bönmo Tso, whose
name means "the female Bön practitioner [of the] lake."[33] Their conversation is in effect a debate between female representatives of an
early shamanic and a later, more individuated form of religious practice. These two styles of practice, and the historical periods associated
with them, form the cultural matrix in which Tibetan social and
philosophical constructions of selfhood emerged. Though fully identified with the Buddhists, Yeshey Tsogyel (unbeknownst to her, perhaps, and certainly unacknowledged in her "autobiography") strad-
dles older layers of Tibetan culture as a preserver of the Great
Completeness tradition, which is the one major system of thought

and practice shared with Bön by Tibet's earliest Buddhist religious tradition.

Tibetans regard Yeshey Tsogyel as a Buddha who takes the form of an ordinary Tibetan woman so that people of her country might more easily form a relationship with her. Tsogyel's concern is especially for ordinary people, meaning most people, "who, for the time being, do not see her Vajravarahi form as a fully perfected deity. Among the practices of the Guru [Padmasambhava] especially intended for Tibetans there are many whose chief deity is Yeshey Tsogyel."[34] Nyingma liturgical tradition adds the title Great Bliss Queen to her name and has developed rituals of considerable importance around her.[35] Yeshey Tsogyel is revered as an enlightened figure in her own right and as a manifestation of Sarasvati, the Indian goddess of sound and muse of learning and literature. She is also identified in some texts with the Bodhisattva Tara.[36] In her most resplendent form, Yeshey Tsogyel is Vajravarahi (the "Adamantine Sow"), whose magnificence is not accessible to ordinary folks.[37] Like all male and female enlightened figures in the Indian and Tibetan Buddhist pantheons, the Great Bliss Queen is a manifestation of wisdom and compassion. These qualities are inviolable, yet express themselves in a variety of ways.

She displays whatever emanation form will tame
Any given [person], just as, for example, the full moon in the sky
Emerges as [various] reflections in different water vessels.[38]

Her "essence" therefore is not in her appearance or activities as Yeshey Tsogyel, but rather in her wisdom and potential to appear in various guises in accordance with whatever needs arise.[39] At the same time, her female body and her ritual's explicit emphasis on womb and vulva as symbols of enlightenment welcome women into the divine circle in ways that male figures do not:

She has one face and two arms, and
The color of her body is red.

Naked, her feet evenly on the ground with one foot forward,

[An expression of] great passion and a laughing face.[40]

What might this red figure, so obviously rooted in ancient Tibetan traditions, have to do with the dichotomies under debate by contemporary feminists? This discussion will unfold in the following chapters, but here I want to say something about Yeshey Tsogyel's role in my own discovery and development.

The Great Bliss Queen and Me

I continue to negotiate all the divides and fissures within the Buddhist and feminist conversation, as well as the uncharted spaces between them. The Buddhist traditions that see one as already enlightened and the traditions that say one needs to construct the qualities leading to Buddhahood suggest quite different relationships with oneself. Am I more a sculptor or a gardener? Can I be both? When I find I am not what I would like to be, is it my task to tap into a potential that already exists, or am I to create new qualities, a different self?[41] Put another way, when should I make more of an effort, and when rely on self-acceptance and relaxation?

Throughout the 1970s and much of the 1980s, I studied intensively with several Geluk scholars in the United States and India. Starting in 1977, however, I also became increasingly engaged with Nyingma mentors, ideas, and practices, even though my scholarly attention continued to focus on Geluk. Geluk is the order most closely associated with the Dalai Lamas of Tibet, and until the Chinese takeover it was the most politically powerful and populous of all five traditions of Tibetan religion. With the flourishing of their monastic universities, Geluks became renowned for their scholarly discipline, skill in debating, and philosophical rigor. They were sometimes stereotyped as overly intellectual at the expense of practice, whereas they accused Nyingmas of lacking the philosophical acuity necessary for true spiritual insight. Of course, not everyone in Tibet was rigidly sectarian, and several of my teachers had close connections with the "other," something for which I am extremely grateful.[42]

In June of 1981, I flew to California for my first seminar-retreat with a Nyingma Great Completeness master from Amdo, a region in east Tibet long known for friendly relations between Geluk and Nyingma institutions. It was from this teacher that I first learned about the importance of Yeshey Tsogyel. Two years later, while at Harvard, I began to study and translate her liturgy in collaboration with a Nyingma scholar and to consider what she might mean for contemporary American women. Thus, just at the time when Buddhist and feminist positions had begun to converge in force for me, and just as I had also begun to consider whether I should turn my attention to real women or continue to refine my pursuit of ancient philosophical lore, I made the acquaintance of a female Buddhist figure of enlightenment. Yeshey Tsogyel stands as a luminous red presence, free from the constraints represented by clothing, exuberant with her dancing posture, smiling face, and rhythmic drum. I was especially delighted to find that the major commentary on her was from a Nyingma tradition that used Geluk sutra "developmental" studies to prepare for their practice of the Great Completeness "discovery" techniques.[43] Yeshey Tsogyel thus not only links the forms of Tibetan Buddhism with which I am most closely connected but allows me to address questions about the status of women within as well as outside those traditions.

Until 1993, I had never met a female Tibetan teacher.[44] All my Tibetan or other Asian teachers were male. My own position, whether staying in a Tibetan monastery in India or engaging in discussions with monk-scholars in this country, was anomalous insofar as I had the kind of access to study, instruction, and personal interaction that only males would traditionally have in Tibetan culture. To be a scholar in a monastery is a male role, no matter what kind of body is involved.

In 1993, just as I was completing this manuscript, I learned that

Ani Mu Tso, a Tibetan nun considered an emanation of Yeshey Tso-gyel, would be in New York while I was visiting the East Coast. (Yeshey Tsogyel's mediation between my Geluk and Nyingma con-nections continued: I would never have met Ani Mu Tso if I had not been asked, during the time of her stay in New York, to give a semi-nar at the New Jersey Geluk Center, with which I had been con-nected for more than twenty years.) Through a lucky set of interven-tions, I was able to meet her privately and in that way make a human connection with the mythic figure I had lived with for so long. Ani Mu Tso's own expression was open and touchingly attentive as a child's, yet contained by a mature strength. The second time I met her, I went with four other women.[45] Though we had each been in-volved with Tibetan Buddhism for twenty years or more, this was the first time any of us had met with or heard Buddhist teaching by a fe-male teacher. We tried to tell her how much it meant to us to see a woman in the lama's role. Unlike some Western women, I have had only positive experiences with my male teachers, most of whom were celibate monks; none ever approached me sexually or treated me as anything but a serious student. Still, seeing a woman on the tradi-tional teacher's throne gave me a visceral sensation of connected-ness, a connectedness I had not been aware of missing before but could now see was different from what had occurred with male teachers. When I returned home from New York, I dreamed that each of us had received empowerment from a red, a white, and a blue Yeshey Tsogyel. During the initiation, my dream-mind focused on each of the other women, and I saw with pleasure how she received the blessing. I can remember no other dream in which I so clearly took account of other persons' internal experience. The dream seemed to indicate the possibility of American women being cen-tered in themselves as well as crucially engaged with others.

The Great Bliss Queen is a Buddhist prototype of the successful spir-itual seeker, partly because she overcomes dualistic tendencies that impede simultaneous awareness of self and other. I refer to this as "cognitive nondualism," the experienced dissolution of separation between subject and object. She also expresses the ability of a well-focused mind to experience simultaneously the constructed and non-constructed, the conditioned and unconditioned aspects of the self, which I call "ontological nondualism." Finally, Yeshey Tsogyel embodies the possibility of manifesting one's complete physical and mental potential, which Buddhists call enlightenment. I call the fulfillment of this capacity "evolutionary nondualism" because, whereas mainstream Christians do not seek or expect to "evolve" into a Christ, practitioners of Tibetan Buddhism do expect to evolve into their own enlightenment, a state that fully emulates and is entirely equivalent to the experience of the Great Bliss Queen and other enlightened persons.

The Great Bliss Queen is important for another reason as well. She weaves together intellectual and experiental elements in a way that speaks to other divides implicit in this book, that between the conceptual and nonconceptual, and between the academic and non-academic.[46] These parallel the divide between theory and practice, which is significant for me on both Buddhist and feminist grounds. My main professional activities center around teaching university classes on Buddhism, though I also occasionally teach Buddhist meditation practices outside the university. If it is sometimes difficult to get university students to understand the concept of Buddhism as a practice, and not simply a set of ideas, it is also sometimes difficult to interest new or would-be practitioners in the cultural nexus of the practices they wish to adopt, and to be realistic about the consequent limitations of those traditions in this culture. That is why, in addition to discussing how Buddhist theories and meditation practices speak to feminist concerns, I find it crucial to consider the different cultural understandings of self that come into play when Western women or men begin to appropriate Buddhist perspectives into their lives. Therefore the body of this book does not present a displaced "picture" of the Great Bliss Queen, but rather stresses her engagement in the cultural religious context from which she emerges, even as it places these in conversation with Western feminist concerns.

Although Yeshey Tsogyel is a female enlightened being, her female-ness alone does not make her relevant to contemporary Western women. Tibetans themselves, as I understood from speaking with Ani Mu Tso, are unwilling to consider her gender a significant factor. When, for example, I asked Ani Mu Tso what was the most significant aspect of Yeshey Tsogyel, she replied, after much silence, that it was her preservation of Padmasambhava's Great Completeness teach-ings. Though I believe that the symbolism, philosophy, practices, and imagery associated with Yeshey Tsogyel can be resources for twentieth-century Western women, I do not offer her as a "goddess" or "matriarch" or "role model" who automatically affirms or embod-ies the female character, especially the Western female character.[47] Not only would it be inappropriately essentialist to do so, but I am not at all sure that there is something distinctly and meaningfully "fem-inine" about her as Westerners, or even Tibetans, understand this term. In any case, the cultural significance she had in Tibet cannot simply be transplanted to another context. She cannot model how to be a woman in the twentieth century, how to negotiate domestic re-sponsibilities with a husband, or salary equity with administrators; she cannot settle issues such as whether to focus on a career, whether or when to have children.[48] Nor does she seem to have had the kind of significance for Tibetan women that certain Western women ascribe to goddesses today. It takes a feminist perspective to interpret as sig-nificant *for women* the fact that her female form expresses some of the most profound insights of the Buddhist world view. In any case, the point of practicing the Great Bliss Queen ritual is less to look at her than it is to take a fresh look at one's own potential. In this way, meet-ing the Great Bliss Queen is meeting oneself.

The material in this book is meant for a broad spectrum of women and men of various political, religious, and theoretical persuasions who are concerned with feminist reflections on selfhood across cultures. One could easily devote an entire chapter or book to many of the points considered here. At this early stage in the Buddhist-feminist conversation, however, it is critical to describe the larger landscape before detailing some portion of it.

In the following chapters, I address feminist readers by suggesting a different passage through the essentialist-postmodern debate than can be derived from Western sources alone, and I address Western Buddhists, especially women, by calling attention to the cultural complexities arising for the first visible generation of Buddhists in this hemisphere. Insofar as the conflict between essentialist and postmodern perspectives emerges from the same cultural and historical processes that have produced the ideas of personhood that contemporary Westerners inevitably bring to their understanding and practice of Buddhism, I see the material for these two kinds of readers as inextricably related. Interesting and fruitful as it is to become immersed in Buddhist cultural or philosophical sensibilities, it is vital to step back for a broader look at the kinds of challenges faced by Western women who would actually appropriate Buddhist perspectives or practices. Our next chapter therefore considers the different cultural dialogues that shape Buddhist and feminist orientations, and especially the distinctive constructions of personhood and womanhood they produce. Awareness of these is a crucial preparation for a genuine encounter with the Great Bliss Queen.

Chapters 3 through 5 consider Buddhist views on mind, self, and relationship as described in developmentally oriented systems and their relation to feminist thought. More specifically, chapter 3 explores Buddhist understandings of mindfulness and its implications for feminist discussions of the self and subjectivity.[49] Chapter 4 reflects on the interplay between self and other found in Buddhist practices of compassion, and offers a feminist analysis of this, asking what might distinguish empowering from disempowering forms of compassionate engagement. Chapter 5 examines how Buddhist and feminist understandings of self speak to and bypass each other, with special attention to the relationship between "Middle Way" Buddhist understandings of an interdependently constituted self and postmodern feminist theories that emphasize the self's dependence on cultural contexts. All three chapters speak to the possibility of maintaining personal coherence while recognizing that an incoherent and unmanageable array of data conditions our sense of personhood. The structure of these three chapters also reflects the chronology of my own movement through their subject matter, namely, an initial foray into the Buddhist material as traditional texts and native scholars have expounded it, and then a stepping back to consider how this material sits in the wider framework of a cross-cultural conversation.

The final chapters bring the discussion back to the figure of Yeshey Tsogyel, the Great Bliss Queen, and the discovery-oriented practices associated with her. Having looked at ways that traditional Buddhist discussions are sometimes in tension with and sometimes capable of contributing to Western feminist theory and its cultural context, one is more truly able to meet the Great Bliss Queen both on her ground and on one's own.

At issue throughout these chapters are questions of what it means to be a self, and especially what it means to be a self who is a woman in a particular culture. Mirroring feminism's own concern that "difference" not be lost to "sameness," I am motivated to give equal attention to the consonances and dissonances between Buddhist and feminist voices, allowing neither one to displace the other. The first step is to consider the most basic terms of contemporary and Buddhist understandings of "self." This is the explicit subject of the next chapter and the heart of our concern throughout.

CHAPTER 2

Persons: Then and Now, Here and There

> The Western conception of the person as a bounded,
> unique, more or less integrated motivational and cognitive
> universe, a dynamic center of awareness, emotion, judg-
> ment, and action organized into a distinctive whole and set
> contrastively both against other such wholes and against a
> social and natural background is, however incorrigible it
> may seem to us, a rather peculiar idea within the context of
> the world's cultures.
>
> Clifford Geertz, "From the Native's Point of View"

A Western woman carries both dominant Western assumptions
about selfhood and individuality and her own reservations about
those assumptions. It is thus important to remind ourselves of these
male-oriented understandings of selfhood, especially the uniquely
Western ways in which choice, narratives, and individual responsibility shape modern individuals. Although these themes are familiar
to students of Western culture, they have rarely been placed in conversation with Buddhist thought and culture or considered in the
context of Western women's relationship to Buddhist traditions. After
reviewing Western notions of the individual, we turn to feminist revisions of these characterizations of individuality, using the issue of
mortality as a touchstone for male and female differences. In the latter half of the chapter, we move to a parallel consideration of Tibetan
culture and the place of women in it so as to highlight significant cultural elements implicit in the Buddhist-feminist conversation. This
makes it possible to consider issues of personhood and gender from
several mutually illuminating perspectives.

Throughout, I use the term "individual" to indicate persons, especially in the West, for whom idiosyncratic traits, personal choices, and unique accomplishments are crucial to their identity. I use it also to suggest that a major project of such persons is to separate themselves, by virtue of their unique traits, from the larger society. As I suggested in chapter 1, Tibetans, like many Asians who have grown up outside strong Western influence, do not cultivate individuality in this sense. I am not saying, of course, that creative, idiosyncratic, or altogether unique persons have been absent in Tibet or any other traditional Asian culture.[1] My point is that "uniqueness" has not been a widely held cultural value and expectation. Moreover, Tibetans are often extremely independent in their personal and work relationships, much less prey than contemporary Westerners to the kind of psychological enmeshment that often troubles relationships between contemporary "individuals." This is a key difference to keep in mind as we discuss various ways in which the boundaries associated with Western-style personhood are not operative in Tibet.

THE WESTERN SELF

The Western construction of persons as unique and special gained particular prominence in the sixteenth century. Persons were no longer equated with their social roles, so that these roles were no longer considered part of a person's essence. Thus, a person came to be understood as "an individual unity with a separate existence independent of place in society."[2] This developing sense of individual uniqueness and personal choice is reflected in changes in the meaning of the English words "individual" and "self" over the past five centuries. In the fifteenth century, "individual" meant "indivisible." It could be used to describe the Trinity ("indyvyduall Trynyte") or a married couple, who were "individuall, not to be parted as man and wife."[3] Since at least the seventeenth century, however, the term "individual" has emphasized the separateness of persons rather than their connection. As Peter Abbs puts it, this inversion of meaning, "moving from the indivisible and collective to the divisible and distinctive, carries quietly within itself the historical devlopment of self-consciousness . . . that change in the structure of feeling which during the Renaissance shifted from a sense of unconscious fusion with the world towards a state of conscious individuation."[4]

In the late Middle Ages in Europe, "self" was a noun representing something to be denied in favor of God and all he represented. Only in 1674, writes Peter Abbs, following the *Oxford English Dictionary*, did "self" take on its modern meaning of a "permanent subject of successive and varying states of consciousness."[5] With this, the center of meaning was no longer situated in the wider external sphere—in God, society, or nature—but came to rest more completely within the narrow boundaries of the individual himself. The Protestant reformation and the rise of capitalism combined to place persons in an individuated rather than mediated relation to text and God, just at a time when the development of a new class structure and the proliferation of land ownership encouraged the assertion of exclusionary boundaries, particularly between men. "Consciousness," literally meaning to "know with," took on its modern meaning of self-awareness in the seventeenth century. Numerous related terms also entered the language during this period: self-sufficient (1598), self-knowledge (1613), self-made (1615), self-seeker (1632), selfish (1640), self-interest (1649), self-knowing (1667), self-determination (1683), self-conscious (1687).[6]

By the eighteenth century, an emphasis on a person's unique qualities was further amplified by the idea that each individual has a unique "potential." During the Romantic period, creativity became particularly valued as a manifestation of that potential, which was understood to emerge from a deep interiority filled with emotion and unique feelings that yearned for expression.[7] This unique individual was nevertheless still connected to the wider world, in that nature was seen as a reflection of the individual's mental and emotional state.

Following the Romantic period, however, society was increasingly perceived as an inhospitable environment against which the individual must struggle to fulfill his or (sometimes) her potential.[8]

The link between individuality and personality, which in the twentieth century is taken for granted, was still to come. In the eighteenth century, these concepts were still quite distinct. Individuality had to do with one's identity and purpose separate from that of the social realm; personality counted much less and referred to personal attitudes, dress, and relationships. Biographies of the period focused almost exclusively on the general chronology of a person's life; "personal" material, if included at all, would be gathered in a final chapter, often with an apology for offering such trivia.[9] By the nineteenth century, personality had become a strong focus of personal narratives and a major form of creative expression; today personality is "at the center of modernist concerns," its power grandly magnified in the form of the public persona, the movie personality, the media star.[10] The masks through (*per*) which to sound (*son*) are now larger than life, sometimes capable of replacing "real" persons, even as the "real" person herself has come to be identified with self-knowledge and a psychological consciousness.[11]

Unique individual expression requires novelty, and modern persons are groomed to be innovators, experimenters, and pioneers. Persons who free themselves from the past most successfully are so much the ideals that genius has been defined as "the capacity for productive reaction against one's training."[12] The reverence for creative genius and inventiveness in Europe and North America takes on an added significance if we reflect that the word "create" stems from the Latin *creare*, "to make" or "to produce," and once referred only to that which had been created by God. Augustine wrote that created human beings could not themselves create, a perspective that remained key until the sixteenth century, when Torquato Tasso was able to claim, "There are two creators, God and the poet."[13] We still speak of genius and creativity as being inspired, a phrase that harkens back to the medieval Latin sense of genius as "guardian spirit." Most significant here is that persons in contemporary middle-class Western culture see the expression of their unique individuality and personality as an important goal.

The growing sense of individuation over the past few centuries in Europe and North America can also be associated with the increasing distance of these cultures from their oral roots.[14] Speech engages one with others; reading and writing are solitary endeavors. Print could create community by providing the same books to a wide audience but was also arguably a significant factor in developing the sense of personal privacy and privilege that marks contemporary Western individuals. With the rise of print culture, texts began to be presented as if they were the sole creation of the single author whose name, with increasing regularity, appeared prominently on the title page. In this way, despite the indebtedness of any text to the inspiration and context provided by previous writings and conversations, print culture is especially associated with romantic notions of "originality" and "creativity," and thus with quirks of personality and a concomitant interest in the personal history "behind" a given work. Individualism brought to the fore a conception of persons who, like texts, present themselves as wholly original, self-contained, and independent intelligences.[15]

In the West, the move from an oral to literary orientation has been part of a more pervasive movement toward localizing power and authority, as well as thoughts and feelings, within the physical frame of an individual person. All this has had the effect of drawing more tightly the boundaries around such individuals. Charles Taylor's characterization of this process is particularly apt for our discussion: "The modern idea of a subject as an independent existent is just another facet of the new, strong localization. We can now think of ideas as being 'in' this independent being, because it makes sense to see them as here and *not elsewhere.*" But the importance of personal choice is now crucial in the formation of self. One makes major life choices based on one's own preferences, personality, and power. Taylor goes so far as to say that "we are selves only in that certain issues matter for us."[16] As a result, modern Western women and men are powerfully inclined to think of the human mind primarily in terms of its contents, that is, in terms of thoughts and feelings the mind acquires through schooling, acculturation, and personal interactions. Postmodern analyses of subjectivity thus are very much concerned with how social, historical, racial, and other factors give rise to particular ideologies or choices.

The difficulty of constructing a coherent self with a coherent narrative increases in direct proportion to the range of choices. Taking on the responsibility for making those choices is a hallmark of modern Western constructions of selfhood. Children are trained to make choices at a very young age. Parents ask their three-year-olds, "Do you want Cheerios or Corn Flakes? Do you want a red or blue T-shirt? Make up your mind; tell me what you want." This training is absolutely necessary, because the range and urgency of choice will be a significant aspect of the child's adolescent and adult life. In contrast, Linda Bell, a psychologist who has done extensive work in Japan, notes that a Japanese girl attending kindergarten in the United States was stymied by the teacher's request that she name her favorite color. "What's our favorite color?" she later asked her mother. Her mother, in turn, called the school for help in responding to this surprising question.[17]

The particular weight of personal responsibility for choice in the modern West derives not only from modern European and North American constructions of individuality but also from the smorgasbord quality of living in a pluralistic and, in the twentieth century, an electronically interconnected world. At the same time, the multiplicity of choices and the individual responsibility for creating a life from those choices adds to the sense that each person is "special." This has several mutually reinforcing ramifications. It makes narrative coherence a greater challenge than in cultures with fewer choices, and it increases the sense of isolation among persons, except to the extent that they can share their "individual" qualities and perspectives.

In addition, in the monotheistic religions of the West, which find it possible to revere only one supreme being, religious identity is exclusionary in ways it is not in much of Asia. The "problem" of pluralism is not a theological problem in, for example, China or Japan.[18] Monotheistic religions are far more difficult to reconcile with pluralistic realities than a religious tradition like Buddhism, which grants the existence of innnumerable enlightened beings. The early Jesuit missionaries in Tibet told the stories of Jesus walking on water and rising from the dead. They found no argument among the Tibetans, who readily identified Jesus as a Bodhisattva. They believed easily and were virtually impossible to convert. They were not burdened by the need to make a choice.

WOMEN AND THE NEW ECOLOGY OF RESPONSIBILITY

The localization of power and authority in individuals that began in the sixteenth century has given rise to a new kind of social ecology, changing the individual's sense of self, and changing also relationships between individuals and between individuals and their surroundings. In this context, choice becomes more and more a matter of personal responsibility, and more explicitly part of the definition of a person's unique character. The late eighteenth- and nineteenth-century European enchantment with individualism that forms the deep background of contemporary Western feminisms was also associated with a positive assessment of women's innate values, framed as the "necessary anchor for male individualism."[19] Until very recently, the traditional expectation that they would be receivers rather than innovators forced women to neglect their personal inclinations

and accept collective (male) wisdom of what women are. Women today of course seek more individual power over their lives even as they
question the "norms" of individuality based on male roles and inclinations. This is the unique internal dialogue modern women bring to
an encounter with Buddhist thought, and through which they can
create a new ecology of responsibility that is neither as rigidly autonomous as that of men nor as limited as it has been for women in the
past.

It is in some sense ironic, in another sense probably inevitable,
that the possibility of reconfiguring women's identity comes at a time
when all firm identities are in question. "Why is it," writes Nancy
Hartsock, "just at the moment in Western history when previously si-
lenced populations have begun to speak for themselves and on behalf
of their subjectivities, that the concept of the subject and the possibility of discovering/creating a liberating 'truth' become suspect?"[20] It
should be remembered that despite the creative adaptation of postmodern theories by many feminists, postmodernism is by definition a
dialogical response to the classic male figure defined by the Enlightenment. Thus, the current questioning of individualism is useful, but
it should not lull us into thinking that men and women are necessarily struggling with the same issues when they question it. Modern or
postmodern, the internal dialogues of men and women are different.
For example, in a sociohistorical analysis implicitly related to the
essentialist-constructionist debate, Elizabeth Fox-Genovese notes
that Western women continue to understand rights as deriving from
the individual's innate being, so that society is perceived as existing
for the individual, not the other way around.[21] Women also typically
adopt the language of individual rights in making a feminist case. Yet
contemporary Western women and men mix in different proportions
the experience of being an individual in the older sense of being (relatively) "indivisible" from others and the newer sense of being quite

distinct from them. Persons of different races and cultural backgrounds living in the West also mix these in a variety of ways. The feminist essentialist-postmodern debate can be seen as a struggle to recognize that persons are in fact "individuals" in both senses, that is, we are both isolated from others and inextricably connected with them, internally divided and yet whole, different from our contexts and yet a product of them.

The emphasis on uniqueness and increased sense of "specialness" of persons also means that death, the great equalizer, marks the loss of something utterly irreplaceable, the end of a singular destiny. At the same time, the existential psychologist Irvin D. Yalom suggests that an exaggerated sense of one's own specialness is often associated with a failure to accept mortality, and that this can result in an inability to complete meaningful tasks—jobs, intimate relationships— in the real world.[22] The ultimate expression of the Western individual—the hero—does not, however, come to terms with death or sacrifice his sense of specialness; rather, he creates a unique role for himself through his achievements, seeking thereby to vanquish the limitations imposed by death. In this way, as Ernst Becker observes, death gives life to the hero, allowing him "to earn a feeling of primary value, of cosmic specialness, of ultimate usefulness to creation, of unshakable meaning." "What characterizes modern life is the failure of all traditional immortality ideologies to absorb and quicken man's hunger for self-perpetuation and heroism. . . . Modern man cannot find his heroism in everyday life any more, as men did in traditional societies just by doing their daily duty of raising children, working, and worshipping."[23] The heroic stance against death described by Becker is thus closer to male than to female experience in modern Western culture, and Becker's depiction is increasingly undermined by feminist and postmodern understandings of selfhood. In short, we all die, but we do not all problematize death in the same way. The reasons we do not are indicative of the differently constructed positions of women and men in relationship to individuality, choice, and life itself.

Where did "man" get this hunger for heroism? Did he ever actually spend two-thirds of his life's energy raising children and worshiping? Where are the women in modern life, and what hungers do they have? Becker does not consider them. His focus is on the male individual who constructs his character and heroism as a bulwark against the intolerable assault of mortality. For women, I want to suggest, the issues are very different. Heroism is, for example, taken to task in the writings of Annie Leclerc: "It is death that raises the hero's temperature, not life, [which] leaves him cold. . . . Heroism is played out in the face of death. . . . It is in the region of death and in the fight against death that life wins its spurs."[24] A definition of the heroic depends a great deal on how one constructs life's challenges and gender identity. Many women would agree with cartoonist Gail Machlis, who defines a hero as someone who cooks six meals a week for four people without losing her mind.[25]

Few women writers characterize their own deaths as a significant issue, though many, for example, Mary Daly, Susan Griffin, Joanna Macy, Carolyn Merchant, and Rosemary Ruether, are concerned about the death of life-sustaining capacities in our society and environment. At the same time, Mary Daly describes a female nature that seems to have no place for death. She calls women's true nature "biophilic," a creative be-ing, and a rejection of spiritual or political stagnation, which is deadening.[26] Yet her emphasis implicitly rejects the need to confront mortality. How do we understand this?

On the one hand, women live closely with signs of their mortality and shifting stages of life: monthly bleeding, the palpable presence or absence of pregnancy, and menopause.[27] On the other hand, the powerful conflation in Western cultures of women, vulnerability, and nature gives feminist writers reason to distance themselves from the

mortality that is an inextricable part of "nature." Partly for these reasons, perhaps, feminist reflection does not dwell extensively on physical death, but focuses more on the threatened demise of women's position as individuals of their own construction. Males, more than
mortality, are seen as the limiting factor.[28]

The male hero, bearing the burden of his own choices, violently
opposes the forces that threaten him. As Simone de Beauvoir has observed, "It is not in giving life but in risking life that man is raised
above the animal; that is why superiority has been accorded in humanity not to the sex that brings forth but to that which kills."[29] There
is no question which endeavor is better researched, better funded, and
more linked to "productive" careers in Western culture. Killing, like
birthing, breaches the boundary between mortality and immortality,
and makes an irrevocable difference in the relationship between self
and other. But only killing, which ends relationship and responsibility to another, is considered concordant with heroic individuality. To
the extent that Western culture suspiciously regards relationality as a
threat to "genuine" autonomy, birth, mothering, and nurturing are
likely to be denigrated. Women raise children and are experienced by
the very young as all powerful; later these same children "blame
women for their malaise and do not face the more general existential
dilemma: our fate as a species."[30] The all-encompassing embrace of
motherhood is conflated with the annihilation of death, and women
are absurdly blamed for the disquiet one feels in facing mortality.
Thus, the autonomy prized in male development and crucial to the
heroic lifestyle entails repression of having been "of woman born."[31]
As D. W. Winnicott puts it, this conflation of women and death "is related to the fact that in the early history of every individual who develops well, and who is sane, who has been able to find himself, there
is a debt to a woman—a woman who was devoted to that individual as
an infant and whose devotion was absolutely essential for the individual's development. The original dependence is not remembered, and

therefore the debt is not acknowledged, except insofar as the fear of *woman* represents the first stage of this acknowledgement."[32] Not only is this unfair to women, but it means that core existential issues of vulnerability are not confronted.[33] It also means that the nature of self-other relationships are grossly distorted. The individualism of classic heroism has severe limitations.

In a skillful reinvention of "heroism," Maxine Hong Kingston has imagined a warrior woman who is also a wife and mother and who deviates from many of the "heroic" elements of Western (and, apparently, Chinese) culture. Fa Mu Lan does not carve heroism out of her character alone, she is parented into it by a wise man and woman, and death is not what motivates her. Like Psyche, she dips into the waters of life and strengthens connection with the world around her. Her deeds are aimed at gaining love by avenging wrongdoing against her family. In return for her vast effort, she seeks only the respect and entitlement that would naturally have been hers had she been born a male. After the publication of *The Woman Warrior*, Kingston told an interviewer, "I don't actually like warriors; I wish I had not had a metaphor of a warrior, a person who uses weapons and goes to war." But, as King-Kok Cheung observes, Kingston's book is not about fighting: it is a struggle against "silence and invisibility."[34] Kingston's consummate role model, whose appearance and example ends her book, is not a warrior but a poet and musician who spent time among a foreign people, learned their songs, and then returned to play them to her own people where "they translated well." This "heroine" is grand, not because of conquest, but for her creative living: she weaves her new discoveries into her native tongue. Her unique contribution is to forge a new relationship between the cultures and persons who participate in her own personal history. She does so, not as a monument to herself, but because it is her lot to live in the nexus of those connections.

Contemporary women, and many men as well, require ways to be strong without being heroic, ways to rely on internal resources without cutting themselves off from wider social connections. In short, they need ways to be individuals who are neither overly essentialized nor so fractured that strength and coherence are undermined. This is true for Western women who take up Buddhist practices as well as for feminists interested in the possible theoretical resources Buddhist materials might provide.

To sum up, in the West, "individuation" has by and large meant the emergence of consciously chosen activities and attitudes. In modern cultures, unlike traditional ones, the chasm between childhood and adulthood roles is enormous. The road to adulthood and personhood is marked by a range of choices unknown in traditional societies, and the individual's responsibility for those choices is great. "You wonder where you get authority for introducing new meanings into the world, the strength to bear it," writes Ernest Becker.[35] Divorced from cosmic forces, human purpose must be deliberately chosen, and human agency is now seen as separate from a larger meaningful order. For women, the question is even more complex, as they explore how to combine the capacity for personal and creative choice with the capacity for connection, in order to share yet fully participate in both authority and strength.

The challenges and definitions of Tibetan personhood are very different, and yet they also suggest a dialogue between separation and connectedness. The personal boundaries that result from Tibet's cultural dialogue are formed through an amalgamation of its people's attitudes regarding their relationship to society, natural environment, and the cosmos, and to the privileged authority of the past.

THE SELF IN TIBETAN CULTURE

Buddhism entered Tibet in force in the eighth century, competing fiercely and finally successfully with indigenous spiritual expressions. Stan Mumford argues persuasively that the history of the Ti-

betan people is reflected in their internalization of two different perspectives: a socially embedded shamanic sensibility stemming from
the earliest phase of Tibetan culture, and an individualistic sensibility associated with the rise of Buddhism.[36]

Social cohesiveness in traditional Tibetan communities is based
on shared horizons and small-scale clans or villages. Terms indicating continuity such as mental continuum (*tantra*, *rgyud*), life continuum (*samtāna*, *rgyun*), and lineage (*gotra*, *rigs*) are at least as significant elements of personhood as terms indicating separateness.[37]
With an emphasis on continuity rather than origins, the term "creativity" in the sense of unique personal expression has little place.
Overall, identity comes as much or more from family, class, and lineage as from personal endeavors, remarkable though they might be.
Even the Great Bliss Queen is identified in her liturgy as the
"Karchen daughter." In villages and nomadic communities, social
identity comes through "natural indices" such as family of origin, not
individual achievement. For example, Tibetan peoples of northwest
Nepal still distinguish their social strata on the basis of *rü* (literally,
"bone"), considered part of one's physical inheritance.[38] Social position in Tibet is not seen as culturally constructed but in some sense as
given, much as social rank was once considered a de facto element of
medieval society in the West. Although some choices and social mo-
bility exist, especially in the context of monastic or other religious af-
filiations, most associations come about through family of origin
rather than individual preference.

When Buddhist traditions came to Tibet, their increasingly numerous adherents were encouraged to take responsibility for their
own "karmic career" and were taught that their future well-being
would be determined by their own actions and religious practices.[39]
At the same time, *karma* (meaning simply "action" and referring to
the idea that all persons experience the effects of their own good and
bad actions) itself implies extensive connections, most especially with

one's own past, but also with a world that embodies the collective actions of innumerable living beings.[40]

Like Tibetan culture, classic Buddhist formulations of identity are dialogical. In the Indian texts foundational to Tibet's Buddhism, André Bareau finds two constructions of personhood: (1) identity that is retained across a series of existences, for which the term "being" (*sattva, sems ba*) is used, and (2) the identity of a specific existence (*pudgala, gang zag*).[41] Thus, one simultaneously possesses two kinds of identity, one embedded in a wider system of rebirths, the other pointing to a certain kind of personhood in this life. (The karmic theory to which such dyadic identity is wedded is a far more significant doctrine in Indian and Tibetan forms of Buddhism than in the Ch'an/ Zen and Pure Land traditions that have predominated in East Asia.)

Traditional Jewish and Christian cosmologies understand God as the creator of the world, and the world itself as material. By contrast, the theory of karmic cause and effect, which appears to have been an indigenous Indian concept, understands the external world and one's place in it to be created by one's own and others' past activities of thought, word, and deed. Thus, Western peoples live in a world not of their creation, a world composed essentially of matter. Tibetans live in a cosmos they co-create, and that is itself alive and, in some of the older strata of Tibetan literature, sometimes even speaks. In the Great Completeness literature, for example, the cosmos is described as an unfolding process of awareness rather than a creation of worlds or creatures.[42] In the person of Samantabhadra, "the All Good" speaks and tells its own story.[43] Samantabhadra pervades and is the cosmos. Samantabhadra is even seen as indicative of the kind of subjectivity to be discovered in oneself. Likewise, karmic theory situates one as subject and co-creator of this world, meaning that the cosmos that each person experiences takes shape according to her own and others' actions.[44] In all these ways, the cosmos is a natural creative process. It is not something to be explored as if by a stranger;

nor is it controlled by anyone.[45] Neither Samantabhadra nor any other Buddha is a giver of commandments that have to be obeyed, and in this sense a Buddha is not the kind of authority figure one would seek to rebel against. Tibetan "personhood" is not constructed as a revolt against metaphysical authority (rebellion being of course an important expression of individuality in the West). No one in Tibet has yet declared that "Samantabhadra is dead." In the West, by contrast, we are encouraged to distinguish ourselves from the masses of both past and present—in other words, to individuate.

Although karmic theory emphasizes that actions and their effects accrue to particular persons, traditional Tibetans do not understand themselves as "individuals" in the contemporary Western social, economic, or psychological sense. Further, they are rarely, if ever, alone in the sense that a Westerner in an apartment in a city to which she has just moved and knows no one, is alone. Tibetan renunciates, who may meditate in solitude for years in the Tibetan vastness, or others who leave home to make extensive pilgrimages, model forms of autonomy difficult to replicate in the West, yet even they are still embedded in a traditional context. No matter how isolated, even high in a solitary cave, one remains part of a community of values, and of people and spirits also. Family or villagers offer moral and practical support to retreatants. Although the "karmic career" emphasizes a certain autonomy of action, it does not cut one off from the collectivity. We see here in ideological terms what we have already noted in philosophical form, namely, that Tibetan Buddhists understand a coherent sense of personhood to be compatible with a complex view of causality in general, and the self's constructed nature in particular. Their extensive social connectedness, combined with an ideology claiming, in effect, that the individual person, with even a single intentional action, is a powerful force in making the world he or she inhabits, may also foster personal autonomy and forcefulness.

Much of the traditional Tibetan world view is passed from generation to generation through face-to-face conversation, fostering a sense of familiarity with the cultural arena in ways difficult for Westerners to imagine. Knowledge stored in books can be avoided; the expressions of one's immediate companions cannot, and every live oral interaction immerses one in the larger group's world view.[46] At the same time, oral traditions, unlike texts, adjust to circumstances without leaving obvious records of that adjustment. The relevance of the past for the present can more easily remain unquestioned, even when it is recognized that times do change. Moreover, in traditional Asian contexts such as Tibet, the past is venerated. Even the most exceptional Tibetan philosophers and practitioners did not so much lay claim to new spiritual territory as to insights well hallowed since ancient times, hence their creativity was always implicitly in the service of embellishing ancient verities. "Reaction against training" was not their goal.

Buddhist teachings, whether oral or written, are considered a primary expression of the past, and this gives them extraordinary authority. Tibetan Buddhist traditions typically exhort one to listen unwaveringly, "without the perceiving faculty of your ears straying to some other sound."[47] To forget what you have heard is "as if juice is poured into a pot with a leaky bottom—however much you pour, nothing will remain there."[48] And Yeshey Tsogyel is made to say by Daktsam Dorje, the eighteenth-century male compiler of the "autobiography" describing her eighth-century life: "I became the King's priestess . . . living with my Guru, spreading the Buddha's teaching. [The Guru] bestowed them all upon me, retaining nothing, just as the contents of one vessel are poured into another."[49] Male students of Buddhism also are constructed as receivers, but the woman Yeshey Tsogyel is a receiver par excellence, since she preserves the teaching for all future receivers when she transcribes and buries the words of Guru Rinboche so that "like timely messages" they will reappear when circumstances warrant.[50]

Consonant with this, the person to whom the major Buddhist texts, practices, and rituals are directed is construed primarily as a receiver rather than an innovator, and as a hearer rather than a reader. This construction is linked in turn with the close interplay of oral and literary orientations in Tibet. Unlike in the West, where print culture has largely replaced oral orientations, in Tibet, Buddhist literary traditions have continuously been enfolded by oral commentative scholarship and debate, by the recitation of memorized texts, and by chanted mantras and liturgies in *sādhanas* or meditative rituals by which practitioners physically, vocally, and mentally embody the meaning of the texts.[51] Thus, Tibetan culture, which has produced one of the largest religious literatures on earth, nonetheless maintains a strong oral orientation. It is likely no coincidence that its religious practices are characterized by the twin and often simultaneous processes of chanting and visualization.

Some years ago, an eminent Geluk scholar visiting the United States was giving a technical exegesis on the stages of death, when he deliberately turned from his classroom lecture to tell an elaborate tale of a monk who had left his body one night to wander in spirit form through uncharted regions, encountering many strange beings, including one who carried a beating heart.[52] This scholar's lack of self-consciousness about any rift between the textual commentary, replete with classic Buddhist terms and philosophy, and the story he told of spirits made it obvious that he felt equally comfortable in both areas of reflection.

Similarly, in the 1970s I studied with a Geluk scholar renowned for rigorous reasoning, skill in debating, and mastery of a wide range of Buddhist philosophy. When he became ill during his first visit to the United States, he called for flour, mixed it with water, and from this dough molded an image of himself approximately eighteen inches high, carefully sculpting the folds in the robes and delicately positioning the individual fingers of the raised left hand. His illness was ritually transferred to this figure, which he then asked a student to dispose of by casting it away near water, so that no one would find it. Such ritual contacting, propitiating, or bargaining with invisible beings related with illness has no formal basis in the classic Buddhist philosophy in which he was trained; however, such practices are universal in Tibetan culture, and very similar practices are detailed in texts of the Bön tradition.[53] The presence of spirits is for Tibetans associated with special links between materiality and the sentient world. Rituals for preventing hail, for example, state that in addition to traditional Buddhist contemplative practices of visualization and recitation, the hailmaster needs certain substances to counteract the power of the beings who bring hail. The "antidote" for planetary demons (*gza' bdud*), for example, is soil from a place struck by lightning; the antidote for the earth demon (*sa'i bdud*) is water from melted hail; and the antidote for earth deity leaders (*sna dren*) is soil from a place where there has been fighting. This is an odd yet oddly moving list, not least because of the mysterious connections between things it suggests.[54] In virtually every Asian Buddhist country, belief in ubiquitous spirit-beings was in place long before Buddhism arrived, and these beliefs proved extraordinarily resistant to change. A world view that includes spirits implies a very different ecology of responsibility, or distribution of agency, than does Western individualism, where the main locus of power is in oneself. In the West, Buddhism for perhaps the first time enters a culture without such widespread beliefs.

This more open boundary between persons and their environment suggested by Tibetan cultural understanding is complemented by an equally open boundary between the psychic and physical. In Tibetan medical understanding, diseases are associated with elements, much as in the medieval West they were associated with humors and with spirits. As Charles Taylor has observed, when the line between the psychic and the physical is not sharply drawn, when, for example, bile is not simply a cause of melancholy but the embodiment of it,

magic becomes possible, because magic relies on the notion that certain powers have their seat in certain substances or in certain speech
acts. Magic, says Taylor, did not just fade away before the majesty of
science in the West; it lost its power owing to profound changes in how
people understood themselves to be situated in the world. The boundaries the West draws so tightly around individuals, or between self
and cosmos, also apply between material objects. The nature of a
stone, to the modern Western imagination, is in that stone, and no
where else.[55]

The social and cosmic embeddedness we have already discussed
suggests that in Tibet persons' identities are not "localized" as they
are in the West and the boundary between self and cosmos is far more
permeable. This is possible because self and cosmos are equally alive,
and equally populated by myriad invisible beings, some of whom
bring disease or crop-damaging weather.

In 1991, a group of eight Tibetan monks from India gave a performance of sacred dances and chants at Rice University. The next day,
at a meeting between the monks and a group of faculty members (two
groups that reflect my own crucial internal divisions), one of the pro-
fessors asked who, under normal circumstances in Tibet, would be
the audience for such practices. The response was instantaneous:
"Do you mean human or nonhuman audiences?"[56] Animal and
other nonhumans are felt to be fellow participants in the life process.
Moreover, in rebirth, one may move from one category to another. Indeed, several Tibetan terms, for example, "sentient being" (*sems
can*), "person" (*gang zag*), and "creature" (*skyes bu*), apply equally to
all six states of rebirth, only two of which—human and animal—are
normally visible to us.[57] Persons do not spring to life in one individual
form only, but are embedded in a series of lives, as well as in the social,
spirit, and natural networks. And life is everywhere; there are no
empty forests, no wholly inanimate objects. The boundaries to the

self in Tibetan cultures can be fluid indeed, as is implicit in Tibetan philosophical terms for persons.

Traditional Buddhist Terms for Persons

There are numerous important words for "self" and "person" in the Indian and Tibetan philosophical literature. In these we find a meaningful play on the constructs of separateness and connectedness that are so important to Western and Western feminist understandings of persons. The Sanskrit term *puruṣa*, meaning "man" or "human," is a prime example.

The first syllable, *puru*, is derived from the root *pṛ*, meaning "to fill," and *puruṣa* appears to be associated with this root in two dichotomous ways.[58] *Puru* itself means "much abundant" and is also associated with *purī*, meaning "city, town, citadel, king," all forms of desirable abundance.[59] However, the significance of "abundance" moves in the opposite direction as well. From the root *pṛ* is also derived *pṛthivī*, "earth." This meaning gives rise to terms such as fillings, heaps, and crumbling earth, hence dirt and excrement. Thus *puriṣya* means at once "being in the earth," "rich in land," and "excremental."[60]

Persons themselves are seen as having both desirable and undesirable forms of abundance. This can be seen in the two-syllable Tibetan term *gang zag*, a translation of the Sanskrit *pudgala*, meaning "person." *Gang (pūrṇatva)* means "full," and *zag (āsrava)*, which can mean "contaminated," here has the related meaning of "disbanded" or "disintegrated."[61] The combination of these syllables, according to one gloss, signifies that the faults and good qualities in the continuum of any living being are now plentiful, and now disbanded.[62] This fluctuation is the central characteristic of all living persons other than fully enlightened Buddhas.

Puruṣa is translated by two different terms in Tibetan, depending

on context. In the classical language of Buddhist texts, *puruṣa* is usually rendered as *skyes bu* (pronounced *gyey-bu* to rhyme with "hey
you"), literally "the born" or "the produced," and translated here as
"creature." This creature is of course "produced" by its own karma,
not by Buddha or any other being. *Skyes bu* is the generic and male
term, *skyes dman* (rhymes with "amen") signifies the low born, the
women.[63]

The word *skyes bu* is glossed in a twelfth-century Tibetan work by
Gam-po-pa (1079–1153) as "one who has power or ability," especially
the capacity for enlightenment.[64] The word identifying humans as
those who are abundantly nourished thus migrates toward a por-
trayal of them as possessed of the most positive results of nourishment, which is to say, power. When Buddhist texts set this term in the
context of their own religious narrative, a human person is defined in
terms of the power to change his or her status as conditioned by
karma. Unlike Western religious and cultural constructions of humanity, Mahayana Buddhism sets no limits to what can be accomplished: this is another flexible boundary.

The Stages of the Path (*Lam rim*) literature, a genre that Geluk
made famous, uses the same term in its famous tripartite division of
persons (*skyes bu gsum*) based on their motivation. Human creatures
in particular are categorized according to the type of religious attain-
ment to which they aspire. The lowest seek a good rebirth, the mid-
dling freedom from cyclic existence, and the highest aspire to become
fully enlightened Buddhas in order to help others find their own enlightenment. Indeed, so significant is one's projected spiritual development in defining one's present personhood that the literal meaning
of "ordinary creature" in Pali (*puthujjana*), Sanskrit (*pṛthagjana*),
and Tibetan (*so sor skyes bu*) is "a creature who is separate"—separate from the developmental states and superior rebirths that, potentially, lie ahead. However, in a manner somewhat parallel to the evolution of the English word "individual," both in Pali and, to a lesser

degree, in Tibetan, "a creature who is separate" comes to mean simply "one of the many-folk" or "one of the masses." That is, the emphasis is on what is included rather than what is excluded.[65]

We can say, then, that ordinary creatures and thus ordinary persons are by definition divided from what proper use of their powers, nourished by religious practice, will bring about. This is the most significant internal boundary in Indo-Tibetan Buddhist traditions, yet it is not an indelible one, not an "essence" of human beings in any sense. Through development or discovery, persons bring about their own enlightenment. The relationship of practitioners to a Buddha like the Great Bliss Queen, for example, is predicated on the idea that performing her ritual will enable one to become a Great Bliss Queen oneself. Ordinary persons can become Buddhas, and Buddhas once were ordinary persons. By contrast, in mainstream Jewish and Christian traditions, the ordinary creature cannot be or become God because of the powerful boundaries between person and world, psyche and soma, created and Creator. To this extent, Western religious heritage "fixes" a person within the cosmos in ways that Buddhist traditions do not. The bounded identity that anthropologist Clifford Geertz identifies with contemporary Western culture can thus be associated with the strict demarcations between human and divine inscribed into most Jewish and Christian religious traditions and to the human limitations foundational to much of psychological theory.

The most famous philosophical term associated with persons is the "self," or *ātman*. This Sanskrit word is translated into Tibetan as *bdag* (pronounced "dock"), which means "self" or "I" or, with an added suffix, "owner" (*bdag po*), and it refers to an ontologically overbearing sort of self, one that is imagined to be much more substantial than it actually is. This kind of self is variously described in Buddhist texts as permanent, independent, self-sufficient, true, or inherently existent. No one and no thing, neither Buddhas nor enlightenment nor any other phenomenon, has such qualities. Unlike the other terms for "person" discussed thus far, *ātman* is a category of which there are no instances, a point I will dramatize by saying no more about it just now.

How have these Buddhist cultural and philosophical constructions of selfhood affected the lives of Tibetan women? Did Buddhism's powerful female imagery, here exemplified by Yeshey Tsogyel, have positive ramifications for the social realities of women or men? In what significant ways were women's lives constructed differently from the lives of men in their culture? Taking account of Tibet's dramatic geographical variations as best we can, let us examine women's status in pre-Chinese Tibet.[66] This should help us understand some of the huge differences between the kinds of relationship Tibetan and Western women have with Buddhism, its symbols, or with figures such as the Great Bliss Queen. Awareness of such differences is crucial for a meaningful conversation between Western feminists and Buddhist voices.

THE WOMEN OF TIBET

If there is any country where religious perspectives seem likely to mold social realities, it is Tibet.[67] Since at least the eighth century, Tibet's culture has been steeped in religion. Traditionally, every home, however poor, had a shrine where offerings and prayers were made daily, and the enormous intellectual, literary, and artistic energies of the population were focused almost exclusively on the religious sphere.

The Tibetans have an adage, "Every doctor has his own medicine, every lama his own religion." We might well add, "and every valley its own customs." Given the rough terrain and lack of roads or vehicles in Tibet, it could hardly have been otherwise. Any village might be days or weeks by horse or foot from the next, and people in each area had their own ways of doing things. This diversity makes it impossible to generalize about Tibet as a whole. My focus here is on the Kham and Amdo regions, which were the stronghold of Nyingma Buddhism and the area where Geluk and Nyingma influences combined in the literature on the Great Bliss Queen. Approximately half the population of these regions is nomadic. I refer also to Lhasa, the largest city, site of the main Geluk monasteries in Tibet, seat of the early Tibetan kings, and capital of Tibet since the seventeenth century. What were the lives of women in these areas like?

Women outside the Home

During the century before the occupation of Tibet, if not earlier, there was considerable parity between women and men in the area of work. In east Tibet, nomadic families traveling with their yak-hair tents and grazing animals shared a hard and simple life. Their staples were a rich tea made with salt and butter, *tsampa* (parched barley), yogurt, cheese, and meat when available. Clothing made from wool and animal skins was sewn by men, and among nomadic and other peoples both men and women spun yarn.[68] Men and women dressed alike, their garments equally suited for active work. Women were primarily in charge of the "white," or milk products, the nutritionally crucial cheese, milk, and yogurt.

Tibetans are famous for trade, and women of all classes appear to have been active in this sphere. Among the horse herders of east Tibet, men were typically unwilling to conclude a sale, however favorable, in the absence of their wives. Western and Chinese foreigners encountering this phenomenon were amazed. One traveler put it this way: "By what means have these women gained such a complete ascendancy over the men, how have they made their mastery so complete and so acceptable to a race of lawless barbarians who but unwillingly submit even to the authority of their chiefs, is a problem worthy of consideration."[69] In Lhasa, too, women were the family shopkeepers (unthinkable even today in most areas of India), and some had their own businesses. At the same time, a preference for male offspring did exist. In Lhasa parents followed the custom of slipping a ring onto a son's penis as soon as he was born, lest some mischievous demon change him into a girl.[70]

Mores governing public modesty were also egalitarian. Unlike neighboring India, where women often risked kidney infections and other diseases because of the impropriety of relieving themselves in public and the lack of private places to do so, men and women were equally free in this regard. In Lhasa and elsewhere, the *chuba*, a long dress worn by women, made relief possible without exposure. Thus, there was nothing to prevent women from heading to town for trade or to circumambulate the temples. Women were free to strip to the waist at public bathing spots, since breasts were not regarded as shameful or sexual, this particular taboo being reserved for legs, which both men and women were required to keep covered.

The traditional monastic universities—major institutions of religious and political power—have always been closed to women, and so monastic literature could implicitly exclude women, even while maintaining their equal access to enlightenment. In Geluk oral commentary, it was sometimes indicated that being male was an advantage, though Nyingma teachers occasionally say that women have the advantage in certain tantric practices.[71] However, few Nyingma and no Geluk women are recorded as having achieved significant religious or political power in Tibet. Indeed, wherever hierarchical power structures were emphasized, as they were in Tibet's monastic order and theocratic political system centered in Lhasa, women were excluded. Women shared with men the unbounded identity between self and cosmos and spiritual potential, but they occupied far narrower boundaries when it came to secular power and authority.[72]

Thus, there is a powerful contrast between an egalitarian Buddhist vision on the one hand and the institutionalized hierarchies of Tibetan life on the other. Tibetan Buddhists, like most Mahayana traditions, emphasize that everyone is capable of experiencing enlightenment and that the well-being of each and every person is equally important, just as in the United States everyone has the right to "life, liberty, and the pursuit of happiness." However, in neither case do these principles express themselves in a leveling of social or economic difference. Tibetan society, especially in those relatively few but significant areas where political and economic power accrued, was intricately hierarchical.

Tibetan language itself is hierarchical, particularly as spoken in centers of power like Lhasa. Most nouns and verbs have honorific forms, usually entirely different in sound and spelling from the non-honorific forms, and these must be used whenever one addresses someone socially, economically, or spiritually superior to oneself.[73] The most widely used word for woman (*skyes dman*) literally means "low born" and is also the nonhonorific word for "wife." A man might use this term to refer to his own wife, or he might call her *chung ma*, literally, "little woman."[74] But he would always use an honorific for the wife of someone of rank greater than his. Other terms are less explicitly offensive. Women are known as those not to be put out (*bud med*) because a woman is not to be left outside the house at night. Another less common phrase is *lus phra ma*, "female of slight body."[75] Other synonyms, also relatively rare in ordinary speech, are *gnas byed*, "maker of a dwelling" or "maker of stability"; *mi mo*, "a female person"; and *mtshams ldan ma*, perhaps a pun, which can be understood either as "one who has a boundary" or "one who has an intermediate space." Other epithets include *'dzin ma*, "female grasper," and *lan bu can bcas*, "one who has long plaits [of hair]."[76] These terms fall into two main groups, those associated with a woman's more "essential" physical characteristics, and others with her community or family position.

Religious Vocations

Women who wished to devote themselves to religion could, like men, become either celibate nuns or *tantrikas*, religious practitioners not vowed to celibacy. Usually of the Nyingma or Gagyu orders, these tantrikas might marry and were likely to spend much of their lives on pilgrimage, receiving instruction from isolated or monastic tantric teachers, or in retreat. In outlying areas, nuns and female tantrikas of the Nyingma order might study and sometimes live within the monastic confines. These options were open to women of all classes. Most typically, nuns lived together in nunneries, institutions that tended to be small and did not offer either the educational opportunities or access to wealth and political power provided by the more well endowed monasteries.[77]

In nomadic communities, some unmarried women were known as *ka-ma*, "hearth ladies," because in their youth they slept by the family hearth and, like young brides, did the dairy work.[78] Not as highly regarded as Buddhist nuns or tantrikas, the *ka-ma* nonetheless eventually received a certain respect as religious practitioners. They dressed like Buddhist nuns, although they were not obliged to shave their heads as nuns did. In their later years, they would join the monks' circle of tents and concentrate on religious practice, supported, as were the monks, by their families.[79]

Another religious vocation, documented mainly in the Lhasa area, was to be an oracle. Oracles are persons who in the course of the appropriate ritual receive into their body the deity with whom they are connected, so that the deity's voice speaks through them and in this way can be consulted on important matters. A female oracle married, and on her death her daughter became an oracle in her place.[80] Other important religious roles, such as the hereditary tradition of hailmasters, who protected summer crops from destruction by hail, were always male. A successful hailmaster was a politically powerful person in his community and was richly rewarded for his many years of training. Khetsun Sangpo Rinboche, who himself was a hailmaster for three years before leaving Tibet, and who taught me some of the basic principles of this practice, observed that there was no reason why a woman could not successfully protect an area from hail; it was just that in Tibet women never did.

We cannot say precisely where and how religious egalitarianism fails to translate into social egalitarianism, but clearly the amalgamation of social, political, and economic power is an obstacle.

Families

Marriage structures derived primarily from local economies rather than from gender roles as such. Monogamous marriages were the rule, but polyandry and, secondarily, polygamy were not uncommon in pre-Chinese Tibet. The issue was not personal preference but the logistics of inheritance. A farmer with three sons and insufficient land for each might arrange for a single woman to be their common bride. This custom was especially prevalent among herders in the northern plains and western Tibet.

Likewise, parents with several daughters and insufficient inheritance for each might arrange for a single man to be their common husband. Polyandry was most widespread in the Tsang area, outside Lhasa, where soil was poor and estates large, requiring many people to look after them. Polygamy by some accounts was an option only for rich men who could afford two or three wives.[81] In the case of divorce, child custody practices varied. In some areas, boys stayed with the father, girls with the mother; in others the mother most commonly took all the children. In the case of illegitimate children, at least among nomads, the father was required to make a one-time payment to the mother if neither desired to marry.[82]

Weddings were arranged by parents and other relatives of the prospective bride. Among nomadic peoples, a father or uncle of the groom visited the girl's home and requested both parents to give their daughter in marriage. The girl was not likely to be consulted in the matter, though the prospective groom would probably have had a say. Typically, the girl's parents would not agree to the initial offer. Their flimsy reasons for refusing, however, were understood by the petitioners as an invitation to pursue the matter further. The girl's parents often required the request to be made three times (as is also the custom when requesting religious teachings from a lama), thereby establishing the esteem in which their daughter was held and, possibly, eliciting the best financial offer. Depending on their economic status, the groom's family would give items such as silk cloth, silver, horses, or multicolored cotton fabrics.[83] Once the girl's parents had given their consent by accepting gifts, often with a show of reluctance, the match was made. Among the Lhasa nobility, a gift known as the "breast[milk] fee" (*nu ring*) was given to the girl's mother, thereby acknowledging her special relationship to the bride.[84] The bride's family in turn would give gifts in measure to what they had received. Thus, although numerous accounts speak of Tibetan wives being "bought," this was not precisely the case, at least among nomads, since each family received an equal share of goods.

The central feature of the nomad wedding ceremony was the Yogurt Vow. Yogurt is considered an auspicious food; the bride's vow thus referred to the dairy work she would do after marriage and was meant to ensure that she would make good yogurt. The presence of this ritual underscores the fact that even if women were not essentially understood as nurturers, they were required to take on this role at the time of marriage.[85] There was no ceremonial equivalent for the groom, suggesting that the husband's work roles were not as closely linked to gender as his wife's. Thus, whereas women might conduct trade as the men did, men did not make yogurt. In short, the ritual emphasized, as did the special fee paid to her mother, a woman's role as nurturer and sustainer, qualities also attributed to Yeshey Tsogyel in her supporting role as preserver of Padmasambhava's teachings. Yet yogurt making by no means fully defined the role a woman would play in family life, nor would marriage necessarily rule out the possibility of a woman's religious vocation at some future time, most often after her children were grown.[86]

The women and men of pre-Chinese Tibet grew up with paintings, statues, and stories of female figures like the Great Bliss Queen.

These well-known images displayed the variety of manifestations of enlightened personhood. It was not the case, as with goddess worship among modern European or North American women, that devotion to a female figure registered a protest or in any way bespoke a challenge to the prevailing religious order. Devotees of female Buddhas were as likely to be male as female.[87]

Positive female imagery and the importance of female deities helped to welcome women into religious life, even if their numbers, status, and economic base were less than those of males. Women who entered the religious life might eventually be identified with female embodiments of enlightenment and recognized as adepts in their own right. Female figures such as the Great Bliss Queen were more prevalent in Nyingma than Geluk areas, and the opportunity for women practitioners was also greater there. Their families might object, but women were welcome in all Buddhist orders as nuns, and in less heavily monastic orders, it was possible (though not common) for women to achieve considerable status as practitioners or teachers.

I have been told by a Geluk teacher that nuns were not scholars but were often known as great meditators. I have also been told, however, that a particularly obscure set of debates found in Geluk textbooks was developed by monks as a way to best some nuns who had so far proved invincible in debate. This story seems apocryphal; all other sources indicate that nuns were not schooled in debate. In any case, the Geluks have not, to the best of my knowledge, produced a single woman teacher of record. Still, it is not entirely clear whether women teachers were as unusual as the written records indicate.[88]

In all walks of life, for both women and men, social cohesion (not to be confused with social harmony) was a given. The greatest life-choice for women was whether to enter a religious life or to marry. There was no "public sphere" to speak of that might tempt her away from home; the greatest pull away from domesticity would be a wish to devote herself to religious practices as a nun or tantrika roaming the Tibetan vastness with her companions, certainly a life of considerable freedom and personal independence.

Even this brief survey demonstrates that women's challenges in Tibetan cultures have been very different from those of contemporary Western women. Women, especially the white middle-class Western women who are usually a majority in Western Buddhist communities, must make many more choices than did the women of traditional Tibet and must seek forms of self-knowledge and self-empowerment appropriate to that task.[89]

It seems natural to suppose that dilemmas of selfhood peculiar to our time and place are part of what brings Americans and other Westerners to Buddhism. Buddhist thought and practice does, in some measure, speak to these issues, but in order to make best use of its resources it is important to be clear on the ways it does *not* explicitly address them. The Buddhist spiritual journey is very different from the Western psychological journey, to which it is often too swiftly compared. "Finding oneself" in the contemporary Western sense means identifying one's unique talents, limitations, and place in the world so as to make choices consistent with this identity. Buddhist practices, by contrast, are celebrated for their ability to access universal faculties such as clarity, focus, or an experience of the unconditioned. Unless this difference is clear, one is in danger of recreating the experience of a California woman who after many years of Zen practice observed, "My concern now is that I used Buddhism as an escape from growing up."[90] This can happen, but it need not.

Can Buddhist theories or techniques respond to the uniquely contemporary and Western pulls of essentialist and constructionist positions on selfhood? Can Buddhist material suggest a way to express or shift one's personhood as a woman while negotiating the constructions of the world that name, frame, and demand particular ways of being women? For all that Buddhism is famous for asking questions about self and identity, its questions are not these questions. Yet as we explore further, we will find that Buddhist traditions can indeed speak to the dilemmas described by Western feminists. In particular, they do so by providing a way of understanding subjectivity that bridges the divide between essentialist and postmodern sensibilities, and by not assuming the types of narrow boundaries that in recent centuries have characterized both male and female forms of self-reflection. It is to a description of this kind of subjectivity that we now turn our attention.

PRACTICE AND THEORY

CHAPTER 3

Mindfulness and Subjectivity

> Without mindfulness there will be no reconstitution of al-
> ready acquired knowledge and consciousness itself would
> break to pieces, become fragmentary.
>
> Soma Thera, *The Way of Mindfulness*

Feminists frequently emphasize the need to find new ways of understanding and experiencing the self, but feminist theory provides
little in the way of techniques for doing so. Looking through my Buddhist lenses, I find that most feminist reflection on experience focuses
on the *contents* of a woman's mind: what she knows, how she feels,
how she understands and differentiates herself. But what most feminists lack, from a Buddhist perspective, is an understanding of how
the mind *is*. The question of how the mind "is" emerges as an important topic in all the forms of Buddhism we consider here. Buddhist
epistemologies, while clearly articulating the profound intertwining
of language and subjectivity, also emphasize that one's mind has a dimension that is neither primarily gained nor governed through language. The mind's capacity for clarity, for example, is simply part
of its collateral or natural dynamic.[1] Mindfulness enhances clear
awareness of present experience and facilitates new levels of mental
calm, compassion, or self-acceptance. Such mindfulness is understood to emerge through a chosen trajectory of discovery or development. It does this, not by bringing forth new ideas about the self, but
through a new sensibility about subjectivity.

In most Buddhist traditions, mindfulness and the calm and concentration to which it gives rise are subjective states that are not ordered by language, concepts, or emotional response (though they are

not necessarily incompatible with these constructions). Subjectivity that has a dimension not rooted in language is virtually ignored or even disdained in feminist and other Western analyses. But from the perspective of most Buddhists, to ignore the mind's multidimensionality is a bit like studying a dancer's moves merely to discern how the limbs are positioned, how much weight they can bear, or how they pertain to ancient patterns of choreography without looking at the internal tension and the material processes of the limbs, ligaments, and blood vessels themselves. Buddhist traditions aim to correct a form of ignorance considered anterior to language, an ignorance said to occur in newborn children, and in animals, as well as in adults.[2] These traditions are also predicated on the conviction that the mind can become entirely still, undistracted by thought. Perhaps only a tradition that considers internal silence possible can feature its objective analogue, the unconditioned, as part of a path to liberation. In talking here about mindfulness, we emphasize the subjective aspect; in chapter 5 we will discuss the special "object" known as the unconditioned emptiness to which a concentrated mind alone has access.

Practices of mindfulness (*smṛti*, *dran pa*) are used to develop new subjective states and to discover hitherto unnoticed aspects of oneself. Classic Buddhist definitions of mindfulness call it a remembering, defined as nonforgetting. In some contexts, this means a remembrance of one's past, such as the Buddha's recollection of past lives on the eve of his enlightenment.[3] Sometimes mindfulness simply suggests a continued focus on what is now present before one's mental or physical senses. This is its primary meaning in meditation practice and the one that occupies us here.[4] The most salient characteristic of such mindfulness is its capacity to maintain clear and stable observation of a chosen object, whether a visualized image or some aspect of one's own body or mind. This clarity (*samprakhyāna*, *gsal ba*) is one of the defining characteristics of mind in Indian and Tibetan Buddhist traditions.[5] Though the notion of clarity is familiar enough in the West, it is not part of dominant Western discourse on mind.

Mindfulness and associated states such as calming or concentration provide a way of describing a person's subjectivity in terms of the mind's own characteristics, not only in terms of its relationship to an object. Thus, the category of mindfulness makes it possible to consider the state of the subject without referring to its contents. For example, the subject can be described as "clear," "stable," or "intense," and one can have these qualities with respect to any thoughts or emotions.[6] Moreover, clarity, stability, and intensity are subjective states that one can either discover or choose to develop.

BUDDHIST TRADITIONS ON MINDFULNESS

Mindfulness as Subjective Style: Theravada and Tibetan Developmental Models

In ancient India, surgeons had to pass a simple test of manual dexterity. Presented with a leaf floating on water and a sharp cutting instrument, they were to sever the leaf without sinking it. Too strong a stroke and the leaf was submerged, too timid an effort and it remained uncut. The balance of the surgeon models the balance required in mindfulness.[7] Balance is also valued in the Tibetan story of a musician named Shrona, who complains to Buddha that he cannot meditate:

> Buddha asked, "When you were a householder, surely you played the lute well?"
>
> Shrona answered, "Yes, indeed."
>
> "Was the sound right when you tightened the strings very strongly, or when you loosened them very thoroughly?"
>
> "Neither. I had to do it with moderation."
>
> "In the same way," Buddha told him, "you have to moderate the tightness and looseness of your mind in order to meditate."[8]

With such balance, new insights, as well as new states of subjectivity, are possible. One's mind becomes, in the words of the renowned contemporary Theravada teacher Ven. Ledi Sayadaw, "that which is firmly established." Being firmly established leads to calm attentiveness, so that one can place attention on the breath, for example, for as long as one wishes, and the mind will remain clear and fixed on its object for that period. Ledi Sayadaw gives this example of the challenge and benefits of mindfulness:

> A mad-man who has no control over his mind . . . does not even know the meal-time and wanders about aimlessly from place to place. . . . After eating five or six morsels of food he overturns the dish and walks away. He thus fails to get a square meal. . . . Persons who are not insane but who are normal and have control over their minds, resemble such a mad person having no control over his mind when it comes to the matter of *śamatha* (calming) and *vipassanā* (insight). . . . These normally sane persons find their attention wandering because they have no control over their minds.[9]

To control one's mind is much emphasized in developmental traditions, not only for the benefits it brings to oneself, but also for the way it protects others from being harmed by one's own carelessness or worse. In this way the cultivation of mindfulness can be said to have a social dimension, as is illustrated by one of the many story-vignettes attributed to Buddha:

> An acrobat climbed his bamboo pole and called to his pupil: "Now, boy, climb the pole and stand on my shoulders." When the pupil had done so the master said, "Now, boy, protect me and I will protect you, by thus looking after each other, we will show our tricks, earn money, and come down safe from the pole." The pupil, however, said, "No, master, that won't do. You protect yourself, and I will protect myself. Thus, self-protected and self-guarded we will show our tricks, earn money, and come down safely from the pole. That is the method."[10]

Buddha, in telling this tale, sides with the student and comments that "protection" is maintained through cultivating mindfulness. Such protection rests on a dexterous balance between inattention and a too forced or overly localized attention. The effects of mindfulness thus go beyond the boundaries of one's own mind and body. At the same time, I might add, mindfulness makes very clear what those boundaries are, both physically and mentally.

In Mahayana Buddhism, mindfulness is above all a practice that brings one into the world. As Geshe Ngawang Dhargyey once observed, "It is no wonder to have it [mindful attention] when you are in peace and quiet; you must have it amid hustle and bustle."[11] The classic instructions on mindfulness, however, were in their original contexts directed primarily at monks, nuns, or others whose lives were devoted to meditation. Only in recent times have these practices been taken up by persons who combine them with numerous professional, business, and family responsibilities.[12] This, along with the increased participation of women, is the most significant change in recent Buddhist history. Women in the West thus are dealing not only with a tradition from another culture, one that was, for much of its history, primarily directed at men, but also with meditation practices and philosophical reflections—especially in the case of Theravada and much of Tibetan Buddhism—that were once the province of those who devoted their entire lives to them.

Re-Membering the Self

The heightened awareness associated with mindfulness allows one to note objects more clearly and to stay focused on them longer, setting in motion a process of discovery that can change the experienced structure of self. The *Foundations of Mindfulness Sutra* is a classic source for mindfulness practice.[13] This text and the meditative traditions associated with it teach mindful observation first of the breath, in order to stabilize attention, then of the body, mind, and their existential attributes such as impermanence or emptiness. Once strong mindfulness is accomplished, it becomes obvious that whether one places attention on breath, body, or mind itself, that object seems to dissolve. For example, my arm usually feels solid and constant. During a Theravada meditation course, it came to feel only like an ongoing flux of mini-sensations with no overarching "arm" at all. This, in Theravada understanding, matches the actual way the arm *is*. The mind, too, can be experienced as a mere flux of thoughts, images, or feelings. In other words, changes in one's own subjective state (more concentrated) affect how mind and body are experienced (less substantial). As Buddhaghosa vividly expresses it, "all formations [e.g., the person's mental and physical constituents] which keep on breaking up, [are] like fragile pottery being smashed, like fine dust being dispersed. . . . Just as a man with eyes standing on the bank of a pond or on the bank of a river during heavy rain would see large bubbles appearing on the surface of the water and breaking up as soon as they appeared, so too he sees how formations break up all the time."[14]

The profound steadiness associated with focused mindfulness is also accompanied by a powerful experience of unalterable flux. With training, one notices the paired arising and ceasing of a physical sensation, and then the fading away of the moment of noticing that cessation. Mind and body are nothing but a great disappearing act.[15] Dismayed at such flux, the mind naturally seeks a peaceful state beyond this, a state made possible in part by its own steady concentration.

Because mindfulness is physically centering, it provides a visceral sense of personal continuity in the midst of clearly observed flux. (This is not to say that a sense of dissolution is not sometimes overwhelming. During ten-day Theravada retreats, I have seen meditators cry out, weep, or—in my own case—tremble violently as a result of the simple practice of mindfully observing the body for as long as fourteen hours a day. The stereotype of meditation having only calming effects is far from accurate.)

The experience of mind and body as only a seething flow of sensations is a dismembering of the self. But there is also a re-membering, a bringing together, in the sense that mind and self are reconstituted for one's experience. Re-membering steadies and integrates. Paradoxically, the more one's mindful concentration develops, and the more grounded one is in present experience and in the steadfast flow of consciousness itself, the clearer one is about the fragile and constructed nature of mind and body. I say "paradoxically," but the tension of paradox is there only in description, not in the experience.

The steadying effect of mindfulness is associated with the "collateral energy" of attention itself. Collateral energy is described by Gregory Bateson as "the energy already available in the respondent, in advance of the impact of events."[16] For example, in kicking a stone, energy is imparted to the stone, and it moves with that energy alone. It has no collateral energy of its own. (Bateson is speaking, of course, about the modern West. In Tibetan and many other traditional cultures, there is nothing that is not somehow alive with its own collateral energy.) On the other hand, continues Bateson, when a dog is kicked, "it responds with energy got from metabolism." I would add that if the dog runs down the street as a result of this encounter and then starts to chase its tail, that chasing (especially as time goes on) has less and less to do with the instigating kick, and more and more to do with the dog's own internal processes. Similarly, as the practice of mindfulness moves away in time and experience from the instructions that initiated it, what meditation reveals has more and more to do with the characteristics of one's own mind. Thus, mindfulness "re-members" the self as it reorients mental geography.

One of Theravada Buddhism's most interesting claims is that the geometry of mind is such that certain groups of wholesome qualities always occur simultaneously.[17] Thus, even a moment of mindfulness brings with it an entire cluster of salubrious attributes: confidence, a lack of desire and hatred, mental balance, mental and physical buoyancy, tranquility, proficiency, and flexibility. These qualities crisscross the mental, physical, psychological, spiritual, and emotional rubrics. Buddhist discussions of awareness are more properly theories of perception than of the psyche.[18] Neither Theravada nor Tibetan texts discuss mindfulness in contemporary psychological terms—that is, taking account of a person's particular emotional life shaped, for example, through family upbringing or social positioning. The mind's collateral qualities do not depend on external stimuli. For example, "pleasurable interest," one of the more interesting qualities associated with mindfulness, is a sense of joy or delight in what one is doing, even if it is as simple an act as observing one's breath. Obviously, this joy does not derive from any entertainment value associated with the object; it arises simply because of the mind's own stable flow of attention.[19] Such pleasurable interest can also make simple activities like knitting, raking leaves, or polishing wood satisfying and engrossing. Being in the present is always interesting.

Mindfulness facilitates a centeredness and internal coherence akin to "essentialist" forms of strength and at the same time is compatible with constructionist or postmodern sensibilities because of its intense awareness of the flow that constitutes mind and body, including itself. In this way, mindfulness and its associated states can ameliorate the tension between essentialist and postmodern perspectives in feminist contexts. Some feminists make a case for referring to "woman" as an essentialized category when this is useful for political purposes, even though they recognize this term as a fiction. In contrast to such strategic essentialism, Buddhist theories and practices envision a subject for whom groundedness *and* a sense of the constructed nature of self can be simultaneous, so that there is never a necessity to "choose" strategically between them. There is place and possibility for both.

Stabilizing Meditation

Theravada practice is unique for the kinesthetic experience of impermanence it facilitates. However, virtually all schools of Buddhism emphasize the understanding of impermanence and, in particular, of its most dramatic instance, which is death. Here, too, the capacity for focused concentration plays an important role. For example, the Tibetan tradition teaches a conceptual reflection on death and impermanence.[20] In this style of meditation, one considers three basic facts about death: it is definite, its time of coming is indefinite, and when it does come neither friends nor fortune but only spiritual development will help. In what is known as analytical meditation, one mentally embroiders these three themes, thinking, for example, "I don't know when death will come; what will truly be meaningful to me at that moment?" Analytical meditation ceases when it really comes home that "Yes, oh, *yes*, it's not just something they talk about; I am definitely going to die and I have no idea when." One experiences, perhaps for the first time, a visceral sense of one's own mortality. This vivid internalization, no longer encrusted with words, begins and is sustained in the stabilizing phase of meditation. Here the capacity for mindful concentration is key. It makes possible a fluid movement between conceptual and nonconceptual experience, thereby undermining Western polarizations of body and mind that have denigrated women and all subjective states not dominated by "reason."

Stabilizing meditation has been defined as "meditation in which the mind remains unwaveringly on its object."[21] The more concentration develops, the less conceptual thought impinges on or affects the mind—which is not to say that thought ceases, but that it ceases to tug the mind in its direction as is common in, say, daydreaming or brainstorming.[22] The same type of alternation between analytical and stabilizing meditation is used by Geluks for the cultivation of compassion and wisdom. Whereas Western scholars have given considerable attention to the theoretical and ritual aspects of Buddhist traditions, there has been little concern with how nonconceptual categories such as mindfulness and concentration shape or presuppose Buddhist views of mind and self.[23] In some practices, mindfulness becomes a crucial catalyst for dissolving the distance between subject and object, or between mind and body.[24]

Mind and Body

In Theravada practice, the usual sense of physical solidity may shift to a palpable experience of physical lightness, the usual sense of mental continuity to an experience of the sequential emergence and disappearance of individual thoughts and mental states. In Mahayana descriptions, too, a state of considerable concentration known as calm abiding is associated with intensity, clarity, stability, and with physical experiences such as a lightness of body and a special pliancy of mind and body.[25] In all these traditions, mindfulness creates visceral coherence in the face of change through its groundedness in the body and its collateral qualities of mind. Visceral coherence, grounded partly in sensory experience, is quite different from the narrative coherence, constructed through stories, that postmodern feminists despair of achieving. A person's narrative is never complete, since it can always be expanded, and it is rarely, if ever, entirely coherent, since it inevitably includes conflicting plot lines and perspectives. Visceral coherence, grounded in mind *cum* body, is not beholden to a story line.

Whatever claims Buddhist traditions make about the mind, and no matter how rarified its concentration, the human mind is explicitly located in a body and affected by it. At the same time, unlike the localized mind of recent Western understanding, this mind is not lim-

ited to the flesh and blood of the body.[26] For example, the subtle consciousness that departs the body at death is described as riding on a
very subtle physical form, known as *rlung* (pronounced to rhyme with
"Jung") in Tibetan, *prāṇa* in Sanskrit, and *ch'i* in Chinese and variously translated as wind, air, subtle breath, or energy. The point is,
consciousness is always associated with a kind of physicality, though
it is not necessarily bound by the body's coarse physical form.[27] These
connections between mind and body are also important reminders
that meditation is not a disembodied process or an escape from physical reality.

   Mindfulness reveals mind and body to be in constant communication, each shaping and responding to the other. As Buddhaghosa
picturesquely describes the situation: "The drum and the sound are
not mixed up together, the drum is void of the sound and the sound is
void of the drum, so too, when mentality occurs having as its support
the materiality . . . the mentality and materiality are not mixed up together, the mentality is void of the materiality and the materiality is
void of the mentality; yet the mentality occurs due to the materiality
as the sound occurs due to the drum."[28] Specific physical sensations
are associated with subtle alterations in subjective experience, especially in deep concentration. The more esoteric traditions also teach
a variety of physical postures to enhance particular meditation
practices.

   Because of this communication between mind and body, and because their collateral qualities are physical as well as mental, the categories of mindfulness, calming, and concentration are states that re-
sist Western mind-body dualisms. Anger, for example, is associated
with a subtle physical sensation of heat, and focusing either on the
physical or emotional aspect of anger causes both to dissipate. A variety of sensations indicate other kinds of feelings; it is also possible to
recognize kinesthetically the presence of a new idea, even before one
knows exactly what it is. (This book began as such a kinesthetic feel-

ing.) Physical and mental processes are not two halves of a whole, but two avenues of access into the fully integrated complex in which they participate. Nor are they themselves entirely distinct; rather, mind and body are a kind of Möbius strip, for if you follow either far enough, it brings you to the other. From a feminist perspective, these connections are significant. If mind and body are directly experienced as interactive, then there is no basis for framing an opposition that allies men with reason and mind and women with bodily experience. Even more to the point, there is no basis for devaluing body/emotion/female and valorizing mind/reason/male. A hierarchical construction of these connections can give way to reciprocity.

A Discovery Model of Mindfulness:
The Great Completeness (rDzogs-chen)

The Great Completeness tradition speaks of an innate awareness (vidyā, rig pa) considered the mind's natural condition (sems gyi chos nyid). Innate awareness is in this sense the ultimate collateral energy of mind and body.[29] It participates in but is different from the workings of the conceptual mind, and the meditator's discovery of it is central to Great Completeness practice. Unlike either the mindfulness or concentration discussed above, innate awareness is always a nondualistic state, and one that can only be discovered, not developed.[30] For this reason the Great Completeness traditions distinguish carefully between the more effortful, developmental forms of mindfulness and the mindfulness that occurs when one relaxes into one's already present innate awareness.[31] Ma-ji-lap-drön (Ma-cig-lab-sgron), one of the most widely known female lamas in Tibet, concisely states the point:

> First tighten with tightness,
> Then loosen with looseness.
> The essence of the view is here.[32]

Khetsun Sangpo Rinboche, a lama in the Nyingma Great Completeness tradition, describes the initial tightening this way: "Beginners
like ourselves need [such mindfulness] when we are sleeping, walking, standing, eating and so forth. . . . Until one reaches the point of
never forgetting [one's object of attention,] thought is bound by a
stringent mindfulness. . . . Through this type of mindfulness becoming steady, the mind is kept tight. Then, let the mind relax."[33]

To accomplish the discovery of innate awareness, one must learn
well what to loosen and how to loosen it. Some forms of looseness and
relaxation are centering; others are merely fragmenting or passive.
When, as the Great Completeness traditions advise, relaxation is
such that thoughts continue to circulate without disturbing innate
awareness, a strong sense of physical ease emerges as another form of
collateral coherence occurs. The innate awareness itself remains un-
wavering (*ma yengs byed mkhan*), and there is a natural settling of the
mind described as a "mindfulness of actuality" (*dharmatā-smṛti,
chos nyid kyi dran pa*). As with other forms of mindfulness, one's
breath is calmed, and there may be strong, even sensual, experiences
of physical comfort throughout the body. Innate awareness is literally
a "knowing" said to free the mind from its sense that subject and object are separate. This innate awareness is a kind of "essence," insofar as its qualities are not alterable by either external or internal conditions. Whether one recognizes it or not, whether one is enlightened
or not, it is the same. This is an important principle in discovery
orientations:

> Buddha is neither found in meditation
>
> Nor lost without meditation:
>
> Continuously remain in non-distraction.[34]

For the Great Completeness traditions, this suggests an expanse of
mind that is beyond ordinary causes and conditions.[35] A variety of
meditation practices, including visualization, chanting, and silent

sitting, are taught as a means to facilitate (or develop the capacity for) discovering this aspect of mind. Mindfulness is crucial at every stage. A teacher works with a student to identify an initial form of this experience, so that she can later recognize it herself. To experience innate awareness is also to know what some Great Completeness traditions refer to as the "single sphere" (*thig le nyag gcig*), a recognition that mind is expansive beyond measure. Iconographically, the single sphere is the dwelling place of the Great Bliss Queen, and the Great Completeness ritual associated with her is a way to recognize and enter this sphere. There is great freedom in this recognition, and in coming to understand that the mind need not be conceived as a container that gets filled up, but can be experienced as an open possibility where something more may always take place.

What is the relationship between the mindfulness discussed earlier, which takes some effort, and the innate awareness of the Great Completeness, which one discovers by relaxing into it? Once having experienced innate awareness there is, strictly speaking, no need to depend on effortful mindfulness. Yet even exemplary teachers in the Great Completeness tradition continue to practice the more stringent style of meditation. In a poem written in 1991 during a serious illness, with a lifetime of experience and a considerable reputation as a master in the Great Completeness tradition, the Nyingma lama Khetsun Sangpo exhorts himself in this way:

> Not forgetting mindfulness and introspection in any kind of activity
> Always make effort regarding what should be done and not done.
> Khetsun, when you sleep, sleep within awareness and introspection,
>   do not leave them behind . . .
> The great Bodhisattva Shantideva also
> Again and again praised the guarding of mindfulness and
>   introspection . . .
> It is also praised in [Nagarjuna's] *Letter to a Friend*[36]
> Saying that when mindfulness deteriorates, all practice is

destroyed . . .

Also Pa-trul Chö-kyi-wang-bo said

Mindfulness and introspection sustain the paths of sutra and
mantra.

The word of Guru Pema and the words of [his root] lamas[37]

All mandate its implementation again and again.[38]

Here Khetsun Sangpo Rinboche recalls two of the greatest Indian
teachers of the developmental path as it became known in Tibet (Nagarjuna and Shantideva) and links them with two major figures of the
Great Completeness tradition (the Nyingma master Pa-trul Rinboche and Padmasambhava, teacher and consort of the Great Bliss
Queen).

The innate awareness of the Great Completeness also brings
about a variety of collateral qualities, including those already mentioned in connection with other Buddhist traditions. Still, it is my experience that Theravada and sutra Mahayana Great Completeness
techniques produce different, though often compatible, insights or
sensations. (Whether they ultimately culminate in similar forms of
"enlightenment" is beyond my experience and the frame of this
conversation.)

All the mindfulness practices discussed here are similar, however, in their ability to combine an experience of centering with a keen
awareness of change. In Theravada, a steady mindfulness of the body
reveals its constructed and fluctuating nature. In sutra Mahayana,
mindfulness remains watchful amid the various activities it observes.
In the Great Completeness, numerous functions of the mind can
continue without fragmenting innate awareness. In all cases, its capacity to be both still and responsive to change suggests that mindfulness can bridge the gap between constructionist and essentialist
orientations.

"Experience," though problematic as a category, remains a cen-
terpiece of feminist reflection.[39] Essentialist feminists give special at-

tention to the physical difference of being a woman, and many find women's "essence" in that bodily experience. For postmodern feminists, experience is formed through a complex and gendered interaction of one's own senses and sensibilities with the historical, political, and social context in which one is situated. A woman, therefore, is defined not by any essential attribute but by her particular position in historical time and political reality.[40]

Narratives created from social, historical, and other such particular data are rarely coherent. Many modern lives encompass culturally hyphenated identities, multiple roles and complex positionings. These do not make for a cohesive, unified story. A coherence that is not necessarily a narrative coherence, that does not depend altogether on words and concepts, is a possibility claimed by feminist essentialisms, yet as we have seen, it often comes at the expense of particularity. Mary Daly, for example, suggests that all women, whether they know it or not, possess a "radiant sunrise," which they can come to know through a "burning away of false selves."[41] Postmodern feminist understandings emphasize particularity, but that emphasis often precludes an experience of coherence. It need not. The centering associated with mindfulness develops from the ability to retain a focus on flux and particularity. It is not, as in narrative coherence, sustained by a thematization of diverse elements that sustains such coherence, but rather by the collateral coherence of a focused mind. With mindfulness, one cultivates or discovers new ways—not just new data—of understanding and experiencing oneself. Of what significance might this be for modern-day Western feminists?

MINDFULNESS AND WESTERN WOMEN

I have suggested that Buddhist discussions of mindfulness characterize mind as other than just its contents and as capable of maintaining a continued attentiveness amid an awareness of flux. Mindfulness also brings a number of wholesome mental and physical functions into play, all of which are important for how they are, rather than for what they know. Most significant, mindfulness is a subjective dimension possessed of a collateral coherence rather than a narrative or cognitive coherence. All these qualities are relevant to the following considerations.

The Idolatry of Ideals

Both feminists and Buddhists seek to improve their lot, whether in terms of self-understanding or practical or political changes. This desire often gives a certain utopian, even idealistic, tinge to their reflection. Idealism has its place, yet if it gets out of balance, one all too easily finds oneself living in an abstract future, dreaming of an idealized self that is yet to be. Idealism is problematic from a Buddhist perspective when it pulls one out of the present. It is problematic from a feminist perspective when it overlooks women's genuine needs and circumstances, demeans her present self, or exacerbates any tendency toward self-hatred. Ideals beckon and inspire, which is precisely why someone lacking a strong sense of self may be engulfed by them. Ideals are thus an excellent way of controlling those who can be persuaded they should live up to them. In this way ideals can alienate one from one's feelings, if those feelings do not measure up to the ideal with which one prefers to identify.[42] But personal change cannot occur in an emotional vacuum.

The paradigm of struggle against self is well known in religious and secular practice.[43] For women the struggle for self-knowledge is all the more difficult in a male-centered world that is more than willing to tell her who she is or should be. The less sense a woman has of her own wishes, the easier it is for society to drive home its culturally expedient message. This is problematic in at least four ways: an unbalanced enthusiasm for ideals can hinder self-knowledge, demean the self, provide a means for manipulation, and foster an oppositional or divided sense of self. This is true whether the ideal in question is a male-centered "normalcy" or a feminist agenda. Moreover, a struggle toward ideals is, as Judith Plaskow observes, a practice for those with a certain kind of strength.[44] The idealist struggle virtually requires an oppositional style of identity. Mindful awareness, on the other hand, simply sees, accepts, and is present, even as one is aware of alternative possibilities due to the infinity of interconnected events and constitutive elements comprising any given moment.

I once overheard a conversation between two American Buddhist practitioners. An excited newcomer asked a more seasoned student, "How has meditation changed you?" She appeared to expect a triumphal story of vanquishing unwanted personality traits by embracing a more ideal style of personhood. Responding not at all to her air of anticipation, the other student said with mild surprise, "Change? I don't want to change. I just want to *be* there."

Wanting to "be there" counters the impulse to be somewhere else. Ideas about how one should or would like to be can encourage one to hide from oneself and to overlook qualities or feelings that, however deeply felt, do not match one's ideal. And as Susan Griffin observes, "The very act of hiding *proves* to the self that what is hidden is terrible."[45] Engagement with ideals can distract us from self-understanding, directing attention to what is wished for rather than what is. Being present is the antithesis of being overwhelmed by ideals of what one should become.

Letting go of ideals is both a cause and an effect of mindfulness. To the extent that one can be in touch with oneself and one's surroundings, one is grounded in the present, not lost in the mists of the future. The Vietnamese Zen master and poet Thich Nhat Hanh suggests how mindfulness enhances even an activity like driving, whose most obvious purpose seems to be getting somewhere else rather than being here where one is.

> As you drive, you want to *arrive*. This is why you sacrifice the [act of] driving. You believe that at the point of arrival, things will be better. But that is not true. . . . Therefore, every moment we drive, we have

to live in that moment and *not think* of arrival. Next time when you
are caught in a traffic jam, you will know what to do. You don't fight.
If you fight, you destroy life in the present moment. Sit back and
breathe mindfully. When you encounter a red light, you look at it,
and you smile at it. Before it was your enemy; it prevented you from
arriving. But now it has become a *bodhisattva*, helping you to go
back to the present moment. . . . An irritating moment becomes
a pleasant moment. And the red light becomes a bell of
mindfulness.[46]

Self-knowledge, like driving, can be much hampered by the overwhelming presence of a goal to be reached. Mindfulness suggests a
way of cultivating the self that does not operate via oppressive ideals.
There seems also to be an association between self-care and mindfulness: "If you hold yourself dear, watch yourself well," says the
Dhammapāda.[47]

A number of women have written about the importance of mindful clarity, and I believe it is a quality that has special significance for
women. In a landmark article, Valerie Saiving persuasively suggested
that distractibility and diffuseness, the lack of an organizing center or
focus, is often seen in women, largely because women are socialized
to pay attention to others' activities, and to be responsible for multiple
tasks simultaneously. Likewise, the wandering that Mary Daly
chronicles requires immense awareness and self-knowledge.[48] Doris
Lessing, herself influenced by Sufi meditative traditions, makes
awareness the starting point of Martha Quest's spiritual odyssey in
The Four-Gated City. Martha learns how to make herself "alive and
light and aware"; she knows the advantages, walking in the London
rain, of having "her head cool, watchful, alert." She knows, too, the
sense of "a quiet, empty space, behind which stood an observing
presence."[49]

Mindfulness is self-empowering, a way for women and men to relate to themselves and others that neither opposes, judges, nor tries to

change what it observes. Mindfulness fosters a clear observing awareness that permits self-knowledge without the crippling presence of an ideal against which one inevitably falls short. A contemporary Theravada commentator describes mindfulness as "an impartial watchfulness [that] does not take sides."[50] The *Foundations of Mindfulness Sutra* describes the activity of mindfulness this way: "When anger is present, one knows: 'Anger is in me,' or when anger is not present, one knows: 'There is no anger in me.' "[51] What mindfulness does *not* do is go on to make the judgment "I am wrong to have this anger."

Mindfulness departs from the urge to master, override, rein in, or otherwise manipulate the self. It avoids treating the self as a territory to be conquered, governed, or colonized by ideals. Insofar as the relationship to oneself sets the tone for one's relationship to others, it is crucial to have models of self-engagement that do not denigrate or otherwise oppress. A mindful person is attentive, interactive, and nonoppositional. She is also autonomous in that she need not depend on some external goal to galvanize her mindful collateral energies. Yet no matter how salubriously engaged, mindfulness has its limits. It, too, can become an impossible ideal; it can be misapplied or too stringently interpreted. Mindfulness will not necessarily clarify new directions of endeavor or strategize needed political and economic reform. In addition, too much fascination with internal situations can drain energies from other important activities.[52] It is a matter of balance, and balance is an art.

The relationship between mindfulness and idealism is an important part of the significance mindfulness has for contemporary feminist contexts. Buddhists do not explicitly pose mindfulness as an alternative to idealism. But being nonjudgmental toward oneself has special significance for women in a culture where self-hatred is an issue, as it apparently was not in Tibet. Indeed, in a recent discussion among therapists and the Dalai Lama, it was very difficult to get across to this highly sensitive and much acculturated teacher the meaning of "self-hatred." The idea was virtually incomprehensible to him. But self-hatred, and related matters of esteem, doubt, and the difficulty of self-care are often problems for Western women.[53]

A person who is mindful is present, accepting, focused, and clear. This is a state in which all the self's various voices can be heard. To be mindful thus is to acknowledge and accept plurality without being disrupted by it.[54] When mindfulness is a meaningful category, therefore, the subject cannot be reduced to a "site of competing discourses," as it often is in feminist and other postmodern descriptions.

Protected from disruption by plurality, and capable of accepting what she finds, a mindful person also undermines the ideology of bigotry, which itself is a rampant urge for sameness fueled largely by an unwillingness to accept the unacceptable in oneself.[55] Difference itself is not conflict; it takes an ideology of sameness to configure it that way. Further, being aware (but not critical) of weakness, defect, or confusion in oneself or others relieves the strain caused by trying to fight it or pretend it is not there. Similar to what psychologists call "owning one's feelings," such a move empowers the conscious self. Growth takes place, not without effort, but without the kind of fight that can divorce the self from its own source of strength. When all the voices of self are fully owned, they are less likely to be projected onto others. In this way, self-acceptance translates into acceptance of the other.

Mindfulness is helpful in other ways as well. It reduces dependence on others' attention, partly because one is so alive within oneself, and partly because "keeping up" with the present moment means there is less energy available for getting stuck in one's own or others' idealized projections. A state of focused mindfulness is thus the opposite of what has popularly been called "co-dependence," which above all is characterized by the attempt to live in the minds of others. (Hence the cruel but revealing quip: When death approaches the co-dependent sees someone else's life flash before her eyes.)

In all these ways, mindfulness simultaneously demonstrates the self's constructedness and its identity. This is not just a theoretical issue, but perhaps the fundamental existential oxymoron: All my life I am changing (getting older, dying) and at the same time remaining the same (retaining a sense of identity). Because mindfulness allows one to become centered in one's changing self, it is both a physical and mental grounding, and this grounding is the beginning of constructive personal strength. In short, mindfulness offers a model of individual power that can also support deep communication with oneself and with others.

Mindfulness and Silence

How can we situate the language of this text with respect to the silence that is its origin and end?

Barbara Johnson, *The Critical Difference*

In some forms of mindfulness thoughts are stilled; in others they are not. But the explicit function of mindfulness, I want to emphasize again, is not to alter, access, or restructure the contents of the mind, but to change the *tone* of consciousness by manifesting collateral qualities not based on thought or language. In many forms of meditation, as much attention is paid to one's state of mind—distracted, lethargic, peaceful, clear, intense—as to its contents. Attention is also given to other aspects of existence, such as impermanence. Therefore, mindfulness is a category of subjectivity somewhat apart from what is commonly discussed in Western psychology, epistemology, cognitive capacity, or literary theory.

In its function as a witness, mindfulness is a silent observer of voices, saying nothing, but potent and effective in other ways. In this it resembles the "evenly hovering attention" of a psychoanalyst.[56] The silence of mindfulness is, of course, a subjective state. It is not the textually inscribed silence to which Barbara Johnson refers, nor that of Jacques Derrida, nor even the disembodied and wholly disengaged muteness sometimes attributed to mystics, though it may share some qualities with all these silences.[57] The silence of mindfulness comes from a capacity of mind, not a failure of speech. This capacity, moreover, can be intentionally, deliberately, cultivated. The point is not that the mindful subject *is* silent—incapable of expressing herself— but that she deliberately *has* silence as a possibility. This potential for silence must be strongly distinguished from the hegemonically hushed voices of the Orientalized Asian or of women and minorities. It is neither an inability to speak, nor an avoidance of speech, nor even an inexpressibility of the subject matter.[58] Nor is it a silence of the senses; indeed, it is the sensory realm keenly observed. It is the ability to not speak, a chosen state with its own purpose. Buddhist traditions carefully mark out specific and describable silent states that have both depth and breadth. There are moreover concrete, replicable techniques for experiencing such states. For example: "Focus your mind on the breath, count each inhalation and exhalation as 'one' and proceed up to twenty-one, and then repeat. If you become distracted, simply resume where you left off, or, if you cannot remember, place your mind on the breath and begin again with one." Or a more subtle technique in Theravada: "Pay attention to the movement of air over your top lip as you inhale and exhale." In the Great Completeness, one might discover some aspect of awareness through uttering a sudden sharp sound, or through deep chanting, or by directing the gaze in a certain way.[59] These representative techniques assume that what will be gained is not an "idea" but a different experience of subjectivity, of mind itself. If Western feminism is to help women expand not just the variety but the style of subjective experience, such exercises may be extremely helpful.

Unlike Derrida, Buddhists do not ask "how to avoid speaking," though they do reflect on the different meanings silence can have when it is one person's response to another. When the Bodhisattva householder Vimalakirti rebuked Shariputra for his limited understanding of meditation, Shariputra, by his own subsequent account, "was unable to reply and remained silent." This failure to respond is not the silence we discuss here. Nor is it the thunderous silence of Vimalakirti, who, like the Buddha, was deemed to express the inexpressible when he chose not to respond to naive questions put to him.[60] The silence of mindfulness is not a means of communication, not another form of speech, but a deep listening.

Being There: Presence with a Difference

Postmodernist narratives about subjectivity are inadequate.

Jane Flax, *Thinking Fragments*

According to Jacques Derrida, whose work is often appropriated by postmodern feminists, "mind" refers primarily to constructs produced through their difference from other constructs. From a Buddhist perspective, this is an excellent description of thought, but a strangely disembodied notion of mind, precisely because there is no category that takes account of the *state* of the subject, apart from the constructs that are its contents. Derrida's argument, and that of many feminist postmodernists, concerns a consciousness occupied primarily by words, though words can never be fully complete and present in themselves.

In feminist postmodern literature, as in postmodernist thought in general, little or no attention is paid to the multidimensionality of the subject, its depths of calm, or its potential distance from conceptual activity. This picture of consciousness is inappropriately flat, and its flatness is a crucial factor in making the postmodern self seem too "thin" or insubstantial to be a basis for feminist agendas. On the other hand, if subjectivity is not seen as limited to conceptual functioning, another source of personal power opens, an additional arena from which to connect with the world. In this way, mindfulness eases the sense of being caught "inside" oneself, of being isolated from the wider world. Its subjective space is not confined inside the body, because to go deep enough "inside" is also sometimes to touch a point that connects with a vast neither-external-nor-internal-world.

The cultivation of mindfulness or concentration depends primarily on the force of stability and attentiveness, rather than on the amount of information it gathers. Who would deny the significance of knowledge? Neither Buddhists nor feminists, certainly, but Buddhists do not define a human subject only by what she knows. Moreover, the Great Completeness discussion of innate awareness suggests that no matter how much information—thoughts, feelings—it does access, the mind can never be fully characterized or dominated by these. There is always room for something else. The fact that ordinary objects of the senses can never be fully known is something on which most Buddhist and postmodern theories agree. Buddhists, like postmodernists, reject naive theories of representation or "pipeline" models of meaning wherein a word or thought is considered to express or convey "fully" what it names or describes.[61] However, this inability of the conceptual mind to know an object fully carries different weight in postmodern theory than in Buddhist traditions. Buddhists will understand the mind as fully present to its object, regardless of whether or not that object is fully "known."[62] Postmodernists do not accept presence because no matter how broadly the boundaries of a person or object are drawn, there is always something included and something excluded. For feminists like Hélène Cixous, such uncircumscribability is even a cause for celebration of woman's "endless body, without 'end,' without principal 'parts.' "[63] Descriptions can always be further supplemented; they are never complete.[64] Buddhists and postmodernists would agree that in this sense being fully present to an object is impossible. But the point for Buddhist traditions is that there is power and a meaningful kind of completeness in being fully attentive and in that sense present. The ocean of one's focused attention remains a coherent dimension amid all its waves of deferred differences.

For Buddhists, silence and the categories of mind most closely associated with it—mindfulness, calm, and concentration—allow the subject a sense of proceeding beyond the play of voices (without necessarily hushing them) into a different dimension of subjectivity. What is important about Buddhist descriptions of subjectivity in connection with mindfulness and meditation is the possibility of a subjectivity not wholly governed by words, and therefore not susceptible to the kind of fracturing associated with feminist postmodern or constructionist perspectives. Buddhist understandings depict a self that is strong, not limited or overgeneralized by essentialist or other concepts, and a type of coherence not marred by recognition of the self's constructed nature. It offers the subject a sense of her mind as an extensive, even inexhaustible, resource of strength and fresh perspectives. This subjectivity is of particular interest to women, because women are today explicitly concerned with finding modes of expression and reflection that are as free as possible from the internalized cultural restraints on women's being.

The issues of presence and the problem of ideals thus converge. Both are predicated on mastery; both are philosophically problematic. To adopt any overly simple relation to an ideal, or to think that any ideal can become fully present, is to assume a unitariness incompatible with feminist and Buddhist orientations alike. It is also to suggest that the ideals in question are already fully conceived when they are not. In contrast to many Buddhist traditions, feminists explicitly understand their goals to be very much in progress.

While it can be a refuge, the interior dimension to which mindfulness gives access can also become a distraction. It is important to be clear that mindfulness, or any meditative practice, may bring to awareness issues that should be dealt with on their own terms. Meditation is not therapy, though it can be therapeutic. It opens a dimension of mind and self that psychology, individualistic enterprises, and intellectually oriented culture often omit, but in the modern West it cannot be a substitute for real psychological work.

I would emphasize, too, that there is nothing intrinsically "Buddhist" about mindfulness. Many women and men who are neither Buddhist nor meditators have this quality, though they do not always have words for it or a method to strengthen it. I have used Buddhist sources to call attention to a function of the mind that often goes without name or recognition in contemporary Western culture, and that has as many possible uses, contexts, and strengths as mind itself.

Several feminist writers describe uncommon forms of self-experience or new ontologies of selfhood, but offer very little clarity about how such experience is accessed. I am thinking, for example, of Daly's call to "the Original lustrous radiant sunrise of our be-ing"; or Irigaray's admonition, "She is neither one nor two. She cannot, strictly speaking, be determined either as one person or as two"; or Cixous and Clément's proclamation, "She surprises herself at seeing, being, pleasuring in her gift of changeability."[65] Evocative yet vague, these descriptions are in danger of becoming impossible ideals, new versions of the "angel in the house" criticized by Virginia Woolf.[66] We need an expanded vocabulary capable of describing subjective states congruent with feminism's theoretical insights, as well as methods for cultivating those states we find desirable.

Traditional Buddhists find mindfulness central to their sense of the examined life, and they would agree with Plato that the unexamined life is not worth living—or rather, that it causes one to go on living, life after life, endlessly and unsatisfactorily. At least one Tibetan teacher defines mindfulness to include awareness of what practices are suitable for oneself under what circumstances.[67] Postmodernists in general and feminist postmodernists in particular have opened up an enormous intellectual space through which to reconsider the relationship of self and knowledge. Feminists have integrated gender concerns into this space as well. But a subjective experience that moves from textuality to a different style of subjectivity altogether is not available in postmodern thought as currently constituted. The possibility of a subjectivity not anchored in either language or oppositionality suggests how the strength and agency associated with essentialist perspectives can be integrated with a full acknowledgment of the complexity of a woman's identity in the contemporary climate. Identity need be no less powerful though it changes with context, as do relationships with others, including relationships with one's own or other traditions. Mindfulness, too, is not the same for everyone, and not always the same for oneself. One can proceed well only by noticing the differences produced through the processes of reflection or meditation.

On a similar note, Roland Barthes observes that the internal difference of a text only emerges through rereading.[68] This alone saves the text from repetition, for those who fail to reread are obliged to read the same story everywhere. For Buddhists, one who fails to reconsider assumptions about mind is doomed to remain "the same" in ignorance. For feminists, a failure to reread Western assumptions about gender and subjectivity is to remain limited in familiar ways. For Western practitioners of Buddhism, a failure to reread Buddhist traditions is to be confined to what seems to be the "same" Buddhism, but that actually fits neither contemporary needs nor the supposed patterns of the past. Such rereadings will call on all our resources of intellect, awareness, emotion, intuition, self-respect, humor, and plain goodwill. These are all qualities that can enhance one's connection with various dimensions of oneself, and, therefore, with others.

CHAPTER 4

Gain or Drain? Compassion and the Self-Other Boundary

> For as long as space endures
> And for as long as living beings remain,
> Until then may I too abide
> To dispel the misery of the world.
> Shantideva, *Guide to the
> Bodhisattva's Way of Life*

The expression of compassion or resistance to it crystallizes many of the issues we have discussed so far. Is it possible to have a compassionate connection to others and still retain a powerful sense of self? In the West, women have long been thought of as more naturally, or essentially, compassionate than men, a claim many feminists reject. In Buddhist traditions, compassion is something to be cultivated by both women and men. Moreover, in Tibetan Buddhist traditions, compassion is often understood as male, and a sense of relatedness is considered magnificently self-empowering. Why should this be? Is it just a sentimental notion? Is it simply an exercise by which monks— among the most numerous practitioners of these techniques for developing compassion—justify their privileged vocation?

The first part of this chapter describes a Buddhist method for cultivating compassion; the second considers assumptions embedded in this method from a feminist perspective, looking especially at the kinds of boundaries it suggests or erases between self and other, as well as between autonomy and independence, and reason and emotion. In examining these boundaries, we also will examine Western cultural assumptions that combine to denigrate women, compassion, and relationships. We need to understand as precisely as possible which personal and cultural circumstances help to make compassion and relatedness empowering and which do not.

ENLIGHTENED COMPASSION: PREPARATION AND SEVEN STEPS

One of the most prominent techniques for developing compassionate connectedness in Indian and Tibetan Mahayana Buddhism is a meditative practice known literally as "the seven precepts of cause and effect" (*rgyu 'bras man ngag bdun*), so named because each step is considered to give rise naturally to the next one. After the preparatory cultivation of equanimity, the seven steps are (1) recognition of all others as mother; (2) mindfulness of their kindness; (3) wishing to repay their kindness; (4) cultivating love, here specifically a wish for the happiness of others; (5) cultivating compasion, here specifically a wish that others be relieved of suffering; (6) combining love and compassion in the "unusual thought" to take responsibility for others' happiness and the alleviation of their pain; and (7) the compassionately loving aspiration to enlightenment (*bodhicitta*).

The Seven Unfoldings is still in wide usage among Tibetan Buddhists. It is an especially important practice in the Geluk order, which regards it as having originated with the Buddha, passing from him to the Bodhisattva Maitreya (whose name, from the Sanskrit *maitrī*, means love or friendliness). Maitreya is believed to have taught it to Asanga, and so it continued from teacher to disciple until the practice was brought to Tibet by Atisha in the eleventh century. The Seven Unfoldings practice also draws inspiration and a conceptual basis from Candrakirti, a major seventh-century Indian commentator on Nagarjuna.[1]

Also important in Geluk and other traditions within Tibet is Shantideva's fourfold cultivation of the compassionately loving intention to enlightenment. This method is also said to have been brought to Tibet from India by Atisha in the eleventh century, and to have originated with the Buddha's instructions to Manjushri, the Bodhisattva of wisdom, who passed them on to Nagarjuna. The four steps are (1) the equalization of self and other, (2) seeing the faults of self-cherishing, (3) seeing the benefits of cherishing others, and (4) exchanging one's intense concern for oneself and relative indifference to others for an intense concern for others and relative indifference to oneself.

Among Geluks, these two techniques are often combined in a practice known as the Eleven Rounds of Tsong-kha-pa.[2] In the chart below, the numbers on the left indicate the steps of the Seven Unfoldings, and the numbers on the right indicate how those steps are combined with Shantideva's practice in the Eleven Rounds.

Preparation: Equanimity	1
1. Recognition of all others as mother	2
2. Mindfulness of their kindness	3
3. Wish to repay their kindness	4
[Making self and other equal—Shantideva]	5
[Seeing the faults of self-cherishing—Shantideva]	6
[Seeing the benefits of cherishing others—Shantideva]	7
4. Cultivating love [exchange of self and other—Shantideva]	8
5. Cultivating compassion [taking on others' suffering—Shantideva]	9
6. Combining love and compassion: the unusual thought	10
7. Compassionately loving aspiration to enlightenment (*bodhicitta*)	11

The Seven Unfoldings must be preceded by the cultivation of equanimity (*upekṣā, btang snyoms*), here specifically understood as an evenmindedness with respect to friends, enemies, and neutral persons. The initial three steps after equanimity have the dual purpose of cultivating a sense that one is close with all living beings and that they are likable. The next two meditations, steps 4 and 5, involve the cultivation of love, the wish for others to have happiness and its causes, and cultivation of compassion, the wish for others to be free of suffering and its causes.

At the sixth step, these meditations culminate in a powerful determination to bring about happiness and alleviate pain. A practitioner with faith that this is possible simply goes on to the seventh and final step, the aspiration to accomplish the enlightenment that will empower her to help others limitlessly. If the practitioner is more responsive to reasoning than faith, she must first reflect that because her mind is unrestricted by inherent limitations, no achievements are precluded. To understand the mind this way means to understand its emptiness, its lack of being fixed in its present limitations. Once this empty aspect of the mind has been experienced, one can wholeheartedly make a commitment to achieve enlightenment in order to help others. This commitment is called the "mind of enlightenment," an aspiration classically characterized as "having the nature of emptiness and compassion."[3] At the culmination of the seventh step, the practitioner vows to seek enlightenment for the sake of all and becomes a Bodhisattva. Even with the great Buddhist emphasis on flux, conditionality, and essencelessness, a practitioner is considered able to maintain this vow over many years, even lifetimes. Even though there is no substantial, much less permanent, identity, it is possible for a stable mind to reproduce attitudes like compassionate connection consistently. Thus, from a Buddhist point of view, intentionality and purpose do not fall by the wayside of a "constructed" perspective, as some feminists fear it might do. Let us now consider more closely the substance of these reflections and their points of intersection with our concerns.

Equanimity: Relationality and Autonomy

The cultivation of equanimity is a preparation for the love and compassion to follow. It is meant to ensure that such love and compassion will be unbiased and radiate equally to all. "If, prior [to the seven steps] one does not remove the partiality of having attachment for some sentient beings and hatred for others . . . whatever love and compassion one does develop will [also] be partial," writes Tsong-kha-pa.[4] Geluk oral tradition likens this preparation to leveling the ground before building a house: unless this is done well, the house will be lopsided. Thus, one evens out the emotional terrain by removing strong attachments and aversions. On this level foundation, one builds the mansion of unbiased love and compassion.

Tsong-kha-pa defines equanimity as a separation from desire and hatred and an equal-mindedness toward living beings.[5] He also emphasizes that equanimity is not stupidity; it does not make one unable to distinguish friends from those who wish one ill. Such distinctions themselves do not impede equanimity. What obstructs it is the "mind of partiality," the emotional disdain or zealous attachment that often accompanies such distinctions. Equanimity is neither neutrality nor indifference, but an evenness in the way one responds to others.[6] Because equanimity frees the mind from being merely reactive, it protects one from being emotionally overpowered by any given situation. In these ways, the cultivation of equanimity, like mindfulness, encourages a certain independence of mind.

Equanimity is appropriate in terms of both other's and one's own perspectives. Others are fundamentally similar—to each other and to oneself—in wanting happiness and not wanting suffering. Given this profound similarity, it is a mistake to wish some well and others harm. Such uneven responses usually come because, from one's own point of view, it seems that some persons are friends and always kind, while others wish solely to cause harm or are simply neutral. But relationships are not static; they are infinitely variable. Thus, one is encouraged to reflect on how, over time, spouses and lovers may become enemies, and enemies sometimes become loved ones. Because no one is once and forever fixed as "friend," "enemy," or "neutral stranger," equanimity is appropriate.

Through innumerable rebirths, moreover, every sentient being has been in every possible relation to oneself. The present relationship cannot provide the ultimate cue as to how we should behave or feel toward another. This point is often illustrated by a brief tale that I have heard in some version from virtually every Tibetan teacher I have studied with, Geluk or Nyingma:[7]

> A clairvoyant yogi approaches a young mother giving meat to her child, whom she cradles on her lap. At the same time she vigorously kicks away a dog trying to snare some of the meat. The yogi sees that the child she attends so lovingly had in its previous life killed the woman's father, who has since been reborn as the animal whose flesh she is eating. The woman's own mother has taken rebirth as the dog she is kicking within an inch of its life.

From a Buddhist perspective, taking cognizance of rebirth means that whatever the relationship is now, it is only a brief episode in our long history together, making it unsuitable to single-mindedly designate someone as "friend" or "enemy."

The theory of rebirth is surely for most Westerners the strangest of the Buddhist doctrines. Yet insofar as there is to date no proof (whatever that would mean) of life beyond death or the lack of it, we should be humble in the face of this unanswered question. On the other hand, it should also be noted that the idea of going to heaven or hell after death—a belief that, whether one personally holds it or not, seems "normal" in Western cultures—is very strange to outsiders. While I was in graduate school, our department invited a renowned monk-scholar who, after escaping from Tibet in 1959, had lived in a small compound at the center of a Tibetan community in India. When Lati Rinboche came to Virginia in 1975, he had had very little contact with Westerners and so was, in many ways, an emissary from an ancient world. And he was curious about ours. He listened attentively when, by way of practicing conversational Tibetan, I attempted a rough outline of Protestant Christianity's understanding of the afterlife. "It is believed," I said, "that after death one goes to heaven or hell and remains there forever." I will never forget his sudden look of astonishment. "What!" he sputtered, "They believe in only *one* rebirth?!"

For Buddhists this is indeed incomprehensible. If the mind can move apart from the coarse body once, why can it not return to another body, again and again? Buddhist logic argues that just as a wooden table must have wood as a primary source, and can never be fashioned from iron or clay, so consciousness must have a previous consciousness as its primary source. It cannot arise solely from the material conditions of the egg and sperm of mother and father. In the absence of a Creator deity, the only possible source for mind is a prior consciousness in a prior existence. Passing from life to life, we have all been the best of friends and worst of enemies.

But one does not have to accept the theory of rebirth to cultivate equanimity toward others, for connections in this life also support an equanimous regard. One can, for example, consider the great numbers of persons, known and unknown, on whose efforts life depends each time one travels in a plane, or the benefits received from medicines discovered long ago.[8] You can also practice equanimity by imagining that a person on your right strokes your arm gently with a feather, and someone on your left pummels you malevolently, while you attempt to maintain a balanced attitude toward each.[9] In both cases, the point is to get past the kinds of obvious differences that seem to justify different attitudinal responses. This is done by cultivating an awareness of the more subtle but ethically more significant similarities that ordinarily go unnoticed.

The Theravada tradition has a particularly emphatic way of expressing the equanimity gained through a practice known as "breaking down the barriers" between self and other. Suppose, says Buddhaghosa, a person sits with three others, one who is dear, one neutral, and the third an enemy. Bandits approach and demand that one of these four be handed over to them. They make it clear that this is a death sentence. Does a person who has broken down the barriers offer himself? Does he choose one of the others? Insofar as oneself and others are the same in wanting happiness and disliking suffering, each one's needs merit equal attention. To choose either oneself or any of the others means one has not effectively broken down the barriers of discrimination: "it is when he does not see a single one among the four people to be given to the bandits and he directs his mind impartially towards himself and towards these three people that he has broken down the barriers."[10]

Including oneself in the circle of care, an idea that has received much attention from feminist psychologists and ethicists in the past decade or so, is an important step in creating a compassion that is self-empowering.

From Equanimity to Mother Love

Equanimity is empowering partly because it facilitates autonomy, making one less likely to be manipulated or overpowered by whatever person or situation presents itself. As with mindfulness, the individual gains new emotional options because the emotional demarcation separating friends, enemies, and strangers becomes less rigid.

Following successful progress in equanimity, one takes up the first step of the Seven Unfoldings. "Recognizing all beings as mother," begins by considering that whatever the present situation, every living person has over the course of infinite rebirths been one's own mother. A decision to regard everyone as having been one's mother is not, however, even from the most traditional Buddhist perspective, an objective or statistical truth. In the context of rebirth, everyone has also been a most bitter enemy. Nevertheless, one makes the choice to focus on each one's role as a former mother because this will help one to develop compassion.[11]

Recognizing all beings as former mothers, a meditator considers the kindness mothers generally show their children. Textual descriptions on this point are evocative (if essentialist), calling one to reflect how she "rocked me on her ten fingers," and how "though my birth itself caused her great suffering, she was as glad as if she had found a precious gem."[12] From this reflection there unfolds a wish to repay her kindness. Being moved to repay in kind what one has already received in plenty is empowered giving, quite different from giving out of a need for approval, or to fulfill a role one has inherited but not chosen. One is, however, cautioned not to imitate Buddha's disciple Shariputra and give so generously and with such disregard for the limits of one's actual capacity that one regrets it later.[13]

Steps 4 and 5 of the Seven Unfoldings develop the wish that others be happy and free of suffering. With these wishes, one moves from the position of a child, grateful for a mother's kindness, to that of an adult, who now cultivates a mother's care for all living beings. A practitioner imagines that her own love and compassion take the form of light, emanating from her heart in all directions. She extends this light to all living beings, human, animal, and other, good and bad, known and unknown, and as it reaches them it is transformed into exactly what they want. If they want weapons, candy, heat, food, lovers, this is what they receive. After achieving satisfaction in all these material ways, they also receive the complete peace and freedom of enlightenment itself. Then the practitioner reflects how nice it would be if she could actually provide such help to so many persons. What would she have to be like in order to do this? In the traditional Buddhist way of thinking, she would have to be fully enlightened. With this in mind, she determines to experience enlightenment, not for its own sake, but in order to be in a sufficiently powerful position to help others. This determination, known as the Bodhisattva vow, completes the seventh step.[14]

The Fourfold Method

The first move Shantideva suggests is called "equalization of self and other." This step reframes a principle already familiar from the contemplation of equanimity:

> Since the desire for happiness
> Is identical in myself and others
> What is so special about me?[15]

The oral tradition in the person of Lati Rinboche elaborates: "We are dear to ourselves because we want happiness and don't want suffering, and this is the same for others." Therefore, one practices wishing oneself and all beings happiness and imagining that they receive it: Picture yourself this evening, contentedly getting ready for bed; tomorrow morning, joyfully arising; a year from now, peacefully reading; ten years from now, enjoying good health and a happy home. Then repeat the process for others dear to you, then for neutral persons, and then for disliked persons.[16] For Shantideva, acknowledging one's own wish for happiness means naming a quality found in all other persons as well. This recognition, a discovery embedded within a developmental process of reflection, requires a sympathetic understanding of one's own situation, as well as a recognition that it is inappropriate to seek for oneself alone the happiness that everyone wants. However, as traditionally framed by Shantideva and, following him, by much of later Indian and Tibetan Buddhism, this "discovery" also assumes that one did indeed tend to put one's own happiness above that of others. In the West, women are less likely than men to recognize themselves in this description. Shantideva's text does not acknowledge any gendered disparity. Indeed, his assumption that self-cherishing is the central human problem, his enormous emphasis on relinquishing all sense of personal entitlement in order to serve others, is a place of danger for many women in Western culture.

The kind of difference between self and other on which one's asymmetrical relationship to these two categories of persons is based is, from Buddhist perspectives, erroneous. Therefore, in Shantideva's system of cultivating compassion, one deals directly with the erroneous disparity between concern for self and for other. Tibetan oral tradition on Shantideva points out that it is a mistake to understand self and other as independent elements in the way that the colors blue and yellow are independent. One can, after all, discern "blue" without reference to "yellow," but it is not possible to identify "self" without at least an implicit reference to the category "other." Why? "Self" and "other" are like "near" and "far"—it all depends on where you sit.[17]

In 1968 I was struck by a keen desire to go to India. How could I get there? My main problem was that it was so far away. Over the several years it took to arrange the trip, the notions "far" and "India" became completely conflated in my mind. When in 1971 I finally and happily walked off the plane in Bombay, my first thought was, "I've done it; I'm far away." I lived in India for six months before I could experience that "faraway" subcontinent as right here. This is just the sort of simple but significant error that Buddhist traditions find it their particular challenge to undo. So, even as India is itself neither near nor far but in fact can be either, the same person is from different points of view both a "self" and an "other." With no definitive difference between self and other, it is inappropriate to have concern for the pain of the self and not the pain of others. Indeed, Gyel-tsap, a fourteenth-century Geluk commentator on Shantideva's work, observes that if there did exist persons who were simply other, *their* problems could perhaps be dismissed, but all others are in fact also selves, and thus there is no pain that is the pain only of another. Gyel-tsap concludes that the pain of others is therefore of concern to us, even though it does not directly cause us discomfort:

> Because I adhere to myself as "self," my own pain is unbearable. In the same way, other living beings also apprehend "self." . . . It follows that it is reasonable for me to remove the pain of others *because it is pain*, like my own. It is reasonable for me to help others and accomplish their happiness *because those living beings are living beings*.[18]

The suffering of a self, an I, cannot be dismissed. Does it seem impossible that we could ever learn to regard others as we now regard self? Not so, says Shantideva, we have already done so. After all, our own bodies, which we now consider "self," were once other. As he puts it in one of the more dramatic passages of his text:

> Although the drops of sperm and blood [from father and mother]
> Are not actually [established as "self"]
> Just as I come [through familiarity] to know this as self
> So similarly can I regard the bodies of others.[19]

To discuss self is to reflect on its relation to other. Each rubric undermines, contributes to, and plays with the other. If, as Jonathan Culler suggests, one meaning of "deconstruction" is to work "within the terms of a system in order to breach it," then we have to consider that reflecting on "self" as a category inevitably reveals selves to be others, and others to be selves.[20] Until one realizes this mutuality, the attitude of self-cherishing depletes one's capacity to cherish others, and an untoward discrimination between self and other provides the basis for attachment and enmity.

In these ways, Mahayana Buddhists assume that a concern for others is not fundamentally disruptive of identity and purpose. If it is true that the compassion cultivated in the Tibetan Buddhist tradition is empowering, as its most exemplary practitioners give every evidence of it being, can we discern the elements that make it so? Do such elements translate into Western culture? Do they have anything to do with constructions of gender? In other words, what in a contemporary Western context might distinguish personally powerful forms of connection from ones that are draining?

COMPASSION AND RELATEDNESS: THE SELF-OTHER BOUNDARY

This story of the self's difference from others inevitably becomes the story of its own unbridgeable difference from itself.

Barbara Johnson, *The Critical Difference*

In the dominant mentality of contemporary Western culture, "self" is often equated with the autonomous or self-sufficient individual described in chapter 2. Therefore, relationality is in Western cultures often constructed as undermining the "right" or most powerful kind of selfhood. To the extent that personal creativity and individuality are more valued than relationship in the West, to the extent that autonomy is characterized as the pinnacle of psychological and ethical development, there is the implicit suggestion that caring and a relational style of identity make one less than one might be. Thus, compassion is framed in opposition to more singular forms of selfhood.

Before women's connectedness can be valued, connectedness in general must have cultural value. To understand which elements of contemporary culture have undermined relationality is to take an important step toward clarifying how a conversation between Buddhist and feminist perspectives might reconcile a sense of powerful agency with compassionate concern for others. Placing "autonomy" and "relationship" in theoretical opposition to each other is the core problem. As Jane Flax has observed, to define oneself by either one without the other can be disastrous for adults, while Carol Gilligan calls the ability to balance the needs of self and other the defining mark of moral maturity.[21]

This psychological issue is also at the core of the feminist essentialist-postmodern debate. In both cases, questions regarding women's identities are motivated largely by a wish to avoid male styles of identity, which in Western cultures are characteristically oppositional and inclined to project undesirable traits onto others.[22] All class, racial, national, and sexual chauvinisms rest on an identity that, regardless of content, expresses itself primarily through assuming certain unassailable differences between self and others. The ideology that undergirds such an identity requires, in the words of Susan Griffin, the "creation of another, a not-I, an enemy."[23] Some other paradigm of selfhood and relationship is needed. What kind of a self creates strength without rejecting, or withdrawing sympathy from, those who do not share this "identity?" What kinds of relationships are facilitated by an unoppositional self?[24]

If I understand my personhood to be partly a function of our relationship, it is consonant with my sense of identity to be compassionate toward you. If my identity is *only* a function of our relationship, however, there is little within me to draw upon as a resource for extending compassion.[25] If, on the other hand, I understand myself as primarily autonomous, or even if I simply feel that I ought to understand myself that way, compassion for you is antithetical to my own sense of self. To the extent that I experience compassion as thwarting my status as a person or my ability to care for myself, I find it disempowering, and look down on others who would valorize it. Yet surely, as Jane Flax proposes, it is possible to construct views of self in which one does not experience difference as irreconcilable or the existence of others as an *a priori* threat to getting what one wants. As Catherine Keller observes, paraphrasing William James, self is never simply *one*; nor can it successfully maintain a dualistic opposition to the other.[26]

The Buddhist emphasis on learning to consider everyone as a kind mother invites us to consider contemporary Western constructions of "motherhood" in relation to Western attitudes toward compassion and relatedness, self and other. What kind of self and what kind of strength are associated with compassionate concern for others? With these questions in mind we can consider the cultural, interpersonal, and intrapersonal elements that make compassion empowering or disempowering.

Motherhood is a pivotal issue along the feminist divide regarding women's identity. "To what extent," asks Ann Snitow, "is motherhood a powerful identity, a word to conjure with? To what extent is it a patriarchal construction that inevitably places mothers outside the realm of the social, the changing, the active?"[27] Whether or not a woman has children, whether or not she wants to, the possibility of having them and the social construction of her responsibility for them are inescapable. In a culture where identity is fused with the idea of individual choice, the potential for motherhood is often the quality most highly revered and most deeply held against women.

This ambivalence arises in part because pregnancy and motherhood are constructed as lacking deliberateness. Seen as a "given" role rather than an individually chosen project, motherhood is not properly "individualistic." Being "deliberate" has long been conflated with human agency, especially in North America. Thoreau went to the woods "to live deliberately, to confront only the essential facts of life." This is worth considering. "Clearly," writes Barbara Johnson, "for Thoreau, pregnancy was not an essential fact of life. Yet for him as well as for every human being that has yet existed, someone else's pregnancy is the very *first* fact of life. How might the plot of human subjectivity be reconceived (so to speak) if pregnancy rather than autonomy is what raises the question of deliberateness?"[28] In other words, what if "individuality" were reconfigured in ways that took account of women's uniquely gendered capability, as well as of the profound intentionality that accompanies activities regarded as "merely" natural and, in that sense, essential? The essential lacks

status precisely because it is not chosen, yet surely the love and ingenuity that women bring to childrearing and other relationships deserve recognition for what they are, profound expressions of individual creativity.

One of the most significant reasons birthing, mothering, and
similarly nurturing relationships are often devalued in contemporary Western culture has to do with the kind of subjectivity they involve. From a Buddhist perspective, let us note again, it is insufficient
to conceive of subjectivity and selfhood only in relation to language or
mastering knowledge; the insistence on doing so is a particular construction of Western intellectual history. Yet as Jane Flax has observed, philosophy privileges knowledge so exclusively that other al-
ternatives are not explored. Moreover, the knowledge so valued refers
almost entirely to conceptually based knowing, as opposed to the
visceral knowledge of the body, for example, or a capacity to experience feeling vividly. Qualities much like mindfulness, as we have
seen, frequently figure in essentialist feminist discussions that call
for groundedness, clarity, or recognition of being. This nomencla-
ture, like that of Buddhists, reflects an interest in *subjective processes*
as distinct from *subject positions*. Postmodernists, on the other hand,
while focusing on subjectivity or mental experience, still accept
the Enlightenment identification of mind with reason and with
philosophy.[29]

To bridge the distance between these understandings requires
that we name and honor forms of subjectivity that relate to the body
and for which "knowledge" in the sense of information is not the sole
criterion. There are sources in recent Western reflection for such visceral awareness, though they have not often been brought to bear on
the essentialist-postmodern discussion. Flax, for example, points to
Melanie Klein's discourse on an infant's instinctive curiosity that
leads her to explore her mother's body.[30] I would mention also a telling
passage in Emily Martin's description of the subjective state of

women giving birth, a time of extraordinary subjective acuity when what is "known" is not the central experiential criterion. In trying to define what is central to that experience, Martin quotes Michael Odent, whose clinic in Pithiviers, France, has pioneered an especially supportive environment for women giving birth:

> Women seemed to forget themselves and what was going on around them during the course of an unmedicated labor. . . . They get a faraway look in their eyes, forget social conventions, lose self-consciousness and self-control. . . . I have found it very difficult to describe this shift to a deeper level of consciousness during a birth. I had thought of calling it "regression," but I know that the word sounds pejorative, evoking a return to some animal state. "Instinct" is a better term, although it, too, resonates with moralistic overtones.[31]

Indeed, the terms we have are limited. The problem with words like "instinct" is also part of the problem with essentialist vocabularies; they imply the demise of the kind of chosen behaviors and individual personhood valued in Western culture, and they seem to identify the female self with the "acultural" body. Martin herself suggests a more positive frame for what Odent describes:

> Instead of seeing the Pithiviers women as engaged in a "natural" lower-order activity, why can we not see them as engaged in a higher-order activity? The kinds of integration of body and mind fostered by the psychophysiological approach and others, the kinds of wholly involved activity captured by the metaphors of the journey and the trance, could well be taken as higher, more essentially human, more essentially cultural forms of consciousness and activity. Here, perhaps, are whole human beings, all their parts interrelated, engaged in what may be the only form of truly unalienated labor now available to us.[32]

In order to encompass more fully the nature of subjectivity, and to dissolve artificial barriers between essentialist and postmodern positions, as well as between reason and emotion, we need to include among our categories of subjectivity dimensions of mind that are not primarily linguistic or conceptual, and yet (unlike Klein or Martin's examples) are capable of being cultivated and therefore included among "higher-order" and "cultural" human activities. We also need a vocabulary that takes account of subjectivity's relationship to the body and to itself. Expanding our definitions promises to reframe many areas important to women—revaluing birthing and mother-hood, relieving the ancient dualisms of mind and body, and gaining a new perspective on contemporary essentialist-postmodern antago-nisms. If we can honor the subjective state and not just the social sig-nificance of giving birth, it may be possible to reinvent the prestige of mothers and of nonconceptual subjective states.

To reexperience willingly the love one felt as a child for one's mother may, particularly for Westerners, unmask fears of annihila-tion and death, or it may open one to the possibility of an identity that also encompasses death. Birth, death, and subjective states not gov-erned by knowledge all threaten the narrative coherence of autono-mous personhood. Partly because of Western culture's vehement val-orization of individuation, and partly because of the sometimes insuperable difficulties of modern parenting, memories of early child-hood are often conflicted. Against this background, it is not surpris-ing that the relatedness that characterizes much of women's descrip-tions of self often seems disempowering, both to women and to the cul-ture at large. In a striking and persuasive analysis of the way mother-hood and relationality are devalued, Jane Flax suggests that Freud's unconscious fear of vulnerability and dependence made him reluc-tant to recognize what one owes to maternal care, and to relationships in general. As a result, he obscured those aspects of infant develop-ment that depend on mothering. It is both comic and tragic to learn that one of the greatest theorists of our century could not "think of any need in childhood as strong as the need for a father's protection."[33]

The shocking disregard in which the difficult and vital tasks of rearing and educating children are held in contemporary U.S. culture stems in part from an unwillingness to admit how much individuals and societies depend on the work of primary care workers and schoolteachers, most of whom are women. The devaluation of mothering in all its aspects is an important factor in this denigration. Combined with this, I suspect, is a sense that devoting one's life to work that will merely remain in the memory of a few persons seems less "significant" than the kinds of public works, edifices, inventions, art, or books that carry one's individual name into the public arena and the future.[34] In most cultures men can fend off mortality on both counts: they produce children who bear their name and, since the less traceable work of rearing children is mainly the mother's, men also have time for public production. Thus, both men's and women's ambivalent attitudes toward motherhood are deeply associated with the hierarchical evaluation of the public realm and the private sphere. Mothers' importance in the latter does not translate into significance in the former. In a culture like Tibet's however, which lacked the industrial processes that carve life into such separate spheres, the role of motherhood is perhaps more naturally valued, for it occupies the same physical and temporal dimension as much of the rest of ordinary life. The great exceptions, of course, are the monastic universities, where mothers and women are not present, but where they are most likely to be idealized. Further, once consciousness is understood as something that continues, in different forms, for all time, the mind of the child, or any mind, becomes a kind of ultimate surface of inscription. The task of helping this mind to develop, the task of the ordinary mother (*ma*) and the high (*bla*) mother, or lama, is implicitly understood to have more enduring consequences than work on canvas or in mortar and stone.

Whatever its significance for the Tibetan psyche, the emphasis on wishing to repay maternal kindness is for me evocative of Winnicott's observation that a child has a "real need to give to the [real] mother and to have her or his gifts received."[35] It resonates, too, with Nancy Chodorow's observation about the importance of a child's learning to perceive her mother, not simply as an other, but as a subject with desires and an entire constellation of personality traits of her own.[36] There is an important difference between appreciation for what one has received and a willingness to recognize the giver as a person with needs and wants of her own. Both perceptions are necessary if the child is to achieve adequate differentiation. More globally, differentiation is also impeded to the extent that a society does not actively regard mothers as persons with desires and wishes of their own, and this lack of differentiation may further contribute to the association of women with oppressive, annihilating forces. The failure to see mothers and other women as persons in their own right both contributes to and results from this association. The necessity of seeing *any* recipient of one's gifts as having unique needs and desires is a crucial element for Westerners to combine with the Buddhist understanding of compassion.

Various kinds of connections are frequently brought to mind as part of many types of meditation practice. In opening a meditation session, for example, one is often advised in Tibetan traditions to imagine oneself surrounded by male and female family members and friends. One might begin with one's mother and father on either side of oneself, and then visualize as well one's teacher and his or her teachers, each one taking the form of a Buddha whose body, composed entirely of light, vividly appears and then dissolves into oneself, thereby empowering one to accomplish the meditative task at hand. Thus, from the beginning, one practices as a self embodied and assisted by others. Buddhist traditions thus generally see no dichotomy between a sense of relatedness on the one hand and a sense of personal effectiveness on the other.

The male and female enlightened Buddhas at the apex of the Mahayana tradition themselves embody relationality in at least two important ways. First, they attained their Buddhahood in large part through cultivating a close compassionate relationship with other beings. Second, though powerful and active, their "self" is not organized around a conception of dominance or ontological autonomy. Indeed, Candrakirti's famous *Entrance to the Middle Way*, a major Indian source for Tibetan understandings of compassion, opens with a litany of how Buddhahood is attained:

> Buddhas are born from Bodhisattvas.
>
> The mind of compassion, nondual understanding,
>
> And the altruistic mind of enlightenment
>
> Are the causes of those Bodhisattvas.[37]

Compassion for others and thus the persons for whom one has compassion are in the final analysis the *causes* of enlightenment and Buddhahood. This view is very foreign to mainstream Jewish and Christian traditions, where we find a God who, at least in most theologies, is described as self-created and therefore not dependent on any relation for an inherent Godliness. Insofar as the apex of a secular or religious tradition models self-containment as an ideal, veneration of it undermines relationality. While there are important ways in which the Jewish and Christian God does embody loving relationality, the extent to which God has been interpreted as autonomous has been formative in Western ideas of selfhood. By contrast, a Buddhist's effort to foster a sense of deep connectedness does not go against the grain of any larger context. Whatever the reasons for women's lower status in Tibetan culture, it does not, as in the West, seem to arise from their association with relatedness.

Another important difference is that whereas in the West compassion and relatedness are often said to be the province of women, perhaps reflecting women's adaptation to a situation of powerlessness, in Tibet the monastic scholars and meditators were the ones who purveyed and cultivated the compassion they saw as empower-ing.[38] In cultural terms they were powerful *before* they undertook to cultivate love or compassion. Moreover, women in Western cultures who choose to cultivate compassion need also to find ways to increase their capacity for unique self-expression, a form of self-care little noted in Tibet.

Compassionate relationship is also sometimes deemed antithet-ical to "proper" autonomous individuality because it is not seen as a deliberate, chosen response, but an "emotion." Buddhist traditions that cultivate compassion challenge the boundary between thought and feeling implied in this view and the analogous distinction be-tween reason and emotion. Is it possible to choose, deliberately, a car-ing response that expands rather than limits the potential of its be-stower? If so, such possibilities may help us to value a part of human experience that has yet to receive its due in the Western cultural arena.

CHOICE AND THE REASON-EMOTION BOUNDARY

Our compassion is not just emotion by itself, it is based on reasons.

His Holiness the Fourteenth Dalai Lama,
in an interview in *Parabola*, Spring 1984

There is no essential contrast, much less a conflict, between the action being prompted by emotion (at least in the sense in which altruistic emotions are emotions) and its being done for a reason.

Lawrence Blum, *Friendship, Altruism, and Morality*

The cultivation of compassion requires a steadfastness of purpose. A person's decision to cultivate a particular element of compassion, and the persistence required to act on such decisions, mark it as a chosen path of development. The claim that deeply felt compassion can be intentionally developed raises other questions as well. Can we really choose to adopt a particular voice, in this case a compas-sionate one, and make it our own? Is the self's voice in any case only a concatenation of other instructional voices? Are deeply felt re-sponses such as love and compassion beyond the scope of conscious choice? To choose a particular way of responding is quite different from being automatically drawn or socialized into a certain way of behavior. Thus a consciously chosen attitude should not be confused with the descriptions of the behavior of American girls and women in the work of Carol Gilligan and Nona Plessner Lyons, for example. Gilligan says of a young girl: "Her world is a world of relationships and psychological truths where an awareness of the connection between people gives rise to a recognition of responsibility for one another, a perception of the need for response." Gilligan and Lyons assume that the caring they describe emerges through the socialization process, not through choice.[39] Indeed, Gilligan's *In a Different Voice* has been criticized as conservative and as simply perpetuating old proscriptions for women. These concerns are justified, but the Buddhist practices we have considered suggest the possibility of *choosing* the moral perspectives described by Gilligan and Lyons.

In the West, words like "care," "concern," "responsiveness," or "love" belong to the category of emotions, and emotions are highly suspect as resources for ethical behavior or moral action. In a view whose broad outlines are traceable to Kantian thought, emotions are in the West often characterized as capricious, fragile, and unpredictable—too easily thwarted to rely on for moral guidance.[40] Thus, all emotions, positive or negative, are typically distinguished from reasoned principle, with which they are considered to have little affinity. Reason, ever since Aristotle, has been the final arbiter of human meaning in the West; it seems to be "most our own, the only part of the soul that is completely under our control."[41] Seeing control as existentially desirable is thus closely linked with the opposition between reason and passion, sometimes called the central theme of Western philosophy.[42] The contemporary era's tendency to localize ideas and feelings within the mind can make them seem in principle all the more subject to control and thus all the more frustrating when they "escape." Emotions are not "our own" in this view because they are not masterable in the way that reason seems to be. Buddhist traditions see compassion quite differently, for their methods of cultivating compassion are based on the conviction that attitudes can be shaped as desired to become stable and authentic ways of interaction. Love and compassion are therefore qualities that can be developed, not emotions that swamp and overwhelm us.

In short, the status of emotions and their presumed subordination to reason is another cultural assumption that can make anyone's compassionate concern for others seem debilitating to a proper sense of self. If the isolation of feeling from the reasoning process is challenged, the cultural status of both can shift. Today a number of scholars, for example, Lawrence Blum, are rethinking the relationship between reason and altruism.[43] More recently, "postmodern" orientations suggest that emotions, like reasoning, are entirely culturally produced, although the reason-emotion dichotomy remains a highly influential paradigm in the West. Nevertheless, as Joan Cocks observes, the alliance of female with emotion and male with reason has not always been the Western perspective: "While Western culture has always . . . incorporated some idea of a male Self and a female Other, it has not always linked the Self to reason and the Other to emotion. More striking, it has not always treated reason and emotion as exclusive categories."[44]

By putting reason at the service of specific emotions, the Buddhist practices outlined in this chapter question Western oppositions between ordered thought and human feeling.[45] In addition, both women and men are exhorted to cultivate compassion in Buddhist cultures, countering the gendered distinctions, so common in the West, between the male egoist and the female altruist. The reason-emotion debate is simply not part of Buddhist debate. Indeed, at a talk I gave in 1993 at the Tibetan Buddhist Learning Center in Washington, New Jersey, attended by English-speaking Tibetans and Tibetan-speaking Westerners (a cohort that twenty years ago did not exist), a vehement discussion broke out among the Tibetans as to whether there was in fact a Tibetan word meaning "emotion." The Tibetans insisted there was, but offered words like *tshor ba*, which technically only means pleasant, unpleasant, or neutral "feelings." The most eminent scholar in the group put forward a kind of Tibetan neologism, *tshor ba khyad bar can*, literally, "special feeling." The Tibetans were unwilling to concede a lacuna in their vocabulary, though those with more experience in the West conceded the difficulty. On the other hand, the Tibetan-speaking Westerners, including myself, were not convinced that a true equivalent could be found. Certainly there is no Tibetan term with the etymology of "moving out" (*ex movere*) embedded in the Latin root of the English. Thus, there is in Buddhism little sense that "feelings" as such remove one from the center of one's subjective territory, even though conflicts between self-interest and concern for others, or between mental focus and distraction, are clearly recognized.

The Buddhist practices described here assume that one can take a principle learned from an external authority and transform it, through one's own internal decisions and desires, into something authentically one's own.[46] For this to be possible, one must be capable of moving between knowledge and feeling, between one's own and others' voices, between public and private domains, between self and other. (Indeed, it is often what initially feels most authentic, for example, hatred of an enemy or a too-exclusive love for a friend, that must be gradually discarded.)[47] Postmodernists discard "authenticity" as a viable category because in their view the self has no authentic center. From a Buddhist perspective, the possibility for "authentic" responses rests on the capacity to cultivate a certain perspective consciously. What is learned from others can become part of one's self. Constructed authenticity is the only kind possible, but it is also all that a self requires, provided there is sufficient force of mind behind it.

Compassion is said to be cultivated by alternating between analytically and experientially oriented phases of meditation. The result is not an uncontrolled sentimental enmeshment; nor is it an idealized or romantic projection onto others. Indeed, as with equanimity, psychological autonomy is crucial to compassion and utterly compatible with it. The same alternation between analytical and stabilizing dispositions described earlier in relation to understanding mortality also applies to the cultivation of compassion. One may contemplate the appropriateness of intimate concern for others and vividly imagine, through words and mental pictures, that one is able to maintain this concern through a variety of interactions. Or one may reflect, "Wouldn't it be nice if all persons had everything they require, if they could be happy, and wouldn't it be wonderful if I could be helpful to them in some way." These contemplations, according to Buddhist epistemology, are "conceptual" because they involve mental imagery.[48] If in the course of reflection one taps into a strong feeling of compassion, one stabilizes oneself on that feeling. (This is not to deny that analysis is also a form of experience, but to emphasize that there is a shift from *reflecting on* compassion to *experiencing* it.) When a feeling of equanimity, love, or compassion arises, one simply stays with that feeling until it fades away, whereupon one can refurbish it by recalling instances of, or supporting reasons for, compassionate connectedness. Concentration, the ability to stabilize the mind on a chosen focus, is thus a significant element in the process by which conceptual thought flows into nonconceptuality. Indeed, this movement is considered possible in part because conceptual and nonconceptual, or language-bearing and non-language-bearing minds, different as they are, share common ground in being clear and knowing.[49] In this way, moving from conceptual to nonconceptual understanding is not a leap over an abyss, but a simple shift in functioning, like water flowing in one direction or another, but always remaining water. This fluidity between the conceptual, including the rational, and the nonconceptual, including the emotive, is thus a given in this Buddhist practice.

Women in Western cultures interact with knowledge and authority in a variety of ways. The authors of *Women's Ways of Knowing*, a provocative study based on interviews with 135 women, carefully categorize ways in which women interact with knowledge, self, and others. The authors then use these categories to express an ongoing negotiation between experiencing oneself (1) as a vessel for the opinions of others, (2) as a producer of intuitions and knowledge whose integrity is only tainted by listening to others, and (3) as having an ability to integrate one's own intuitive and logical reflections with information received from outside.[50] The ability to integrate outside information entails communication between two selves that neither disappear in the presence of nor take over the other.[51] Similarly, for Buddhists, the possibility of cultivating mindfulness, compassion, or wisdom, rests on the successful integration of one's own reflections, with the information, in the form of philosophical teaching and meditation instruction, received from others. Like the authors of *Women's Ways of Knowing*, Buddhist practices assume that one can create an authentic voice by incorporating others' voices.

Having noted some of the ways that Western and Buddhist valuations of motherhood and relationship are contextualized differently, we need now to consider in more specific terms the kinds of relationship that Western women might create through taking account of the compassionate and loving attitude Buddhist texts describe.

RESPONSIBILITY AND RECIPROCITY IN RELATIONSHIP

In a refinement of her earlier work on young women's experience of themselves and their relation to others, Carol Gilligan and her colleagues, in particular, Nona Lyons, speak of two types of moral-social response to other persons: "reciprocity" and "response to others in their terms." The two approaches of reciprocity and response are traceable to "the two meanings of the word 'responsibility'—commitment to obligations and responsiveness in relationships."[52] Reciprocity is a kind of contractual arrangement between oneself and another who is considered not only equal to but the same as oneself. To regard others this way involves a position of distance and objectivity in which the importance of one's own emotional responses are minimized. As Carol Gilligan writes, "Despite the transit to the place of the other, the self oddly seems to stay constant."[53] In its emphasis on the similarities among all persons, reciprocity is analogous to the Buddhist idea of equanimity and to the equalization of self and other. To the extent that these are predicated on sameness, they invite essentialist views of selfhood. After all, in pointing out the "difference" between self and other, Gyel-tsap and Shantideva noted the confusion that comes from thinking that one's own position as a subject is unique. Overcoming this erroneous sense of uniqueness requires acceptance of an "essentialist" position: (1) Everyone is a self; (2) no self seeks suffering; (3) in this way I am like all others; (4) therefore I should not give those others, who are like myself, what I myself would not want; (5) to do so will bring me suffering in the future; finally, (6) since others are more numerous than myself, I should place their needs ahead of my own. In Gilligan and Lyon's terms, this understanding is more "reciprocal" than "responsive."

The second type of relationality, "response to others in their terms," which Gilligan found to be statistically predominant in girls and women, though not exclusive to them, involves a concern for others based on what others want, rather than on what one owes them. "In a perspective of response," writes Lyons, "The focus is always on the needs of others" as opposed to one's obligations.[54] By their own accounts, persons who prefer the perspective of response experience themselves as connected with others rather than equal to them. Compassionate concern arises not simply from one's own energies or from one's own side, but *in relationship* with others. The cultivation of equanimity in terms of others' wishes for happiness and vividly imagining that they receive whatever they require are consonant with this. The way that Tibetan practices of compassion are taught can also be considered under the rubrics of response and reciprocity. Such teachings may be "given" by a revered if distant teacher sitting on a formal raised platform or communicated informally, through playful and mundane daily interactions, sitting over tea or dinner.

In short, the sevenfold and fourfold methods of cultivating compassion can be seen as containing both categories of relationship described by Gilligan and Lyons, with the important difference, already noted, that the Buddhist interest is in purposefully cultivating certain types of response, while Gilligan and her colleagues emphasize the psychology that shapes the ways girls and women actually behave. Each approach, however, is ultimately directed at understanding the processes of compassionate interaction. The meaningful task does not lie with choosing between two or more styles of relationship, or between the essentialist and constructionist stances Gilligan's categories suggest. Rather, it lies with the artful understanding of which criteria facilitate compassionate behavior in specific situations, and with knowing how to embody compassion effectively. Sometimes it is advantageous to reciprocate like an equal, on other occasions it is preferable to be responsive to a dynamic interpersonal flow. Theory cannot fully define the boundaries of these choices. Theories that would restrict the self to either one choice or the other should be questioned.

RELATIONSHIP IN ACTION

One might assume that to discuss compassion is to discuss relationship. However, Buddhist traditions see compassion primarily as a result of practice, and rarely if ever explain it as a product of one's relationship with others. Indeed, compassion is often understood as simply radiating out from oneself, regardless of how others behave. This suggests that compassion results less from interpersonal dynamics than from intentional cultivation.[55]

Buddhist texts and oral traditions on the Seven Unfoldings and the Eleven Rounds of Tsong-kha-pa emphasize that relationships are the *measure* of compassion, not that compassion is produced *through* mutual interaction. A Bodhisattva needs other people in order to cultivate compassion, but that cultivation depends far more on his or her own efforts in developing certain attitudes toward them than on what actually occurs in interactions with them. Naturally, we expect that the cultivation of compassion will affect relationships positively, but this, too, is different from understanding compassion to result from the interaction itself. The experience of love and compassion, once cultivated, arises from one's own heart, not in dependence on one's particular relationship with others. The lack of emphasis on the interpersonal in Buddhist practice is to be expected, since neither the Indian nor the Tibetan cultures that gave rise to this understanding of compassion emphasized special relationships between unique individuals. The implicit corollary that one is a person who *has* a relationship is quite different from the claim, common in much of recent Western psychology, that one comes into being as a person *through* relationship.[56] For all of Buddhism's emphasis on responsiveness and causality, a development of compassion through mutual interpersonal exchanges is not emphasized in the Buddhist picture.

From a Western and especially a feminist perspective, this is a significant lacuna, for personal interaction "implies the possibility of learning from others in ways that transform the self." That is, the self is no longer an integer, but a dynamic engager of others, "defined not by reflection but by interaction, the responsiveness of human engagement."[57] Furthermore, those others are not merely "objects" that mirror the self and enhance self-knowledge; they are facilitators of growth and self-experience.[58] In a Western context, coming to know others is imagined through what Gilligan describes as a "joining of stories."[59] This process involves a kind of personal, intimate, and psychological connection that is a style perhaps uniquely valued in the modern West. In this context, Western women always have to ask whether compassion is sufficiently responsive to the particularities of a given relationship. The lack of a significant place of personal story and for interpersonal dynamics in Buddhism is a point of tension between Western, especially Western feminist, and traditional Buddhist sensibilities. But women need not give up their stories, or their creative spirituality and personhood, in order to benefit from Buddhist perspectives.

The "sameness" on which equanimity and compassion are based in this Buddhist practice involves a strategic nonattention to the differences associated with varying social, cultural, historical, and racial circumstances. Attention is directed to the "sameness" of wanting happiness or, in some traditions, to the presence of Buddha nature in all living beings. As with essentialist perspectives, "sameness" is these theories' strength and their weakness. There are surely times when it is desirable simply to alleviate another's pain as if it were the same as one's own, when it is not necessary to take account of the different stories that bring persons to their particular desires, or to articulate an interest in the particular circumstances of their pain. But in a synthesis of Buddhist and Western feminist sensibilities, and given Western investment in the uniqueness of each individual, the "getting to know" that is not traditionally emphasized in Buddhist meditative or philosophical literature has an important place.

Buddhist texts often refer to the "skillful means" (*upāya*) by which compassion is manifested according to the needs of a specific situation, but these texts do not encourage or demonstrate a nuanced curiosity about the intimate details of a person's life. Mahayana traditions in particular recognize the need for "different medicines" for different persons' needs, but analyses of personal difference rarely go beyond generalities such as "desirous," "tight-minded," and the like.[60] The sense of the "personal" is, from a Western perspective, missing in Indian and Tibetan discussions of compassion. This is where feminism, as well as psychology more generally, makes an important contribution to Buddhist practice in the West. When particularity is acknowledged, Buddhist methods can cultivate a "response" style of interaction appropriate to Western women's understandings of personhood. Western object-relations theory can also add a relational dimension to the meditative cultivation of compassion.

We must not forget that "relationships" in the modern West and in a traditional Asian culture like Tibet are quite different. Intimate personal exchanges, self-revelation, and analyses of deep feelings are not part of Tibetan friendships or family conversation. Relationships occupy a quite different place in cultures where people are already well "connected" by clan, village, and ideas of the cosmos. On the other hand, successful interpersonal connections are also far more crucial to psychological well-being in the West, where more pervasive forms of connection are often lacking.

Although one-on-one interpersonal relationships do not receive the emphasis in Buddhist culture that they do in the West, family relationships are extremely important. Indeed, the problematic relationship between the family life of a householder and the quest for enlightenment has been a recurring theme throughout Buddhist history. A traditional story of the Buddha shows him casting a last look on his wife and infant son, who are sound asleep on the night he leaves home to pursue his spiritual goals. He could leave with an easy conscience insofar as his wife was, of course, part of an extended family and did not depend on him alone for either her own or their child's needs. But this fact does not resolve more crucial questions about personal relationships in the context of spiritual practice. Indeed, an important dividing line in Buddhist traditions has often been where they stand on the issue of whether or not householders can achieve enlightenment. Motherhood, though highly valued in Tibetan culture, is certainly not formally constructed as part of the path to enlightenment. In the cultivation of compassion, mothers model spiritual love without exemplifying it, and persons who cultivate compassion are not moved to offer this same opportunity to the mothers who inspire them.[61] (By contrast, a conscious effort to include family life in their practice is a hallmark of North American Buddhist communities. Many Western women and men today consider their family life very much part of their practice.)[62]

The modern Western urge to individuate, to be special and therefore isolated, has led to paradoxical self-constructions: a highly individualized self who can only be close to others by sharing her personal story, her unique feelings and perceptions, with them, leading to a psychological intimacy that has virtually no place in traditional Tibetan or other Asian cultures. In addition, intense personal relationships, especially those of a romantic nature, are far more threatening to personal independence in the West than the familial and clan connections of traditional Buddhist cultures. In the West, romantic and other forms of intimacy can be dysfunctional when one becomes more concerned about another's feelings than one's own; this results in a psychologically crippling loss of independence. Shantideva seems in fact to recommend just such a giving up of self when he speaks of the benefits of being more concerned for others than for oneself. Yet given the cultural context in which he lived and the persons he was explicitly addressing, the dangers of codependency would hardly have been uppermost in his mind.

In Tibet the practice of compassion we have described was entered into by those who already considered relationality a powerful principle in their social and metaphysical universe, and who already held powerful positions in that world. No one thought about whether meditation on compassion, or any other contemplative practice, would increase self-esteem or heal childhood trauma. Contemporary women in the West, however, are working toward a widely valorized form of connectedness rather than out of it. It is crucial for Western women and men to incorporate individual strength into their understandings of connection, relationships, and the feelings that go with them. Certainly, the polarization of categories like self and other, autonomy and relationship, reason and emotion, voice and silence all contribute to a devaluation of connectedness, making it more difficult (but never impossible) to find a way of compassionate connection that is empowering for all concerned.

If in the West compassion is felt to be in opposition to autonomous personhood, the Buddhist material understands compassion as the most powerful response a person can make. Buddhist treatments of compassion make it clear that persons matter, that their hopes and fears are suitable areas of concern, that self and other are categories that are only meaningful in relationship to each other. It is this understanding that permeates the radical questioning of the self for which Buddhist traditions are so famous, an interrogation that has striking consonance with essentialist as well as postmodern feminist perspectives.

CHAPTER 5

Self: One Exists, the Other Doesn't

He knows selflessness but does not waste himself.
Vimalakirti Sutra

Without the possibility of a coherent self, liberation
becomes impossible.
Daryl McGowan Tress, "Comment on Jane Flax's
'Postmodernism and Gender Relations'"

The Dalai Lama once said that for him cultivating compassion opened up the possibility of understanding emptiness. Emptiness, sometimes called selflessness, is in classic Indian and Tibetan Buddhism the most essential quality of persons in the sense that it is inviolable and always present. To claim it is compatible with compassion is also to claim that unconditioned emptiness is compatible with activity in the world, with all the endeavors undertaken with, or for, the sake of others.

The issue of selflessness is important for our conversation in other ways as well. Just as the category of mindfulness expands the discussion of mind beyond what is explicitly linked with ideas or feelings, and just as compassion extends a sense of caring and connection beyond its usual compass, so descriptions of selflessness invite a new sense of those who are the objects of one's attention and compassion. Buddhist traditions claim that just as the mind is not thought alone, and just as persons cannot be designated once and for all as "friends" or "enemies," so persons and things have an unconditioned dimension not usually accessed. This dimension is important for our conversation because the unconditioned emptiness is the object that corresponds most fully to the subjective expanse accessed through mindfulness and enriched by compassion.

To understand how these matters relate to Western women, we turn now to a Buddhist discussion of self and selflessness, and especially to the constructed self's possible relationship to what is not constructed. Here our focus is on the theory and practice of emptiness of the Geluk order, whose literature specifically discusses what it and much of Tibet considers the most efficacious understanding of emptiness.

THE SELF IN QUESTION

Rendered into English, the Buddhist term "selflessness" is enormously confusing. The "self" that it denies is neither the modern psychological self nor the unique individual of common Western understanding. It is a self described in terms of its structure rather than its story. As the present Dalai Lama puts it: "There are many different ways in which the person or I appears to our minds. In one way, the I appears to be permanent, unitary, and under its own power; in this mode of appearance the I seems to be a separate entity from mind and body with the person as the user or enjoyer and mind and body as what is used or enjoyed."[1] A more subtle misconception is to see the self's relationship to mind and body as analogous to a chief doctor's relation to her subordinates. A chief doctor is not separate in type from other doctors, but has a unique function as their boss; similarly, the self is sometimes experienced as not really separate from yet still in charge of mind and body.

In identifying one's sense of self, a practitioner thus is not instructed to describe contents or characteristics, but to understand how and where the "I" seems positioned in relation to one's mind and body. Then it will be possible to reflect on whether that kind of self exists or not, for the absence of that self is emptiness. Therefore, the first step in understanding emptiness is for a practitioner to become thoroughly familiar with her ordinary experience of self. This means allowing her natural way of perceiving the self to unfold, and to be mindful of it. The process may seem simple enough, but it is in fact quite challenging because the experience of self is so much taken for granted.[2] The trick is to watch the unfolding process alertly enough to notice it, but not so forcibly that it is interrupted. The Fifth Dalai Lama put it this way: "While the general consciousness remains on the 'I' with distinct force, a corner of the mind should watch its mode of apprehension and analyze the way in which the 'I' is being conceived. For instance, when you are walking with someone on a [mountain] path, your eyes are mainly looking at the path, but with a corner of your eye you are watching your companion."[3]

Weeks or months of observation are recommended. The mindfulness that brings to light this ordinarily unnoticed sense of self is the same uncritical awareness discussed earlier, now directed toward one's customary sense of "I," which it simply observes, without interfering. Identifying one's ordinary sense of self is considered the most difficult phase of understanding what Buddhists mean by selflessness. (This is why, in introducing the term toward the end of chapter 2, I said no more about it until now, when we can carefully identify that "self" denied in the theory of selflessness.) Tsong-kha-pa, who devotes to the topic of identification nearly half of his discussion of emptiness in his *Great Exposition of the Stages of the Path*, observes, "Just as, for example, in order to ascertain that a certain person is not here, you must know the person who is not here so in order to ascertain the meaning of 'selflessness,' or 'non-inherent existence,' you must identify well that self, or inherent existence which [you will later negate]."[4]

What does one observe? At a time of strong physical pain, one may notice that the self or "I" seems to be the body—the throbbing head, the burnt finger. In times of extreme emotion, the "I" may seem to be that mental state alone. When speaking intensely, it might seem that the self is in the throat; when running with all one's force, that the self pervades the entire moving body. When powerful feelings arise—when one is defending oneself against an unjust accusation, for example, or is in a state of fright or exultation—it feels as if the self is those very feelings and nothing else. Mindful observation, says this system of Buddhism, reveals that we usually assume the existence of an "I" that is either wholly independent of its parts or inalienably fused with them. Either of those positions is a misconception of the actual status of the self. It is a misconception that makes the self seem more reified and less open to new possibilities than it actually is.

There are infinite ways in which the self can appear to "be," and these vary not only from person to person but within the experience of a particular person. In a sense, the particulars do not matter. The point is that once one has identified with certainty what the self of ordinary experience is like, one tries to find it. Can any portion of the mind or body reasonably be considered to correspond exactly with one's very strong sense of self?[5] If the self existed as plainly, unambiguously, and unproblematically as it seems to, it should be easy to find. And where would one find it except among the constituents of one's own mind and body? Yet when one looks through the mind and body for the self one has previously identified, one does not find it. The Fifth Dalai Lama compares this searching and not finding with the situation of a farmer looking for a bull (the self previously identified) in his upper and lower pastures (mind and body). Once he has determined that the bull is not in either, he knows the bull is not on his property; that is, he knows the absence of that particular, perhaps very valuable, bull he has been seeking.[6] In the same way, once the self previously identified cannot be found in one's own mind and body, one knows that *this* kind of a self does not exist.

However, one does not conclude from such reflection that no self whatsoever exists, only that the self one had previously assumed and is now looking for does not exist. The danger of confusing the negation of *that* self with the negation of self in general is great. Largely for this reason, questions about how or whether the self exists are typically not raised until Buddhist practitioners have been well imbued with the importance of ethics, the power of mindfulness, and the significance of compassion, a vitally important context that is often overlooked in Western discussions of "selflessness." Emptiness is a topic only for those whose religious and cultural identity is secure.[7] And, says Tsong-kha-pa, emptiness should not be taught to those who will construe it to mean that the self does not exist, or that one's actions and relationships do not matter because there is no karmic cause and effect, no ethical consequences.[8] They would miss the central point that emptiness and selflessness are fully compatible with dynamic personal agency, as well as with material cause and effect.

The absence of the self one has been trying to find, and not absences in general, is called emptiness or selflessness. This specific absence is the ontological analogue to the epistemological silence of mindfulness. With training, this absence is experienced by a mind that is concentrated, free of conceptual thoughts, and also free of the usual sense of subject and object as separate. In other words, a full experience of emptiness entails what I have called cognitive nondualism, wherein subject and object, conditioned mind and unconditioned emptiness, are experienced as fused. The gradual relinquishment of increasingly subtle misconceptions opens up new potential for the practitioner. As Harvey Aronson has noted, in Buddhism "ontologically less is psychologically more."[9]

The mind that conceives of an inherently existent "person" itself depends on the various moments of mind during which this perception takes place, and each moment depends on its submoments. Minds, persons, and all other phenomena exist in dependence on a series of moments and on their own parts. To understand this is to understand persons or things as "dependent arisings," and as existing conventionally, meaning dependently, instead of inherently, meaning utterly independent of causes, parts, or naming. Everything that exists, the entire world and the beings in it, is considered a dependent arising. This status is incompatible with the idea of inherently independent existence that the Geluk tradition says is ordinarily, but mistakenly, associated with our sense of self.

Tsong-kha-pa illustrates this point with the tale of a magician who tricks his audience into perceiving an illusory horse and elephant as real. The *absence* of an actual horse and elephant *exists together* with the illusory horse and elephant. Not recognizing this, the spectators admire and desire the "animals" that do not exist based on an illusion that does. Just as there is no real elephant on the magician's stage, so there is no self-sufficient (*rang rgya thub pa*) or truly existent (*satyasiddhi, bden par grub pa*) self in the area of the mind and body. But although an illusory elephant is not what it seems, it does exist. Similarly, the self, which seems so concretely findable and in charge, is not what it seems. But it does exist, it does function, and people do base actions on thinking it is more real than it is.

What the mistaken sense of self overlooks is its status as a dependent arising. One usually apprehends oneself and others as if they were somehow independent of their form and consciousness. Just as "self" exists only through the relation of mind and body, so mind itself is the name given to a series of infinitely divisible mental moments, and "form" or "body" is designated to a collection of limbs, which depend on flesh and bones, which depend on cells, which depend on atoms, which in turn are designated to a set of electrons and nuclei, each of which have their own constituent parts ad infinitum. Indeed, in Madhyamika philosophy, unlike in some other Buddhist schools, there is no coming to rest on some final small particle or indivisible moment that has no parts of its own.[10] There is no findable essence or essential building block.

Geshe Rabten, among the most eminent Geluk teachers to escape from Tibet in the 1950s, had this to say to a small group of Westerners studying with him in Dharamsala in 1972: "If we search from top to bottom, all the parts of body and mind down to the smallest atom, we will never find the smallest particle that stands for the self. . . . This unfindability is our actual condition. The self exists in a special way, and to find that way is very difficult. . . . We are not the body, not the mind, not nonexistent."[11]

It is the uncaused, permanent, independent, and substantial self that cannot be found. Although the self is neither form nor consciousness, it has no existence apart from them. It exists only in dependence on them. Thus a constructed conventional self, meaning a dependently arisen self, does exist. To understand what that means, however, the Geluk tradition finds it necessary first to identify the subtle though pervasive sense one has of a self that *is* permanent, uncaused, self-sufficient, or independent of its own parts. The absence of such a self is emptiness. Emptiness, itself unconditioned by causes or contexts, is therefore a feature of all persons and things, which, as we have seen, are themselves dependent on causes, conditions, or constituent parts. In this view, the conditioned and unconditioned are fully compatible. We will return to this point shortly.

In the language of Buddhist philosophy, the over-reified sense of self is known as the conception of a "truly existent," or "inherently existent," self. The self often *seems* to be massively existent, unambiguously findable, and concretely identifiable, in the same way that one can point to a rock and then pick it up. These terms signify, in part, the sense of something that is independent of causes or its own parts. The unthinking attribution of inherency to others, as well as the appropriation of it for oneself, is considered to be the lived ontology that underpins all other experiences of selfhood, including the modern psychological selves about which Westerners are more accustomed to reflect. But it is important to understand that "self" does not mean "ego" or "pride" in the Freudian or Western psychological sense. Further, it is not only the powerful or confident who have an ontologically overwrought sense of self. One can feel powerless, or feel that "I don't know who I am" in the contemporary sense, and still have an overly concrete sense of the "I" who does not know.

The self negated in the theory and practice of selflessness is synonymous, not with persons in general, but with a person regarded, however subtly, as independent from the mind and body that is its basis. No such self exists. It cannot be overemphasized that "self" in this context does not mean simply "you" or "me." The self so vigorously denied in Buddhist philosophy must not be confused with an integrated sense of self-worth, which neither modern psychology nor Buddhist traditions (once the concept was explained) would urge one to discard. Although serious practitioners in any culture are meant to find the discussion of selflessness a challenge to their self-conception, those in Buddhist cultures are not also encountering culturally different ideas of individuality and personal psychology in the process.

Modern Western analyses of self or identity pertain chiefly to matters of character, choice, and feeling, or to discussions of social and political positioning. The Buddhist analyses of self focus on existential structure or ontology. Thus, there is no parallel among traditional Buddhists to the contemporary Western concept of a "search for self" in psychological terms or career choices. Lay Westerners, whose lives are filled with such issues, need to be clear that meditation is *not* the proper place to look for certain kinds of healing. When feelings, personal goals, or personal history come to awareness during the cultivation of mindfulness, for example, or during the process of identifying one's sense of self, Buddhist philosophy understands them as secondary manifestations of the core issue on which they focus: the strong tendency to experience *anything* as independently existent. This, rather than any particular personal history, is what most fundamentally predisposes one to experience suffering or impose it on others.

Although the fully enlightened are said to be free of all suffering, it is clear to me that even very advanced meditators are not free from certain kinds of pain that may well be unique to Western contexts. An Asian meditation master once told me that, when he had to give an impromptu panel presentation to a group of strangers (who had not necessarily come specifically to hear him), his "knees were shaking." A Western meditation teacher about to give a public presentation told me, "If I don't recognize you when you come up after my talk, don't take it personally. I get that wigged out at these things." I think it is significant that in each case, the speaker was reacting to events in which their unique "personality" and perspectives would be on display, not to the traditional meditation talks that both were well accustomed to give and of which they unquestionably had deep experience.

It is ironic that Buddhist traditions, developed in cultures that did not exhibit a keen interest in the particulars of personal detail, may in the West become a way of aiding the quest to "find oneself," or "get in touch with oneself," that is, to discover the unique feelings and experiences that construct one as an individual in terms no traditional Buddhist would recognize. (This was not, for example, Yeshey Tsogyel's motivation.)

Partly because of culturally and philosophically unnuanced understandings of "self" (*ātman, bdag*), the theory of selflessness has sometimes had unfortunate ramifications in the West, especially for newer students. Again, the theory of selflessness does not mean the self is not worth attending to. This idea is a particularly Western manifestation of the nihilism Tsong-kha-pa warned against. Both Buddhists and feminists would agree that self-abandoning behavior is wasteful, and Buddhists would further emphasize that it fails to get at the ontological root of the issue. Women, in my experience, are the ones most powerfully and adversely affected by this misinterpretation. In addition, anyone for whom selfhood seems too heavy a responsibility, or who is psychologically troubled, might for all the wrong reasons welcome a philosophy that seems to say the self is not real enough to be a burden. Someone with a painful personal story and an inclination to dissociate from it might well be attracted to Buddhism for its apparent justification of this response.[12] Nor is it uncommon for Western practitioners of Buddhism to go through long phases of shutting down feelings, especially sexual and emotional love, to ignore important psychological issues, or to engage in various forms of stultifying self-denial, all the while thinking that they thereby imitate classical forms of "nonattachment." Women especially are vulnerable to finding in Buddhism a message to discard their personal (as well as social) histories, a message that has virtually no meaning in its native environment.

These are dangerous errors in the translation of Buddhist philosophy into Western culture. Although an understanding of emptiness is recognized in Buddhist philosophy as the ultimate cure for all physical and mental distress—for the entire process of cyclic existence—it would be foolish to see it as a cure for quandaries that are alien to the cultures that gave rise to it. Buddhist teachings do not explicitly address the kinds of psychologically intimate relationships so important to many Western women, and in particular they do not address power differentials in male-female relationships. As one of my students observed, "If a woman is living with an abusive man, someone who beats her, in a situation where she has no independent means of financial support, how is emptiness going to help her?" It won't. But it won't have to either. No doubt one of the crucial shifts Buddhism will undergo in the West is that it will no longer be asked to bear the burden of all personal and social ills, as it did in its traditional Tibetan context. The permutations of this shift are difficult to predict, because Buddhist discussions of self and selflessness, of mindfulness and compassion, have never taken account of gender as a category of analysis. Who within the 2,500-year-old tradition has analyzed Indo-Tibetan theories and practices connected with emptiness in the context of how they do or do not speak to women? As we have seen, the nonhierarchical Buddhist principles were not applied to the social order of Tibet, and Buddhist texts have little to say about the social position or interpersonal particularities of women.[13]

Feminist perspectives can inform and contribute to Western Buddhism's application of the principle of dependent arising in the psychological, interpersonal, as well as the social and political arenas. When Buddhists speak of the self depending on causes and conditions, they reflect primarily on the physical conditions of mind and body, and the most basic elements of warmth, nourishment, and help from others that sustain these conditions. They do not elaborate how the psychological self is constructed through very specific kinds of interactions, and in dependence on various political, historical, racial, and gendered causes. Such elaborations, however, can certainly be seen as an expansion of the meaning of dependent arising.[14]

The introspection for which Buddhist and other contemplative traditions are famous thus means something quite different in traditional and modern contexts. Part of this difference has to do with their very different ways of exploring what "self" is. The modern Western emphasis is on personal story; the traditional Buddhist focus is on the self's structure. How, then, will Buddhist analyses of self map onto Western constructs of individuality? The transition will not always be smooth, partly because of differences between the individuality valued in the modern West and the personal independence often demonstrated in Tibetan contexts, and also because of differences between Buddhist philosophical and feminist postmodern perspectives on what it means to know something, and what there is to be known.

BEING AND SEEING

I once invited to speak in my class at Stanford a Tibetan recluse who had recently emerged from seventeen years of retreat in the Himalayan foothills. In the discussion that followed his talk, a student asked how persons in the most remote areas of Tibet and Nepal, never exposed to things Western, would react on being told about VCRs or computers. Would they believe it? "If they had not understood anything about emptiness, they might not believe it," he said, "but if they had, they would believe it very easily, because they would know all things are dependent arisings, and through different causes many kinds of things are possible."[15]

Emptiness is said by Buddhists to describe how things are. In Middle Way (*Mādhyamika*) Buddhist philosophy, emptiness is considered entirely compatible with dependent arising; indeed, emptiness is said to be what makes dependent arising possible. To what extent can this emptiness be characterized as an "essence," especially since emptiness itself is a dependent arising? How completely can either conditioned or unconditioned phenomena be "known"? These questions bring us to important tensions between Buddhist and postmodern understandings of the mind's ability to know its objects, and to a consideration of the role of language in this process, both matters of great relevance for feminist reflection on selfhood.

Buddhists emphasize that although one fashions a table, no one fashions the table's emptiness. So long as the table exists, its emptiness cannot, like the table itself, deteriorate or be altered in any way. This is true of the self's or any other emptiness. However, even though all emptinesses are the same, mere absences of inherent existence, emptiness is not a Platonic ideal. There is no "ideal" or "generic" emptiness apart from its specific instances—the specific emptiness of the table, for example. Moreover, a table's emptiness depends on the emptiness of its parts—the emptiness of its legs, color, and weight. Similarly, the unfindability of a person depends on the unfindability of the arms and legs of the person. This means that emptiness too is a dependent arising. However, unlike persons, or anything impermanent, emptiness does not depend on causes and conditions. It is unconditioned precisely because it does not deteriorate or change in any way. Therefore, although a person is conditioned, the emptiness associated with a person is unconditioned. Insofar as it is unconditioned, emptiness is an "essential" quality. Insofar as it is a dependent arising, it participates in change and constructedness. Thus, the category of emptiness is connected with both the essentialist and postmodern sides of the feminist debate. That Buddhist philosophy finds it possible for something to be both a dependent arising and unconditioned is a crucial move I want now to contrast with feminist postmodern reflection.

More than any other feature of Buddhist philosophy, it is the characterization of phenomena as dependent arisings that seems to call forth comparisons with contemporary theory.[16] Let us look closely at the apparent similarities. In Buddhist thought, the self exists *only* in dependence on causes, conditions, and its own constituent parts. Its functionality, far from contradicting emptiness, is made possible because inherent existence is absent. Similarly, all dependent arisings are qualified by the absence or emptiness of inherent existence. Dependent arising is in fact the reciprocal meaning of emptiness; ordinary persons as well as Buddhas are dependent arisings, as are all nonsentient phenomena.

For the Middle Way school known as the Consequentialists (*Prāsaṅgika*), no person, no table, no VCR or computer, exists apart from the causal or constitutive elements through which it arises.[17] From this perspective, Buddhists would agree with feminist and other postmodernists who describe the endless play of differences in relation to the self. Teresa de Lauretis speaks for many postmodern feminists when she says that subjectivity arises from a complex of habits resulting from the semiotic interaction of "outer world" and "inner world," the continuous engagement of a self or subject in social reality.[18] Postmodern theorists would agree, too, with Jorge Luis Borges' more colorful observation that there is no proposition that does not imply the entire universe: "To say *the tiger* is to say the tigers that begot it, the deer and turtles devoured by it, the grass on which the deer fed, the earth that was mother to the grass, the heaven that gave birth to the earth."[19] Moreover, the principle of dependent arising describes a self that is both contextually constructed and viable as an agent, a force to contend with, but not the center of the world. In denying persons, as well as things, independence, Buddhist presentations share with Judith Butler, for example, an unwillingness to underestimate the power of the acted upon to be independent of the action that partially constitutes it. After all, Butler argues, to understand identity as an effect of multiple conditions does not mean that it is either "fatally determined" or "fully artificial and arbitrary."[20] In fact, she points out, it is the constructed status of the self that opens up the possibility of agency. To the extent that constructedness is the co-meaning of emptiness, Buddhist traditions would agree. As we have noted, emptiness itself is also a dependent arising. It does not map neatly onto the contemporary feminist debate, however, because although the idea of dependent arising is a valid category for most postmodern theorists, "unconditioned" most definitely is not. Yet the possibility of experiencing the unconditioned is central to Buddhist theory and practice, and the unconditioned realm of emptiness means that there is an objective dimension that corresponds to the internal subjective dimension of mindfulness and concentration.

Middle Way Buddhist philosophy emphasizes what I call ontological nondualism, meaning that emptinesses and dependent arisings are indivisible.[21] In other words, the play of differences, the process of conditioning, is an insufficient description of how things are. Moreover, the conditioned and unconditioned can be experienced simultaneously because conditioned things and unconditioned emptiness are intrinsically compatible (ontological nondualism) and because the mind is sufficiently concentrated to be free from patterning by objects or thoughts (making possible cognitive nondualism). In other words, it is possible both because of how things are and how they are known. (Thus, from a Buddhist perspective, postmodern emphases on the constructed and endlessly diffuse nature of things, combined with its unwillingness to admit of any category outside the process of diffusion, is like talking about dependent arising without emptiness.[22]

The importance of emptiness to the Buddhist tradition is not just that emptiness is considered true, but that understanding it changes the subject in desirable ways, that is, in ways that complement concentration and compassion. This conviction indicates Buddhism's practical orientation, even if its philosophical exuberance sometimes veers in a different direction. This practical orientation stands in contrast to the tendency in Western philosophy to separate epistemology from ontology. Feminist theory by and large both protests and replicates this separation, which at least some feminists see as contributing to the abstractness of modern philosophy.[23] For Buddhist traditions, it is in the interfacing of these approaches that all hope and explanation rests. In Indo-Tibetan Buddhist systems, as we have seen, the attention given to ontological descriptions of persons or things is generally matched by detailed consideration of what happens to the subject who knows this.[24] Knowing emptiness can reorient subjective experience in ways that other types of knowledge cannot.

In developmental strategies such as this meditation on emptiness, the shift in the subject is explained largely in terms of the interplay between conceptual and nonconceptual states. The stabilizing force of concentration balances the sense of destabilization that comes from undoing one's previous experience of the world. Buddhists would agree with postmodernists that the mind and its activities are linguistic in general, but not that mental functioning is irreducibly linguistic. Unlike the textual idolatry of some of contemporary theory, the words that are the starting point for reflection on emptiness and compassion do not continue to govern the subject in the same way throughout the developmental process. The mind is not thought alone; nor is it separate from bodily energies. It is also clarity and knowing.[25] And Buddhists emphasize that this clarity and knowing can experientally be fused with the unconditioned emptiness.

Mental clarity and mindfulness are crucial to the process of accessing the unconditioned. In order to experience emptiness, the mind must be steady and focused. When one fully knows the absence that is emptiness, one knows it with one's full, speechless attention. This complete and fully affective experience of emptiness cannot come about only through language, although language does play an important role. In contrast to much of postmodern feminist theory, Buddhists would contend that language does not have equal influence on all subjective states. Mindfulness and its furtherance as concentration are crucial cases in point. Buddhist wisdom is often praised as "inexpressible." However, the force of this description shifts considerably in a system that valorizes both conceptual and nonconceptual experience. The inexpressible unconditioned emptiness is not nonexistent. Knowing emptiness requires at least some measure of clarity, stability, and intensity. These are subjective dimensions, as we have observed, little attended to in contemporary Western theory.[26]

By the second of the five classic stages of the developmental path to enlightenment, one is able to rest the mind effortlessly, and for as long as one chooses, on an image of emptiness.[27] That mental image serves to eliminate the "self," or inherent existence, that one previously identified. Then the sense of mind and emptiness as separate subsides as one focuses on the increasingly subtle image of that absence, and finally the image fades away completely. This fading away leads to the direct experience of emptiness, classically described in Indian and Tibetan Mahayana texts as utterly nonconceptual, because there is no mental image to separate the mind from the emptiness now encompassed by its understanding. When emptiness is known fully and directly (these terms are synonymous in the Buddhist context), the relationship of mind to emptiness is said in Geluk texts to be like "fresh water mixed with fresh water." Although they are not actually one, in that emptiness is not a consciousness and a consciousness is not mere absence, there is no experienced differentiation between them. They seem utterly fused. This is the classic moment of cognitive nondualism.

According to the Consequentialist system, the most subtle misconceptions overcome by an understanding of emptiness are innate, meaning they are neither learned nor socially constructed, but are prior to and independent of language acquisition. They are embedded not only in the conceptual mind, but in the sensory processes themselves. Things simply look, smell, and taste more solid, findable, and inherently available than they actually are. Although similar to "original sin" in that it is there from the beginning, subtle ignorance can nevertheless be completely overcome. It is neither an essential nor an inalienable quality of the mind that we experience things this way.

Although the wisdom of emptiness is famous throughout the Buddhist world for being inexpressible, concentration bears even less association with verbal activity than does wisdom, primarily because concentration experientially removes one from the influence of one's most immediate thoughts and mental images. Since these thoughts and images are arguably the prime means by which cultural conditioning shapes or affects the individual, concentration is an important part of Buddhist arguments for the possibility of an "unconditioned" state. These arguments, as we have seen, probably represent Buddhism's most serious disjunction with feminist and other contemporary theory.

Geluk and much of Indo-Tibetan Buddhism, like postmodern feminisms and contemporary theory in general, understand language to be a system of imperfect and indirect representation, with no full correspondence between any word and its referent.[28] Words do not describe the actual emptiness, any more than the word "table" fully describes or elicits an image of a complete table. Emptiness cannot be communicated fully through language, but neither can ordinary things. However, when emptiness is known *directly*, thought is absent. At the same time, emptiness, the absence of inherent existence, is fully present to one's experience. Nothing about emptiness is deferred or differentiated from one's own mind. Yet there is nothing particular in emptiness to be assumed present in the first place. It is, as we have said, a mere absence. It has no qualities that can or should be captured by language. From a Buddhist perspective, the contemporary fascination with the incoherent and uncapturable multiplicities that construct self and knowledge suggests an intellectual history that never took sufficient note of the interdependent, constructed, and impermanent nature of things in the first place. Recognition of constructedness does not, for Buddhists, devalorize the unconstructed.

By knowing emptiness, Tibetan and other Buddhist traditions maintain, the subject engages its most quintessential quality, the one that makes all others possible. Its very ability to know depends on the empty and adventitious nature of ignorance. Emptiness, unlike the mind's other qualities, is not subject to change and in this sense is more completely one's own than any other quality. The subtle knowing of emptiness is thus the innermost and most "personal" experience possible; in another sense, however, because all emptinesses are the same, it is a universal experience. This kind of "personal" clearly cannot be conflated with the sense of particular personal and interpersonal history so important in the contemporary West. Like the cultivation of calm and concentration, the experience of emptiness entails a different order of interiority than the textual, content-laden localized and particularized subjectivity associated with contemporary theory and modern psychologizing.

A NEW STORY

Postmodern feminists frequently appropriate Derrida's observation that language's interwoven meanings are never fully present, but always capable of being supplemented by some more complete (yet always incompletable) statement, some further description of context.[29] Also, Judith Butler notes that identity is always an object of language because it is always being signified by language, and also that it continues to have meaning as it moves across various interlocking discourses. She concludes that one cannot solve the problem of agency by seeking out some sort of "I" that exists prior to language. Moreover, language is such that any context is open to further description and any description of limits simply carries attention to what lies outside them.[30] Buddhist understanding of dependent arising is similar to postmodern theory in that parts and causes are recognized as infinite, making anyone's or anything's context boundless and unmasterable. However, there is an important difference in the Buddhist orientation that must not be overlooked in acknowledging this apparent analogy. Although the subject irrevocably infiltrated by language can never be full or complete, the empty subject that is a dependent arising can be complete with respect to knowing its own unconditioned status, its emptiness of being anything other than a dependent arising.

But what kind of "completeness" are we talking about? Not the mastery of infinite detail. Postmodernists have demonstrated effectively that this is impossible, and Buddhists have their own reasons for agreeing. For Buddhists, however, the point is not to lay claim, perceptually or conceptually, to a complete set of information or a seamless context. Rather, it is to develop fully the subject's capacity for nonconceptual clarity, intensity, and expansive, zestful attention. Experience of emptiness requires and strengthens this capacity, until the practitioner becomes capable of resting in this nonconceptual and stable subjective dimension. There is no subjective impulse or objective character by which one is inevitably drawn on to the next incomplete set of details. In this sense, the subject is complete and at rest in ways unimaginable in feminist or other postmodern perspectives.[31]

It is important to recall that Buddhists do not define a subject only by what she knows, or even by what she feels. For Buddhists, silence and the categories of mind most closely associated with it—mindfulness, calm, and concentration—allow the subject to proceed beyond the play of data and detail (without necessarily losing sight of them) into a different dimension of subjectivity. Largely because of Buddhists' emphasis on the capacity for calm focusing, incompleteness is not the issue for Buddhist traditions that it is for feminist (and other) postmodernists.

There is thus a sharp distinction between these Buddhist and the contemporary sensibilities we have described: the crucial Buddhist claim that a subject can engage an object like emptiness "completely" depends, not on the extent to which one fully masters its details (emptiness hasn't any), but on the way the collateral coherence of a consciousness can become manifest. For those who propose language and writing as the governing metaphor of experience, agency and mastery are focal concerns, as evidenced by the near-hysteria (in intellectual dress of course) at the possibility of their dismantling or demise. Why make such a fuss about *différance* except for the desire for complete possession and coherence thwarted by it? The bias toward "mastering" of the master narratives, against which postmodernism poses itself, resurfaces here.

The inseparability between conditioned things and their unconditioned aspect can be seen as a reminder that feminist essentialist and postmodern positions, if never wholly coalesced, are nevertheless intimately entwined across their divide. Why the surge of interest in the constructed nature of gender if not for the sake of women? Why trouble to clarify the meaning of *différance* if not to counter old assumptions and power structures that have kept women on the sidelines? Similarly, those who espouse forms of essentialism must assume that their espousal will make a difference. Why propose that there is a female nature, or praise the revelations of female body or female writing, if not for the conviction that change is possible, that perceptions of the female self and body can alter how women are perceived and the ways they perceive themselves and others? In these ways and more, the essentialist and postmodern positions depend on one another; they are inextricably interconnected.

Certainly, despite the difficulties articulated by essentialist and postmodern feminisms, many women are finding different ways of being powerful, ways consistent with their values. This Buddhist material helps support models of selfhood that are nonoppositional, wherein self and other mutually define, rather than undermine, each other as categories. I take the Buddhist perspectives discussed here as suggesting that contemporary feminist theory, like other postmodern reflection, is severely limited by its inability to take seriously the possibility of something beyond its own constructs, a silence not governed by words, a metaphysical space not conditioned by things.[32] The category of emptiness makes it feasible to consider types of subjectivity that otherwise would not be possible. A clear awareness of emptiness means, for example, that the subject is focused on an object replete with meaning and empty of content. Further, since the calming and other functions related to a full understanding of emptiness are also associated with shifts in breathing, posture, and other physiological processes, it is a knowledge that viscerally unites mental and physical dimensions.

By postmodern lights, Buddhism could be judged naive for claiming that the "truth" that is emptiness can be fully present to consciousness. But what kind of "truth" is at issue here, and what kind of consciousness? Geluk texts claim that emptiness, not having any quality except that of absence, is not subject to the kind of deferral or incompleteness that characterizes most forms of knowing. In addition, the mind that knows emptiness directly is a calm, concentrated, and nonverbal mind. It does not have the same relationship to traces of difference as other kinds of minds. These claims suggest different criteria for meaningful "presence," the measure being not how much of an object one knows—not how successfully one captures the object—but how focused, intense, and clear the knowing mind itself is.

The unconditioned and nonverbal are "other" to the deconstructive network. Is it possible that women, too, are in some sense "other" to this network? Despite the significance of Derridean and other postmodern theory for many feminists, do we not find that women, mother, *mater*, matter, matrix, maternal ground, and foundations are all excluded by contemporary theory? Can this be accidental? Jane Flax eloquently describes how Derrida's system mirrors the exile of "woman," and all she represents, from the world of "man," "culture," and "center."[33] Women, the nonverbal, and the unconditioned are all indescribable through the language and categories of contemporary feminist theory largely because they lie outside this male-ordered fascination with individual agency, legacy, and mastery. This at least is my reading of the "question" behind the "answer" of *différance*, including its insistence on not really being an answer. In questioning the possibility of a coherent self, feminists seem sometimes to confuse all of selfhood with the unitary, masterful, and oppositional self they rightly criticize. The glory days of old when individuality, agency, and truth were enshrined as cultural icons only lend drama to their present dethroning. Due to this fascination with mastery, the unmasterability of the textualized world becomes the most mysterious and interesting thing about it. I agree with Jane Flax that women are by definition outside this story line.

The Buddhist story line we are following is different. It esteems the possibility of subjective silence and objective absence. Subjective silence is not an inability to speak, it is the background of all speech. It is associated with the presence of concentration, an ability to access not only conditioned phenomena, which can never be completely known, but the emptiness to which one can, in the Buddhist sense, be fully present. Objective absence in Buddhism is not nothing; it is the unconditioned possibility of something. Most important in this context, the subjective dimension of silent concentration offers a space for the subject apart from its dominating knowledge, and the objective dimension of the unconditioned gives it an area in which to function. The two cannot be separated. Silence and its analogue, the unconditioned emptiness, are a partnership that contemporary theory as presently constituted does not recognize. Women and others can make claims outside this "story line" by swimming past its boundaries into the deeper dimensions of subjectivity.

Perhaps here lies a clue to a more inclusive philosophical move. By emphasizing the presence of attention rather than completeness of knowledge, the unconditioned can be inextricably included as part of the conditioned. In this way, it is possible to have a story that neither masters, succumbs to, nor even excludes the particular, including its male audience. In this way, we avoid creating a "master" narrative. In fact what we are working toward is not precisely a narrative—it does not lie in the domain of words only—but a posture. With this posture, a nonverbal gesture, it becomes possible to acknowledge connections between the spacious dimension of consciousness revealed by mindfulness and the undominated objective arena suggested by emptiness. In the tradition of the Great Bliss Queen these dimensions are joined completely in the vast single sphere revealed by innate awareness. In all these examples, because dominating, capturing, or naming an object is not in question, the issues of presence, mastery, and coherence lose their force—as does the enforcement of woman's position as object.

᭙᭙᭙ WOMEN AND THE GREAT BLISS QUEEN

CHAPTER 6

Nondualism and the Great Bliss Queen

> If the human consciousness had not included . . . an origi-
> nal aspiration to dominate the Other, the invention of the
> bronze tool could not have caused the oppression of
> woman.
>
> Simone de Beauvoir, *The Second Sex*

> Thought has always worked through opposition. Through
> dual hierarchical oppositions. . . . Everywhere (where) an
> ordering intervenes, a law organizes what is thinkable by
> (dual, irreconcilable, or sublatable dialectical) oppositions.
>
> Hélène Cixous, "Sorties"

Western religious traditions have often supported, or been used to support, dualisms that image women negatively. The active-passive, reason-emotion, and mind-body dyads are primary examples of these. Indeed, religions, or any system energized by ideals, have a built-in propensity for hierarchical polarizations. Models that acknowledge differences without placing them in hierarchy or opposition are thus useful not only to feminist thought and practice but also to the revitalization of religious traditions that through their implication in sexism and racism have sometimes come to belie their own deepest intents.

Ever since Simone de Beauvoir called attention to women's secondary status in Western society, women have struggled to define and counter the polarized oppositions on which this marginalization is often based. Buddhist traditions are also concerned with overcoming various kinds of dualism.[1] According to the Indian and Tibetan Middle Way traditions we have discussed, the dualistic impulse lies deep within the human psyche. It stems in large measure from an unre-

flective reification of the distances between subject and object, self
and other. Even the physical senses seem to be constructed along
subject-object dichotomies, making dualistic perspectives so ingrained that it becomes difficult to imagine anything else.

I have suggested that in Buddhist practice the twin dimensions of
subjective silence and its objective analogue, the unconditioned emptiness, provide a new perspective on the essentialist-postmodern co-
nundrum in feminism—both its theoretical disjunctions and the
real-life challenges of maintaining meaningful personal coherence
while acknowledging and responding to the multiple factors that con-
stitute, create, and change one's sense of self and environment. The
Tibetan literature on the Great Bliss Queen provides another vantage
point on the architecture of duality and a passage through it. Mindfulness, compassion, and an understanding of emptiness are all incorporated into the meanings and practices associated with the Great
Bliss Queen. In her, the categories of the unconditioned and a form of
mindfulness unique to the discovery orientation of Great Completeness traditions coalesce to suggest further ways of undoing dualisms.

This coalescence occurs partly because the advantage of conjoining developmental and discovery perspectives was recognized in important if isolated instances in Tibet. Two major Nyingma monasteries, the Great Completeness Monastery and the Do-drup-chen
Monastery in east Tibet, incorporated Geluk scholarship into their
curriculum as a preparation for the study and practice of Nyingma
esoterica.[2] Their literature on the Great Bliss Queen offers an interesting model of how "oppositional" positions may intermingle. The
Tibetan authors on whose work I have drawn regarding Yeshey Tsogyel are among the most illustrious figures in Nyingma and part of a
major synthetic tradition. They were trying to understand as complementary the developmental and discovery Buddhist models their culture had inherited, and for this reason their work is an ideal resource
as we continue to reconsider the analogous essentialist and postmod-

ern complementarities and disjunctions. In articulating the non-dualism symbolized by the Great Bliss Queen, we are also exploring a traditional linkage between Geluk sutra and Nyingma tantra.

The actual liturgy of the Great Bliss Queen is found in a three-volume collection known as the *Very Essence of the Great Expanse*.[3] Used by a broad spectrum of practitioners and liturgical exegetes, it is an excellent resource for exploring how the more explicitly philo-sophical expressions of Buddhism, which in their most rigorous form were accessible to a relative minority of Tibetan Buddhists, were as-similated to widely known styles of practice.

Our discussion proceeds mainly from two eighteenth-century Nyingma commentaries.[4] Both Ngawang Denzin Dorje and Do-drup-chen III, as well as their monastic institutions, integrated de-velopmentally oriented Geluk-style sutra studies and discovery-oriented Nyingma Dzog-chen practice. Their work casts the Great Bliss Queen as an expression of the interweaving of these two classic Buddhist orientations. The Great Bliss Queen overcomes the dualis-tic tendencies implicated in unenlightened existence. As before, I take "dualism" to signify an opposition that presumes a difference or tension that goes beyond taking account of qualities unique to logi-cally related categories, for example, subject and object, sacred and profane, or enlightened and unenlightened. Such dualisms require hard boundaries, clear contrast, whereas the Great Bliss Queen's symbolism and the ritual centered around her allow the practitioner to emulate her nonoppositional posture.

In synthesizing the iconographic and philosophical discussions of Yeshey Tsogyel, I have earlier identified three nonoppositional dyads that refer to the relationship among objects, between subjects and objects, and between one's present self and future ideal. I call these dyads ontological nondualism, cognitive nondualism, and evo-lutionary nondualism.[5] These are not traditional Buddhist terms; I have coined them to express what I see as central Buddhist assumptions significant for our conversation. Here, I want to reflect on the meaning of these assumptions, and to explore how the figure of the Great Bliss Queen expresses them.

EMPTYING DUALISM
Ontological Nondualism

> Because there is birth from the birthless,
> Living beings are confused.
> Jigmay Lingpa, quoted in
> Ngawang Denzin Dorje, *Ra tig*

In our discussions of mindfulness, compassion, and selflessness, we considered developmental models of practice, especially from Geluk literature. In that context, ontological nondualism refers primarily to the union of ordinary phenomena with their emptiness, or to the relationship between conventional and ultimate phenomena.[6] Ontological nondualism has three significant elements: the mutual pervasion or co-extensiveness of conventional and ultimate phenomena, the dependence of each on the other, and the assertion that one does not in any way contradict or cancel out the other.

Conventional and ultimate pervade each other and never exist separately. In that sense, neither has ontological supremacy. Even to say that the ultimate is immanent within the mundane would be too dualistic if by that one implies that the actual center of ultimacy is elsewhere or that the ultimate is only secondarily present in the mundane. Far from being in opposition, neither the conventional nor the ultimate can exist without the other. There cannot be an emptiness of a person, for example, without the conventionally existent person.[7] Conventional and ultimate phenomena comprise a single indissoluble unit.

Not only are conventional and ultimate phenomena coexistent, but to understand one is to understand the other more fully. That is why the image of the Great Bliss Queen, properly understood, leads also to an understanding of her emptiness. Similarly, by participating in the conditioned aspects of everyday life, one is, knowingly or not, also engaged with the unconditioned that makes conditioning possible. The mutuality between the conditioned conventional and the unconditioned ultimate is the means by which Buddhists include the unconditioned in the stories they tell of how things are. No need, therefore, to turn away from worldly matters to understand their empty nature. Both conventional and ultimate must be understood correctly—one cannot be ignored owing to excessive fascination for the other. Otherwise, there is danger of a nondualistic model *incompatible* with worldly activity, which would only perpetuate the hierarchy between sacred and profane, active and passive, conventional and ultimate. Such a model would be ineffective as a source of spiritual strength in political or other useful endeavors.

Enlightened engagement in the world, like the compassionate activities of the Great Bliss Queen, means one distinguishes one thing from another without reifying or polarizing this distinction. Although physically inseparable, conventional and ultimate phenomena can indeed be reflected upon and cognized separately.[8] To understand how persons and things exist without inherently existing is to walk the fine line of the Middle Way; it is also, in this Nyingma ritual, to cultivate the skylike wisdom through which the Great Bliss Queen moves.

The unconditioned is most ideally accessed by pure, nonconceptual mindfulness and concentration, whereby one becomes grounded in one's own physical and mental experience. This grounded mindfulness collapses the mind-body opposition on which much negativity toward women is founded, suggesting the possibility of an *embodied* groundedness, one that takes its certainty and steadiness as much from a specific way of holding mind and body as from ideas or ideals.

The difference between embodying an idea and thinking it is subtle, but crucial.

Cognitive Nondualism

Dualism structures not only thought, but sensory perception as well. Seeing, hearing, and other sensory processes are the most palpable events in our lives. But cognitive nondualism claims that the apparent bifurcation between senses and their objects is exaggerated and that meaningful activity in "real life" can take place without a hardened dichotomy between subject and object. To say that the deeply ingrained sense of subject-object bifurcation is no more than a rectifiable mistake, even at the sensory level, is among the most radical claims in Buddhism. An enlightened person like Yeshey Tsogyel is seen to function in the world without being drawn into the subject-object dichotomy. Cognitive nondualism also means that, like the categories of self and other, those of subject and object create and depend on each other. Moreover, as with self and other, no one is only a subject or only an object.

Claims regarding nondualistic experience do not get much attention from Western philosophical inquiries into Buddhism, partly because they are not taken seriously and partly because, as already suggested, the epistemological categories associated with them, such as calming and concentration, do not fit easily into Western discourse. But for this very reason, we must examine nondualism closely in the hope of gaining a new vantage point on these issues. Feminism, after all, has been deeply concerned with the subject-object split, though for different reasons than Buddhist philosophy. What is important for Buddhists on cognitive grounds is important for feminists on psychological and political grounds: once subject and object are experienced as mutually defining, "you" and "I" may retain our different identities without becoming the dominated, subjected, or objectified other. Even if one has not had such a nondualistic experience, or doubts that it is possible, the theoretical categories associated with it are extremely useful in expanding the way one structures self and subjectivity.

Evolutionary Nondualism

> Before any Buddhas and sentient beings
> When even the names of these did not exist
> There occurred the singularity, the primordial ancestor, the nature of mind.
> *The Valid Scripture*, quoted in the *Authenticity of Innate Awareness*

Evolutionary nondualism closes the distance between ordinary and enlightened persons. Since the mind of every living being is empty and primordially pure, it has no inherent or immutable defilements, limitations, or hindrances. There is nothing to prevent ordinary human beings from the enlightened state of freedom. Thus, Mahayana Buddhists not only venerate and aspire to a deep rapport with enlightened beings such as Yeshey Tsogyel, but seek such enlightenment themselves.

Classic Buddhist thought, like Freudian psychology, sees the human mind in general as ruled by irrational afflictions. However, Buddhist traditions emphasize that because the mind is not inherently troubled or limited, these tendencies can be eradicated completely, though the mind itself remains. Freud would not agree. His so-called Nirvana principle signifies that the mind's structure necessarily involves a precarious balance of opposing mental proclivities and that this balance is always in danger of coming undone.[9] No contemporary school of psychology takes seriously the possibility of human beings' having complete and perpetual ease of mind, nor do traditional Western theologies.

The radical Buddhist vision of a mind able to divest itself utterly of all problematic tendencies—able to do so because it is empty and primordially pure—is central to evolutionary nondualism. Regarding this, a famous verse of Nagarjuna reads:

> For whom emptiness is possible
> Everything is possible
> For whom emptiness is impossible
> Nothing is possible.[10]

Above all, emptiness makes enlightenment possible. For this reason, the mind or its emptiness is sometimes described as a Buddha-womb or Buddha-embryo (*tathāgathagargha, bde gzhin gzhegs ba'i snying po*).[11] The *Ratnagôtravibhāgavākhya*, an important Indian source for this theory, says that the two-word compound Tathagatha-garbha is to be construed as a womb that is *tathatā*, "a womb that is reality."[12] To know this reality, which Buddhists also call emptiness, is to give birth to enlightenment. In this connection, womb and other female body imagery are central in the iconography and liturgy of Yeshey Tsogyel.

Yet the womb of enlightenment is possessed by all living things, and its fruit depends above all on oneself, not on another, not even Buddha. It is therefore within the province of any person to reap from her own Buddha-womb her own Buddhahood. By contrast, in famous occurences of womb imagery in both the Old and New Testaments, control of a woman's womb is not seen as the province of human male or female, but only of (an apparently male) God.[13]

It is crucial to all three forms of nondualism that in Buddhist thought there is no "In the beginning"—that pivotal moment which informs so much of mainstream Jewish and Christian thought. Creation by the fiat of a singular and apparently male being is far more dualistic than gestation following intercourse with another. When Athena springs from the head of Zeus, when the world arises from the word of God, a "child" is immediately flung forth as separate. There is no nurturing period of gestation during which mother and child are joined in one body.[14] Creation through words in particular favors the art of the mind over the art of the body, undermining the more coherent art of the self by implicitly reinforcing the mind-body polarity (which, like other polarities, is often used to denigrate women). Further, the moment of creation sets up a virtually unalterable dualism in most Jewish and Christian traditions. There is no way for created beings to erase the subsidiary status of their createdness. This status differential, so deeply ingrained in Western consciousness, arguably provides a powerful model for hierarchical power structures.

In Buddhist traditions, as we have seen, the creation process is characterized as cyclic. Innumerable world systems arise, exist, and are destroyed, all because of the actions, speech, and thoughts of their inhabitants. There is even a process akin to the Jewish and Christian Fall:

> At first the land surface was a marvelous substance that someone, through previous conditioning, was led into eating. Until that time, their spontaneously produced bodies had no anus or genitals; for the sake of excretion these now appeared. Gradually, the marvelous radiance of the beings degenerated, and the earth became hard with a corn-like plant growing in abundance. Some, however, were not satisfied with merely taking their portion day by day and began hoarding. Some began stealing; some killed; houses were built to hide the sexual act. Gradually the sins were committed, and the causes of birth in the bad migrations were made. The twenty aeons of formation were finished with the formation of the birth-places for animals, hungry ghosts, and hell-beings.[15]

However, the world is not produced in a one-time-only event. Rather, the kind of process described above occurs again and again. Nor is this cyclic process controlled by any one being. Indeed, an Indian Buddhist scripture entitled *Net of Brahma* (*Brahma-jāla-sutānta*) makes fun of the Hindu god, who, being the first person to be born into a newly emerging world, thinks to himself, "I am lonely; would that there were friends and companions around me." Shortly thereafter, as a result of their own ripening karma, others are in fact born into that world. Brahma, however, understands them to be the product of his own wishes and calls himself the creator of the world. Observing that Brahma was there first, the newcomers too are persuaded he is their creator. But, says the text, like themselves, he was simply experiencing the fruits of his own past lives.

The Great Completeness, which agrees in principle with the beginningless character of cyclic existence, describes "creation" in terms of subjective processes, a movement from the pure experience of Samantabhadra, the primordial Buddha who is also the primordial state of each individual, into delusion. This delusion is due to consciousness failing to recognize itself in the various appearances to the senses. Not recognizing itself, considering objects to be utterly separate from itself instead of its own reflections, consciousness becomes encrusted in duality.[16]

QUEEN OF THE SKY WOMEN

In her ritual context, the Great Bliss Queen is considered the principal Sky Woman, or *dakini*. Doctrinal and iconographical emphasis on the dakini has in Tibet vastly upstaged that of its male equivalent, the *daka*. It is difficult to say why or to assess whose interests are most served by such images. Certainly the image of a beautiful embodiment of wisdom, classically depicted as a fresh, sixteen-year-old girl, is appealing to men; some dakinis are fierce and more wizened; almost none look like real women. Feminists are right to be suspicious about images like these. At the same time, the qualities of courage, nobility, and perseverance detailed in Yeshey Tsogyel's biography dramatically state women's capacity for enlightenment and contribute to the prevailing Mahayana view that women are as suited as men for the most exalted teachings of Buddhism, as well as for Buddha-hood itself.

Dakinis are depicted as moving through the open space of wis-dom. They are known in Tibetan as "space-journeying ladies," or "females who travel through the sky" (*mkha' 'gro ma*).[17] This term, here translated as "Sky Woman" to preserve the poetic brevity of the Tibetan, is also used in colloquial Tibetan (minus the feminine *ma* ending) to signify those other skyborne creatures, birds, whose two wings symbolize the method and wisdom that form a complete path to Buddhahood.

The specific wisdom that defines dakinis is the nondualistic and vibrant knowing of a reality that Geluks call emptiness and that is de-scribed in a phrase unique to Nyingma as "beginningless purity" (*ka dag*) or "primordial freedom" (*ye 'grol*). The dakini moves in space because she fully understands and is active in this great sphere of pri-mordial purity and freedom. Like emptiness, primordial purity and primordial freedom are always present. Their spacious expanse is neither created through meditation nor placed in samsara by any form of divine intervention. It is simply in the nature of things. The Great Bliss Queen did not create this reality; she discovered it, as the practitioner of her ritual is also meant to do.

Sanskrit dictionaries, even of Buddhist Hybrid Sanskrit, merely define dakini as a "female ogre" or a "female imp feeding on human flesh."[18] In Tibetan, the phrase "sky- [or space-] journeying lady" is an abbreviation of a more elaborate term, "a lady who journeys per-vasively in the element of the sky" (*mkha'i khams su khyab par 'gro ma*). The Tibetan term that can mean either "space" or "sky" figures significantly in the discussion of Tsogyel's symbolism, where it also means "womb," by implication a spacelike womb. Her spatial ex-panse is thus empty and occupied, simultaneously vacant and fruit-ful. She has discovered her skylike nature and on this basis continually extends her own capacity for enlightenment and helps others to discover theirs. The spacious realm she inhabits unites compassion and wisdom, conventional and ultimate, subject and object, conditioned things and the unconditioned emptiness.

The great expanse that is both Tsogyel's womb and wisdom is in the Great Completeness traditions synonymous with the womblike sphere in which a Sky Woman is said to move. Her womb and other female organs are emblematic of enlightened wisdom and the state of Buddhahood itself, and are among the most important symbols associated with the Great Bliss Queen. We see here the valorization, not just of female imagery in general, but of female body imagery—a religious use of the very body that in some Indian and Tibetan Buddhist traditions epitomizes defilements to be abandoned.[19] In Nyingma Great Completeness traditions, the womb imagery associated with Yeshey Tsogyel suggests a Buddha nature that is "not merely empty, but has the nature of clear light," a more positive image than the pure absence that is the emptiness stressed by Geluk.[20] Here, the ultimate empty nature itself is filled with positive potential. "Clear light" here refers to a very subtle mind that can manifest, or be discovered, only when the coarser minds and the inner currents or winds (*prāṇa*, *rlung*) associated with them have settled or ceased. This is a settling process that begins with mindfulness and goes on to include mental calming and concentration. Commenting on this, the Nyingma lama Khetsun Sangpo observed that unless one has understood the non-contradictory relationship of emptiness and conventional phenomena, it is impossible to acknowledge this description of Buddha nature and the experience of primordial purity.

Among the numerous liturgical lineages within Nyingma, the *Very Essence of the Great Expanse* forms the basis for discussion of the Great Bliss Queen. As the name implies, these teachings represent the great expanse of enlightened understanding and are as dear to the Sky Women, the enlightened female wisdom beings, as the very essence of their own hearts.[21] Yeshey Tsogyel is praised as the most prominent of the Sky Women, and the essence she and they cherish lies within all beings, awaiting discovery. Indeed, Longchen Rabjam (*Klong-chen-rab-'byams*), the fourteenth-century founding inspiration of this liturgical tradition, went so far as to say that at the initial moment of enlightened understanding one is a "Buddha once again" (*yang sang sgyes*), because, after all, one has been a Buddha since time without beginning.[22]

When Ngawang Denzin Dorje, the seventeenth-century author of this tradition's most extensive commentary on the Great Bliss Queen ritual, expands on Yeshey Tsogyel's status as a Sky Woman, he uses both the typical Nyingma term "reality that is the great primordial freedom" (*ye grol chen po'i chos nyid*) and the classic Middle Way epithet "productionless" (*ajatā, skye ba med*) to indicate the emptiness or lack of inherently existent production, a concept we have already seen in Geluk discussions of selflessness: "The body of one who travels the skies is so-called because instances of her compassionate [activities] entirely suffuse the skylike sphere [which is] her wisdom— that reality which is the great primordial freedom, the fundamental nature of productionless from the very beginning of all the phenomena of cyclic existence and nirvana, appearances and beings."[23]

Whereas the womb or Buddha nature is in Geluk sutric interpretations equated with emptiness, the Great Completeness traditions of Nyingma and Bön describe it respectively as the great expanse (*dhātu, dbyings*) and the single sphere (*thig le nyag gcig*).[24] In the *Great Secret Commentary of Heruka*, Padmasambhava explains, "Because she pervades the element of wisdom and compassion and acts purposefully [for others' welfare], she is called Sky Woman."[25] As a unique coalescence of the active and quiescent, the Sky Woman appears in whatever form is appropriate for practitioners, just as a full moon gives rise to different images according to the size and shape of its reflector.[26] Thus, the Great Bliss Queen unites two domains, that

of conditioned, compassionate activities and that of the unconditioned, the spacelike realm through which she flies. The vast sky,
united with her wisdom, is the arena in which her innumerable compassionate activities take place.[27] The dakini can move in this pure
space because she fully understands the expansive sphere of primordial purity and freedom. But in another sense she *is* that realm; this is
one of several ways in which she overrides the oppositions between
subject and object or active and passive dimensions, as well as other
dualities in which "women" are often cast in the West:

> I bow down to and praise the wisdom Sky Women,
>
> Indivisibly appearing and empty, matrix of all things
>
> Unborn, unceasing, of skylike essence
>
> Showing themselves to any and all disciples.[28]

On this point, Ngawang Denzin Dorje quotes the *Secret Commentary*:

> All manner of magical creations dawn and appear from the birth-
> less sky, the spacious sphere of [the female primordial Buddha] Sa-
> mantabhadri, who is reality. [These creations] dawn and appear as
> peaceful goddesses, fierce goddesses, female Yakshas, and women
> who are the consorts of all six lineages, just as magicians can con-
> jure anything out of nothing. If one realizes the meaning of the
> birthless sky which is the actual reality, the mother [one's own] pri-
> mordial wisdom appears as whatsoever magical creations of
> production.[29]

The sphere that is the "body" or dimension of the Sky Woman is,
like that of any enlightened being, both birthless and of radiant appearance. Though evanescent, it is not mere illusion. Philosophically,
the term "birthless" is in developmentally oriented Middle Way traditions synonymous with emptiness. Let us remember that in the discovery model of the Great Completeness as discussed in the *Secret
Commentary*, the term "birthless" also evokes innate awareness, a
subjective experience distinguished from mindfulness. Unlike mindfulness, innate awareness is not cultivated; it is an ever-present qual-

ity of mind and can only be experienced nondualistically. Hence the need to discover rather than develop it. Recognition allows the already-present innate awareness to manifest (*rig pa mngon gyur*). This manifestation, and the need for a recognition process to set it in motion, cannot be considered "passive." At the same time, it is inappropriate to regard this recognition process as an active "development" in the manner of Geluk sutra practices discussed earlier. In the Great Completeness, rather than moving toward an ideal, one recognizes its immanence. However, just as development always involves some element of discovery, such as discovering the capacity to develop, a discovery orientation is necessarily joined with some form of development, such as developing the capacity for discovery or an ability to bring what one discovers into daily life. Because both elements are present in the literature and ritual practice of the Great Bliss Queen, the antipathy between development and discovery dissolves in her.

It needs to be clear that the "spacious sphere" of the Sky Woman is not an enclosed shape, but an unbounded vastness. In this way it harkens back to characterizations of innate awareness and the single sphere (*thig le nyag gcig*). How would one make a case for the existence of unbounded vastness? One need only call attention to the enormous variety of conditioned and unconditioned phenomena. All that exists, conditioned and unconditioned, "all of samsara and nirvana is . . . the single sphere *because there are many contradictory perspectives.*"[30] Far from undermining variety, the concept of the single sphere finds in the inevitable contradictions of the world proof for its own existence. Put another way, it is precisely being rife with pluralism that validates it as an all-pervasive expanse, and in this sense as single. This single sphere, like mindfulness and concentration, models a nontotalizing, nonmastering form of subjective coherence. Its coherence comes from a certain style of awareness, not from any uniformity among the many perspectives or phenomena that participate in it. Indeed, its very plurality demonstrates its singularity. To feel that one's mind both is and participates in a single sphere means that there is no one feeling, thought, or identity that wholly defines it, and yet it is whole.

The Great Completeness tradition thus puts forward a different style of practice than either sutra or tantra. The chief metaphors of the developmental sutric enlightenment process are abandonment (*spang*) and renunciation (*nges 'byung*). One is encouraged to abandon and renounce nonvirtues and other impediments. The mindfulness and introspection that make this possible are cultivated with considerable effort. In tantra the chief metaphor is that of transformation (*sgyur ba*).[31] In tantric practices nonvirtue is not abandoned but transformed into the qualities of enlightenment by making use of the subtle physical energy associated with afflictions, especially desire and anger. Ethics, concentration, and wisdom increase simultaneously. The Great Bliss Queen ritual can be enacted within this kind of understanding.

Emphasizing neither renunciation nor transformation, though incorporating both into its preparatory practices, the Great Completeness privileges a method known as "self-liberation" (*rang 'grol*), sometimes described as "liberation in its own spot" (*rang sar 'grol*). Liberation takes place in the situation just as it is, because one's mind and all things are, despite powerful appearances to the contrary, primordially pure.[32] If one has not yet made this essential discovery, the Great Bliss Queen ritual can prepare one for it. If one is familiar with the Great Completeness perspective, one performs the visualization and recitation of the Great Bliss Queen ritual entirely within an experience of innate awareness.[33] In either case, the ritual encompasses the three nondualisms already discussed.

One way of accessing the primordial purity so important to the Great Completeness tradition is a practice known as "pure vision." This involves visualizing companions, family, surroundings, and so forth as creations of light, the habitat of an enlightened being. From the viewpoint of the Great Completeness, such pure vision is not an imaginative overlay, but a move toward understanding things as they are. As Khetsun Sangpo taught it, this practice allows you to understand that apparently ordinary things and persons have "been [primordially pure] from the very beginning" so that "you are identifying their own proper nature. Your senses normally misrepresent what is there, but through this visualization you can come closer to what actually exists."[34] In short, by identifying one's body, companions, and world with those of the Great Bliss Queen, one develops the ability to discover what has always been there. This being so, there is no need to renounce or change anything, only to see it more completely. This is the Great Completeness tradition's special mix of ontological and cognitive nondualisms. Unlike the tantric traditions, in which it is necessary to cease the coarse sense and mental consciousness in order for the most subtle mind of clear light to appear, the Dalai Lama observes that "in the Old [Nyingma] Translation School of the Great Completeness it is possible to be introduced to the clear light without the cessation of the six operative consciousnesses."[35] Hence the possibility of "discovering" what is already in our midst. Such discovery reveals a spontaneous presence (*yon dan hlun gyis grub ba*) of collateral qualities such as clarity and spontaneous responsiveness. Thus, comments Longchen Rabjam, "primordially pure primordial wisdom is free in the face of thought and the primordial wisdom, with a nature of spontaneity, abides as primordial radiance, and profound clarity."[36]

Being "free from the face of thought" does not mean thoughts are absent, but that they do not interfere with primordial wisdom. Thought is not a contradiction to the mind's unconditioned nature, but an expression of it. In this way, one maintains the coherence of primordial purity in the midst of the flux of conceptual reflection. The figure of Yeshey Tsogyel embodies this nondichotomous subjectivity.

She unites active wisdom with the primordial and birthless nature of all things. This nature is at once unchanging and the crucial ingredient in all change. Therefore it, and she, cannot be simply passive. Nor can anyone who would emulate her by discovering the nondualistic and primordially pure innate awareness in herself or himself.

NONDUALITY AND FEMINISM

She is beyond all pairs of opposites, all distinctions between active and passive or past and future.

Luce Irigaray, *Speculum of the Other Woman*

We have observed that the most central questions essentialist and postmodern feminists are asking have to do with issues of agency and connection. Where does the power to act come from? How do we acknowledge the infinite strands—of history, society, family, race, class, friendship, speech, body-language, art, and writing—that continuously create us and still feel we can reach inside for something to call our own and rest upon? The opposition between active and passive, a dyad often iterated to women's detriment, is implicitly undermined in each of the nondualisms we discuss. Neither side of the ultimate-conventional, subject-object, or enlightened-unenlightened dyad can unilaterally be constructed as active or passive in relation to the other. Further, all these relationships depend on a state of mindfulness or concentration that itself belies the binary structure of active and passive.

Evolutionary nondualism means that no boundary separates the enlightened from the unenlightened state, nor does one have power over the other. Buddhas neither create, reward, nor punish non-Buddhas. Buddhas, with their origins in compassionate connectedness and wisdom, and their inability to override the movement of karma, are not ultimate autonomous individuals, not deities in the way that the Jewish and Christian God is often understood. Western men have arguably often taken this God's power and uniqueness as an implicit inspiration for their own or, alternatively, have projected their own hierarchical sense onto him. The power and authority attributed to this God is essentialist in orientation. Postmodern Western feminists repudiate this figure, along with the autocracies of meaning and language that define his authority.

More metaphorically, evolutionary nondualism means that there is a path—or even, in the discovery model, an immediate connection—to Buddhahood. There is no gap; there are only bridges between one's present experience of oneself and full embodiment of a more desirable future. One need not wait for a perfect social context or for just the right "subject position" to achieve enlightenment; nor is this an ideal fated to remain forever external or in the future. One can begin exploring one's path, or recognizing one's connection with one's highest purpose, right now.

Ontological nondualism reveals that within the ubiquitous conditioning of dependent arising, there is an unconditioned dimension in objects and subjects. This unconditioned dimension—the inessential essence of emptiness or the primordial purity of the Great Completeness—is most fully accessed by a subject that is also free from the ordinary conditioning of language and thought. For feminists, ontological nondualism can suggest an ultimacy that is not by definition on the far side of an abyss whose near side is occupied by humanity in general and women in particular. Ontological nondualism names the ultimate and conventional, or the divine and human realms, without opposing them, without ceding mastery to either, and thus without providing support for the tendency to correlate females with the mastered or subjugated element of a dyad.

Outside of meditation, the capacity to be compassionately responsive within a nondualistic (or less dualistic) framework counters the assumption that opposition and hierarchy are inevitable when one engages in action or relationships. The descriptions and methods associated with calming, concentration, and nonconceptuality—all of which aid access to ontological nondualism—may be the greatest Buddhist contribution to contemporary feminist reflection. A nondualistic understanding associated with these subjective states adds a powerful dimension to feminist critiques of the culturally assigned position of women as "objects" of the male subject.

The sense of fluidity between active or subject and passive or object positions suggested by cognitive nondualism is akin to the views of feminists like Cixous and Irigaray, with the important difference that Buddhists claim actual experience of this fluid relationship is possible and that a path to that experience is negotiable. Cixous argues that to equate women with passivity and thus with the death of action is to leave no real space for women. ("Either woman is passive or she doesn't exist.") She observes that in a binary pair one term must destroy the other to gain meaning, and she seeks ways of bypassing such formulas.[37] Analogously, the ritual of the Great Bliss Queen images the female embodiment of an agency that breaks through and utterly rearranges the polarities of active and passive, as well as the associated dualities of subject and object, conventional and ultimate.[38] As in the Middle Way and Great Completeness doctrines on which it is based, the Bliss Queen's ritual exemplifies the possibility of drawing from both sides of a polarity simultaneously.

Dualisms and gender biases inevitably involve claims about essences: the essence of truth, the essence of opposites, the essence of power. The question of what kind of essence emptiness might be is answered in different ways in the Geluk and Nyingma material discussed here. In both cases, while emptiness and primordial purity are considered "true" descriptions of how things are, their importance lies in the effect on the mind of acknowledging them and in the qualities of mindfulness, or expansiveness and insight, that enable a full appreciation of them. Moreover, mindfulness, concentration, or a deep experience of innate awareness is associated with physical and mental bliss. Yeshey Tsogyel, after all, is a blissful queen. Unlike the ordinary joys of life, hers is not a bliss *about* anything, but an expression of a natural and inalienable collateral quality of mind.

Because emptiness itself is characterless, and because it does not undermine particularity but makes it possible, emptiness is not the kind of essence that antiessentialist feminists decry. For many women, nevertheless, there will be something distasteful about claiming that women and men share an ungendered "essence." The point, however, is to realize that this unconditioned and therefore ungendered sphere provides the zest with which to participate in all manner of particularity. In this context, Buddhist traditions offer to feminist reflection an understanding of how one's subjectivity may participate in both the conditioned and unconditioned dimensions, and how an inessential essence can form the matrix for multiple possibilities, choices, and configurations. Buddhist thought offers also a model for integrating conditioned and unconditioned, or essentialist and nonessentialist, perspectives into a viable presentation of power, agency, and unconstructed potential. The ritual of the Great Bliss Queen is one way in which these various nondualisms are cultivated.

CHAPTER 7

Becoming the Great Bliss Queen: Her Ritual

> In ritual, the world as lived and the world as imagined . . .
> turn out to be the same world.
>
> Clifford Geertz, *Imagining Religion*

The twenty-fifth day of each lunar month is celebrated in Tibet as the day of the Sky Women. Nyingma lay and clerical practitioners come together to perform a *tshogs*, or Offering Meditation, and to recite the liturgy of a dakini such as the Great Bliss Queen, usually chanting it from memory to the accompaniment of bells and small drums. This ritual succinctly expresses elements of Buddhist traditions particularly useful to Western women and to feminist reflection on identity and subjectivity. Most important, the Great Bliss Queen ritual suggests ways of conjoining a variety of processes that participate in identity and contribute to one's experiencing nondualism.

The traditional purpose of this ritual is to become the Great Bliss Queen by enhancing the mindfulness, compassion, and wisdom that have prepared one to become her. For Western women, the ritual also provides an opportunity to imagine a type of personal coherence that encompasses one's own particular story, including all its contradictions. This middle way conjoining coherence and particularity may be the defining characteristic of feminist appropriations of Buddhist traditions, and of Buddhism in the West. Here we reflect on the traditional form of the ritual and then consider more specifically the challenges it poses and contributions it offers to Western feminists.

One begins the ritual by cultivating an experience of one's environment as the Great Bliss Queen's mandala and oneself as the Great Bliss Queen. The ritual focuses above all on this imagined identification of oneself with the enlightened Yeshey Tsogyel. In tantra, such identification is combined with other meditative techniques involving body and speech as well as mind. In the Great Completeness, this identification enhances the possibility of discovering or deepening one's experience of innate awareness. In both cases, chanting, visualization, and quiet reflection are interspersed throughout. In the concluding portion of the ritual, and in consonance with the opening motivation, one dedicates the merit of this practice to the benefit of all.

REFUGE IN ONESELF AND HER

> I bow down to the Great Bliss Queen
> Actual deity possessing excellence in all aspects
> Mother who births the conquerors who were, are, and will be
> The unchanging great bliss which is the
> Spacious sphere of primordial wisdom.
>
> Lama Gompo Tsayden,
> *Emulating the Quintessence of the Great Bliss Queen*
> (*bde chen gyal mo'i rdza ba'i sgrub pa*)

How does a Buddhist practitioner relate to a being like the birthlessly manifest Yeshey Tsogyel? Ideally, one takes refuge in her with a sense that her mind is no different from one's own. This process is enacted within what the Great Completeness calls the "natural view," that is, within the innate awareness of the natural mind, the spacious arena in which the Sky Woman courses and that is understood to be one's own true nature as well.[1] In the context of tantra, refuge is taken within the union of the stages of generation and completion—that is, within an appreciation of appearance and emptiness, ultimate and conventional, as utterly united. The most ordinary way of taking refuge, to bow with body, speech, and mind to a deity considered external to oneself, is not what is intended here, though undoubtedly some practitioners perform the ritual in this way.

Thus, the ideal refuge is the discovery of the primordial nature of one's own mind. To understand this is to recognize that one cannot newly meet the Great Bliss Queen:

> Having neither met nor parted [with you]
>
> I take refuge in you
>
> The unborn, primordial wisdom dimension of the Sky Woman.[2]

Yeshey Tsogyel is from the beginning of her ritual regarded as identical with oneself, an expression of the primordial purity and spontaneous excellence of one's own mind, even if the actual experience and nature of that identity is at first obscure. This is why meeting the Great Bliss Queen is in a very specific sense meeting the most primal part of oneself. If one does not yet know that aspect of oneself, other practices are required to prepare for this meeting.

In addition, Ngawang Denzin Dorje explains, the great primordial wisdom is unimpededly self-arisen; it is the natural condition of all things.[3] A Sky Woman is a great lady (*bdag nyid ma*) who has dominion over this unfabricated, natural, self-arisen wisdom:

> MA, Mother, essence of this enlightened mind
>
> MO, Woman, the self-arisen primordial wisdom
>
> [Whatever I say, it is your name][4]

Everything is the name and bears the mark of primordial wisdom, an expansive and innate awareness not dominated by any given particular. Even one's present defilements—greed or anger, for example—being adventitious, fail to defile or define it.[5] Regarding this, the present Dalai Lama writes: "Water may be extremely dirty; yet its nature remains just clear—its nature is not polluted by dirt. Similarly no matter what afflictive emotions are generated as the play of this . . . basic mind [it] remains unaffected by defilement, beginninglessly good."[6] This is a central premise of a discovery orientation.

THE VISUAL AND THE VOCAL

> Buddhism is a performing art.
> Stephen Beyer, *The Cult of Tara*

To begin the ritual, one intones the sound *ah* slowly and deeply. This letter sound is important for its symbolic value and for the way one can slowly release the breath while vocalizing it so as to produce a centering effect on the body, as well as a calming and clarifying effect on the mind. Its symbolic significance goes back to Indian Buddhism, and beyond that to the earliest period of Indian religion.

> It is the excellent letter of great meaning
>
> Nothing is born or arisen from this *[ah]*
>
> Free from all verbal expressions
>
> Yet the excellent cause of all expressions.[7]

The sound *ah* stands in the same relation to spoken and written language as emptiness does to all existing persons and objects. *Ah* is the "life" (*jīva, srog*) of all sounds and letters (in Tibet the letter is the sound, not the written shape) because every Sanskrit and Tibetan consonant, unless appended with a vowel signifier, is "naturally" conjoined with the sound *ah*. Thus, all letters and all writings emerge from *ah*, so that *ah* is a condensed embodiment of the entire Buddhist literature as well as the enlightened wisdom this literature expresses. The sound *ah* and the visualized letter itself, often imagined as a glow of white light in the center of the body, is in fact one's own empty innate awareness. Moreover, just as the sound *ah* participates in all language, so mind's natural luminosity participates in all its activities.

Consciousness, like the water described by the Dalai Lama, is never divorced from its purer aspect. Whatever appears to the mind or senses is therefore also associated with primordial purity. The Great

Completeness emphasizes the innate purity of these sensory objects through the practice noted earlier of relating to one's surroundings as a pure realm and one's companions as enlightened persons. Again, Khetsun Sangpo observes that this practice does not mean the blotting out of what is unsatisfactory. Rather, it requires seeing what is really there.[8] Thus, although Buddhism has been called a world-denying religion, from her own point of view the practitioner is not rejecting the world but understanding and seeing it more clearly.

The clarity of consciousness is present no matter what kinds of thoughts or physical sensations arise, both within the ritual and afterward. No amount of anger, for example, or distraction, can detract from this essential clarity. However, anger and distraction do occur and merit attention in their own right. They are as real as dreams and nightmares. Yet since the mind of clear light is an entity of luminosity and knowing, the quality of clear light can be identified even in the midst of a coarse consciousness like desire or hatred. As Do-drup-chen says, the factor of mere luminosity and knowing pervades all consciousnesses and is therefore present even during the generation of strong afflictions. Though afflictions naturally decrease with practice, one need not cease the mind and the five senses in order to experience their primordially pure nature.[9]

Just as sound both emerges from silence and is an expression of it, just as thoughts emerge from primordial clarity and are a manifestation of it, so in the course of the ritual, vizualizations appear from empty space. These visualized images are understood as manifestations of the emptiness or primordial purity of the birthless matrix that is the mind's own essenceless essence.[10] The relationship of images to the birthless matrix parallels the relationship of conventional and ultimate, or conditioned and unconditioned, phenomena and emptiness, thoughts and innate awareness. Just as mind is not simply its contents, so these images are not just their color, shape, and symbolic significance. Just as the mind has a dimension not entirely inhabited by ideas, and just as things in general have an unconditioned aspect not affected by causes and conditions, so the symbols of Tibetan ritual have a dimension not wholly confined to their iconographic meaning. One has to understand them also as displaying the potential of emptiness and primordial purity, as empty of inherent or independent existence, as free from any innate limit or defilement.[11] Thus, the figure of the Great Bliss Queen is itself an expression of primordial purity, emptiness, or innate awareness. In this sense, she is not a symbol. She does not represent innate awareness; she presents it to oneself, as oneself.

> When one understands that from one's very birth there is no inherent
>   nature
> One's own face is the unimpeded dimension of actuality itself
> And even while in cyclic existence,
> Bondage and liberation are not different.[12]

However, in actual performance of her ritual this understanding is probably only realized by fairly advanced practitioners. For most persons most of the time, she is in fact a symbol, a signifier, a path.

How does one begin to experience oneself as the Great Bliss Queen, uniting one's own natural state with the expanse she spiritually traverses and physically embodies? Ideally, within the Great Completeness, one experiences "No thought at all, not thinking of anything/Neither fabricating nor adjusting, set easily in the natural state."[13] Thus, practicing to become the Great Bliss Queen requires a settled, concentrated mind, facilitated in part through chanting the words of her ritual in the prescribed rhythm. This vocalization settles the breath and other inner currents (*prāṇa, rlung*) that affect the mind. In this context, the resonance and not the meaning of words is paramount.[14]

Chanting with others, one is embedded in a social matrix of practitioners and a resonant matrix of sound. The voices of others melt into the experience of self as one kinesthetically experiences the vibration of one's own voice, which one cannot separate from the surrounding sound of others. One is both an individual and part of a unity, and yet not entirely either.[15] The experience of chanting is thus well in tune with a sense of oneself as dependently constructed yet singular, and with selves as interrelational yet independent. At the same time, one is completely attentive and present to that experience. Moreover, the practitioner always experiences herself, not as disembodied mind, but very much as physical being. The ritual alternation between chanting and silent reflection also mirrors the embedded and individualistic layers of Tibetan culture discussed in chapter 2. When the sound fades away, and the images to which it gave rise as well, one is alone in imageless silence, free to take flight in one's own primordial wisdom.[16] This state of consciousness is fundamental to the practice of the Great Bliss Queen's ritual.

THE LADY AND HER MANDALA MANSION

Having cultivated a mind of womblike expanse filled with potential, one is ready to begin experiencing the mandala, or sacred environment, of the Great Bliss Queen. This mandala is the divine circle in which the practitioner appears to her own imagination as Yeshey Tsogyel. The outer band of the mandala represents flaming wisdom, which encircles and protects the practitioner. Within its compass are a series of adamantine walls of red, green, white, blue, and yellow.[17] All are transparent and luminous, composed only of light. The mandala is the ritual evocation of the single sphere (*thig le nyag gcig*), which the liturgy also describes as the entryway to the expanse of reality itself.

The mandala spontaneously emerges from a seed syllable, seen more as its inspiration than its cause, since in the process of visualizing it one understands the birthless nature of the vivid image and, by extension, the empty nature of all sensory objects. The form of the mandala also expresses this: "Its shape is completely round, for it transcends the 'corners' of the eight extremes of the elaborations of production, cessation, permanence, annihilation, and so forth [coming, going, being gone, or many]. Inside, it has the shape of a semi-circle [signifying] the taming of living beings through activities of compassionate engagement. [It contains also] the single door through which are extinguished the enumerated extremes of one and many with respect to the sphere of reality."[18] At the center is a mansion of "flaming bliss," an expression of the generativity associated

Mandala of the Mother, Holder of Awareness, the Great Bliss Queen Dakini

རིག་འཛིན་ཡུམ་ཀ་མཁའ་འགྲོ་བདེ་ཆེན་རྒྱལ་མོའི་དཀྱིལ་འཁོར

with the female organs of the Great Bliss Queen. Her generativity means, among other things, that her identity can never be captured or limited by a single type of being, or even a single form.

The mind-mandala of reality is a womb in that it makes possible all change and activity; it is also a womb because through realizing it one is born into enlightenment. Padmasambhava describes it so:

> This is the basis of all coming and going
> The place of arising of all existents,
> The womb of the mother consort.[19]

The generative quality of the empty expanse—something that receives considerably more emphasis in Nyingma than in Geluk traditions, is further symbolized by the crossed triangles at the center of the mandala. The triangles comprise an ancient symbol common to Hinduism and Buddhism and known in Tibetan as the "source of phenomena" (*chos 'byung*). Its resemblance to the Star of David suggests an ancient connection between Indic and Hebraic traditions.[20]

In the West, longing for or otherwise romanticizing womb-existence is looked upon as regressive. Indeed, Freud was famous for conflating all "mystical" inclinations with this longing for the "oceanic feeling" of the womb.[21] In a similar way, dimensions of experience not governed by language—in particular French feminists' descriptions of the period prior to entry into language—are presented as "regressive" states, never as deliberately chosen ones. Here, however, the womb expresses the ultimate spiritual discovery. How might cultural context account for these very different assessments? Once more, the different origin stories of East and West are crucial. In Buddhist traditions, for example, the womb that is an "expanse of reality" is a ubiquitous matrix, participating in and pervading all that is born from it. It is never left behind as is the maternal womb of contemporary Western description. In contrast, most Jewish and Christian traditions understand God to have created the world *ex nihilo*, that is, from a nothing that, like the maternal womb, is left behind. In Buddhist understanding, there is no dead space left behind when existence manifests.[22] The womb of the expanse is an ever-replenished resource, and the wish to renew association with it is not regarded as regressive but potentiating.

Ngawang Denzin Dorje offers several symbolic interpretations of the crossed triangles that symbolize the womblike source of phenomena. Practitioners of this ritual would have become familiar with all of these interpretations in the course of study, and would be free to recall them during the ritual. Each triangle signifies the female organ (*bhāga*), the opening to enlightenment. The six points of the two triangles signify the six perfections (giving, ethics, patience, effort, concentration, and wisdom) or, more simply, wisdom and virtuous activity. In addition, the points of the triangles, being junctures of two sides, represent nondualisms like the unities of compassion and wisdom or manifest appearance and emptiness. Therefore, like most of the ritual's symbols, the crossed triangles function as visual mnemonic devices, helping the practitioner to recall the various doctrinal points associated with the meditation, above all, that ultimate and conventional, conditioned and unconditioned, do not cancel each other out but abide together.

During the ritual, one is born into a new understanding of the enduring source of existence, ritually embodied as a female organ. The primordial emptiness from which all the ritual's images have emerged is self-contained and inviolable and, at the same time, explosive, capable of manifesting as the Great Bliss Queen or a host of other deities, either peaceful or wrathful. That primordial emptiness is the ethereal but knowable essence of one's own mind.

Having visualized the mandala, one instantaneously becomes the Great Bliss Queen at its center: "On a sun-disc is the chief of all Sky Women, the Actual Dimension naturally free from elaborations, the unborn sphere. She is Samantabhadri [the all-good female reality, source-matrix of cyclic existence and nirvana], the internal clear light, the great bliss which possesses all excellent aspects."[23] This passage again points to the "birthless" nature at the metaphysical heart of Yeshey Tsogyel. Those with pure vision can see her in the glorified form of Vajravarahi, the Adamantine Sow, depicted as a dancing Sky Woman with a head like a sow's just above her right ear.[24] For those with ordinary vision, she emanates in the form of Yeshey Tsogyel and

Displays whatever emanation will tame
Any given [person], just as, for example, the full moon in the sky
Emerges as [various] reflections in water vessels,

So from the Enjoyment dimension, analogous to the moon in the sky,
Appear inconceivable Emanations, analogous to [reflected] moons
    in water.

[Such occurs] wherever water vessels, analogous to disciples, exist.[25]

Yeshey Tsogyel is a skillful teacher whose every activity embodies the essence of her teaching. She is the enlightenment reproduced again and again in every practitioner. She is also the compiler, and in this sense the "producer," of the Buddhist Great Completeness traditions by which one comes to meet her through experiencing one's own birthless nature.

Yeshey Tsogyel's—and the practitioner's own—fusion of wisdom and bliss exemplifies yet again the coexistence of active and quiescent minds, constructed and innate, in a system that finds conditioned and unconditioned dimensions entirely complementary. As the unborn, birthless nature, the Great Bliss Queen is neither merely generative nor merely passive. Queen of the spherical, reigning through an orb of bliss, she conflates and confounds all such flatly polarized epithets.

During the visualization of the mandala and oneself in it as the Great Bliss Queen, one rhythmically chants the liturgy describing her/one's own appearance.

She has one face and two arms, and
The color of her body is red.
Naked, her feet evenly on the ground with one foot forward,
[An expression of] great passion and a laughing face.[26]

Some Buddhas have numerous heads. The Great Bliss Queen's single head here indicates the beginningless, spontaneously established purity present in all phenomena. Knowing this, the practitioner can experience all things, persons, and mental states as "one taste in the nature of reality." Middle Way philosophy understands this "one taste" as the union of the two truths; the Great Completeness tradition understands it as the luminosity inherent in all states of mind. In either case, hers is not a masterful or hegemonic oneness since it does not cancel out differences among objects. Indeed, just as mindfulness facilitates awareness of flux, the wisdom of emptiness facilitates understanding of illusion and change, and experience of innate awareness is compatible with the movement of thought.

The Great Bliss Queen has two hands, signifying the two prerequisites for enlightenment: method, especially compassion and concentration, and wisdom. Her red color signifies her passionate dedication to training disciples. Her nakedness indicates that she has overcome the obstructions to liberation from cyclic existence (kleśā-varaṇa, snyon sgrib) and the obstructions to full understanding of everything knowable (jñeyāvaraṇa, shes sgrib), and that she is free from the clothing of conceptualization that conceives subject and object dualistically. Her manner of standing, with two feet placed evenly on the ground, signifies that she dwells neither exclusively in mundane existence nor in the peaceful disappearance into the nature of reality. One foot is placed slightly in front of the other, an indication of her readiness to act for others.

She is described as having "a desirous expression on her face," indicating the force of her compassion to help all beings. Because all beings are in fact primordially enlightened, she smiles and laughs as she observes that, regardless of their present circumstances, the boundary between the ordinary and enlightened states is entirely permeable; persons are fundamentally free from misery, error, and powerlessness. She takes joy in recognizing that they need only discover this to experience their freedom. The psychological and cultural implications of a passionately happy female deity are so profoundly different from the more somber image of God, both East and West, that they bear much looking into.[27]

But she is not just cheerful, she is noisy also:

> In her right hand is a small drum of skulls
> Which is played, raised up to the ear.[28]

The drum (*damaru*) she holds is traditionally made of the joined backs of two skulls, symbolizing the conjunction of cyclic existence and natural nirvana, a synonym for emptiness. The connecting hollow between the skulls signifies that samsara and nirvana, conventional and ultimate, share the nature of a single reality. The two whiplike appendages that strike the leather stretched over the open sides of the skulls are said to signify the conventional and ultimate compassionate aspirations of those who have and have not cognized emptiness directly.

Her left hand [holds] the handle of a curved blade

Which rests at her side. She stands in a most prideful posture.[29]

Her knife handle indicates the vanquishing of subject and object accomplished when the ignorance binding one in cyclic existence is excised by the knife of knowing emptiness.[30] The emptiness that, as the womb of the great expanse, encompasses all that exists is here symbolized by the curved knife she holds in her hand. The Great Bliss Queen's prideful sexual posture signifies the development of blissful wisdom through the path of secret mantra. In addition to its specific symbolism, each aspect of the Great Bliss Queen embodies primordial purity or emptiness.[31] Ritual identification with her is meant to manifest clarity with respect to the primordial purity and spontaneous effulgence of the practitioner's own mind and its innate awareness.

All these images, formalized and embedded in oral chants and textual inscription, are a kind of illuminated text that is read not just with ears or eyes, but with one's entire being, which itself becomes imaginatively transformed in the process. Given the oral orientation of Tibetan culture as a whole, due to which the external environment is more easily experienced as part of one's own projective sphere, sounds heard and images visualized are likely to be experienced as inextricably related to one's internal physical and mental state. When the visualization of oneself as Yeshey Tsogyel is complete, one imagines that the actual Great Bliss Queen dissolves into oneself. Subsequently, one experiences her compassion and wisdom palpably flowing into one's own mind and body, much as one earlier trained to send such compassion out for the benefit of others' minds and bodies. The practitioner's own body, speech, and mind have merged with the body, speech, and mind of the Great Bliss Queen, thus embodying the evolutionary nondualism at the heart of this ritual. Finally, one dedicates the merit of this experience to the well-being of all and goes about one's daily activities, remaining as mindful as possible of the primordial purity pervading oneself, others, and one's environment.

THE GREAT BLISS QUEEN IN THE WEST

Jonathan Smith has described ritual as "a means of performing the way things ought to be in conscious tension to the way things are."[32] He uses as an example a hunting ritual wherein the hunter enacts a far more gracious encounter with the bear who will be his victim than can possibly be emulated in the rough and tumble of an actual hunt. But for the Buddhist practitioner, the primordial purity that is the matrix of the ritual is also the matrix of all life, and thus the ritual in fact explores the way things *are*, and the way they ought to be *understood*. Unlike hunting rituals, and indeed unlike most rituals important in Western religious traditions, the Great Bliss Queen ritual does not reenact or celebrate a particular communal, personal, or historical event.[33] It claims neither to change the world nor commemorate its activities. This is not to deny the social hierarchies and interactions created by the disjunction between participants and nonparticipants, or the power differential between them. But it is insufficient to understand this ritual, in Smith's terms, as a performance of how things ought to be (though it is partly that), just as it is insufficient to understand its performers as unthinking actors, or in Lévi-Straussian terms, to see the ritual as a way to resolve conflicts between culture and nature.[34] Most if not all rituals result from many different kinds of influences, and the practice of Yeshey Tsogyel may to some extent be all these things. But to leave it at that is to miss the point. It is especially to miss the lasting effect the Bliss Queen's ritual can have on the subjective state of the participant, and on the dimensions of mind not rooted in language. This ritual, rather than being a commemoration or preparation for an actual event, is primarily regarded as a path, that is, a practice that transforms constructions of selfhood in a way that can be maintained outside the ritual circle.

Catherine Bell has elegantly discussed how Western theories of ritual are based on a hierarchized bifurcation between thought and action, so that ritual even becomes described as thoughtless action (not in the sense of nonconceptual, but in the sense of being habitual or mimetic).[35] On the other hand, ritual is sometimes understood as a means for integrating thought and action. In both cases, the dichotomy between thought and action remains. Just as Western theories of mind tend not to invite curiosity about possible nonlinguistic states, so Western ritual theory does not make a clear space for the nonlingual dimension in ritual life. Insofar as passive and active may be understood as analogous to the thought-action bifurcation—thought being comparatively less "active" than ritual—Yeshey Tsogyel confounds both. Her ritual is entered into with a conviction that the way things ought to be is in fact the way they are, and that the ritual itself will help one experience that truth.

The lack in Western thought of the kinds of subjective and objective dimensions assumed by Yeshey Tsogyel's ritual is one reason that it may not translate easily into contemporary Western cultures. There are other reasons as well. For Westerners conditioned to see "the world" as already created and under constant supervision, it is easy to sustain the sense that one is acted upon as one imagines light pouring into one's body, or to feel that the world is an inert recipient of one's gifts when one assumes the role of enlightened deity and sends out multicolored light to pervade and cleanse the world and beings in it. If a practitioner retains, however subliminally, a Western cosmological paradigm in performing this ritual, she will retain also her culturally inscribed position as either a potential "manager" of the world or one of those who is "managed." More natural to a Buddhist cosmology, however, is the image of being a participant in and with the world.

Indeed, the basic moves of the Bliss Queen's practice—sending out sound and light to pervade and heal the physical and sentient universe before they dissolve into oneself—suggest the Tibetan cultural dialogue, and in particular its peculiar interfacing of the oral (aural) and literary (visual) orientations, with the latter always sustained and moved forward by the former.

Persons from orally oriented cultures, writes Ong, tend to project their sensibilities, to see them expressed in the world around them. More widely literate cultures create persons who tend to withdraw for insight into their own personal psyches.[36] Orally oriented peoples may thus be more inclined than persons in print-dominated cultures to set their feelings or experiences in the space around them, including the invisible spirits presumed to occupy that space, and less likely to project these feelings and experiences onto individual persons. In Tibet lineages or sects are the most likely targets of negative projections.[37] Western print-oriented persons are more likely to project their feelings onto other individuals, especially people in significant relationships with them. Unlike Tibet, or the premodern West, the contemporary West tends to identify the mind as the exclusive locus of ideas, feelings, and values. With this localization, the mind becomes "psychic" in a new sense, distinct from bodily soma and from the larger world.[38]

This very different configuration of personhood affects the way Westerners are likely to understand the Great Bliss Queen practice. For example, there is a tendency among Westerners for "visualization" to be a more disembodied practice than it is for Tibetans.[39] The point in imagining oneself as the Great Bliss Queen is not just to re-place one visual image of oneself with another, as if observing a changing scene in a movie theater, but to experience a physical as well as a mental shift from deep inside mind and body. What can this par-ticipation with symbols mean for Western women or men? In the modern West, images tend to be experienced as separate from one-self, and from this tendency follow two possible dangers: one, that a woman simply gives herself over to the image, resting in fascination with it, forgetting her own story; the other, that she does the opposite, and not knowing how to rely on or draw strength from the symbolic, is forced to hold all affects within her own mind and body. If, however, the spaciously empty quality of the visualized image is attended to as much as its particular colors and shapes, the participant is always aware that the image is not only vividly available, but is also empty, primordially pure, as is the dimension of her own mind not governed by thought. Just as one can avoid overidentifying with particular thoughts by releasing attention into a realm of mindfulness or con-centration that is not dominated by them, while at the same time from this vantage point reckoning with whatever issues need to be dealt with, so one can attend to the image in ritual and at the same time not become limited by it. This attention is possible because one heeds the empty expanse that is not only the source of the image but pervades it entirely, even as one scrutinizes every detail of color and shape.

The ritual of the Great Bliss Queen is a form of Guru Yoga, a cru-cially important practice in all Tibetan esoteric traditions.[40] Guru Yoga is a way to join with the guru, who is considered an expression of enlightenment. This connection is accomplished not only in ritual but in one's actual relationship with one's teacher. If there is a danger that the Bliss Queen's ritual might encourage Western woman to for-get or diminish the importance of her own story, that danger is even greater in Western guru-disciple relationships. To understand this danger, we have only to recall some of the chief cultural differences between traditional Tibetan and contemporary Western cultures.

On the one hand, the strength of the traditional guru-disciple relationship lies in the student's willingness to follow all her teacher's instructions and in the guru's never abusing that trust. Ideally, both teacher and student are intent on specific spiritual attainments for the benefit of the student. However, the Western woman often approaches her teacher and ritual practices with a very different set of needs and expectations than a traditional teacher or practice is prepared to meet. In the Western student's "real" life, relationships, family, and career are usually crucial aspects of her identity. But traditional gurus do not offer expertise on marriage or career, and their traditional students often were as free from such worldly concerns as they themselves are. The situation with contemporary Western laypersons is obviously different. The personal story of the Western practitioner must go with her; it is crucial to her identity.

The work of Hélène Cixous provides an interesting counterpoint to this issue of narrative and personal identification. As Toril Moi puts it, "[Cixous'] capacity for identification seems endless: Medusa, Electra, Antigone, Dido, Cleopatra—in her imagination she has been them all."[41] The differences between Cixous' identification and the ritual identification with the Great Bliss Queen crystallize crucial cultural differences between feminist and Buddhist orientations.

To dwell in myth is to dwell in story. To identify with Antigone, for example, is to identify with her deeds, her virtue, her faith, her stubbornness. In standing up to Creon, Antigone defends the religious order in political terms; in guarding the burial site of her brother, she also defies her uncle in very personal terms. She is defined by that particular story of her defiance. In ritually identifying with the Great Bliss Queen, one does not reflect on her story, though one would likely have heard or read it. Rather, one identifies with her inessential essence in order to discover it in oneself and make it part of one's own identity. This is quite different from contemporary Western emphases on an appropriate archetype with whose personality or specific characteristics one seeks to identify.

As we have seen, a Tibetan's sense of self is deeper and broader both ecologically and socially than that of modern Western women or men. This means Tibetans are less likely to "get lost" in a teacher or an image (which are often regarded with equal reverence) even though their powerful expressions of respect and devotion can seem extreme by most Western norms of piety. Moreover, in approaching a teacher, Tibetan women and men do not face challenges to their cultural and familial norms of personhood. Loyalty to persons—to family or clan—is widespread in Tibet, whereas in the West one is taught rather to be loyal to principles (truth, honesty, and the like). Thus, in traditional Buddhist culture, loyalty and devotion to one's teacher is very much an extension of loyalty to blood relations.[42] All this allows Tibetans a sense of perspective that Westerners often do not have. Tibetans may be highly reverential, but they do not necessarily do everything the guru says.[43] Finally, and very crucially, Tibetans are acculturated to the view that the guru is a special being who may behave in ways that ordinary persons should not, must not, emulate. Westerners, acculturated to a more democratic perspective, see exotic behavior in the guru as something to imitate, often with disastrous results in their own lives.

Westerners who participate in Buddhism are likely to be far less grounded in either family or other social structures than traditional adherents. In fact, consciously or unconsciously, Westerners sometimes seek a family substitute through engagement with their Buddhist teachers and communities. Westerners approach the gurus who are the emissaries of Buddhist traditions more as isolated individuals than students from a guru's own culture would do, and Western students do not have the kind of emotional roots in the cultural soil that the teacher, even in exile, still has. They do not go to Buddhist teachers or traditions as part of a consortium of life, including spirits and the elements, or as part of a "we" that places family and community within the boundaries of self. They go alone and have a tendency to place everything they are at the guru's feet, or to put undue hope in a practice. This is often a dysfunctional move, and creates a particularly vulnerable situation for women.

Because idiosyncratic individualism is not at issue in traditional Buddhist cultures, loss of such individuality—as opposed to loss of the kind of inherently existent or self-sufficient "self" discussed earlier—is not a concern for Tibetans; resistance to giving this up can, however, become a potent issue in the West. Some traditional Tibetan teachers see this resistance as an indication of the inferior spiritual quality of Western students. But it is not so simple: there is no culturally hegemonic construction of "personhood," and most traditional Tibetan teachers, even those with wide experience in the West, are not in a position to recognize this.

Specifically in relation to the Great Bliss Queen, it is important to recognize that, carefully described and visualized as her form might be, she is not just an image, not just a symbol. In the context of the meditative ritual centered on her, Yeshey Tsogyel is experienced as a bodying forth of emptiness, manifesting ontological nondualism, the indivisible unity of a form and its emptiness. In the language of the Great Completeness, such an image displays the unity of primordial purity and spontaneous occurrence. In each case, it is a unity of conditioned and unconditioned, of something that is both languaged and imaged *and* has a quality governed by neither language nor images. Even the iconographical detail so carefully elaborated is tamed by this recognition. This is absolutely crucial, because it helps one not to get "lost" in the image or be limited by it, or give too much of oneself away to it. This way of understanding the image and the type of mind involved in ritual invocation of it draws together several of the issues we have discussed already, most especially the different ways in which traditional Tibetan (or other Asian) and modern Westerners relate to images, stories, and themselves.

MIND AND BODY IN A RITUAL CONTEXT

Flying is woman's gesture—flying in language and making it fly.

Hélène Cixous, "Utopias"

Buddhist practitioners engage with Yeshey Tsogyel's ritual in order to embody her. The more one proceeds into the esoterica surrounding the Great Bliss Queen and other tantric or Great Completeness practices, the more descriptions there are of the ways in which physiology supports certain types of subjectivity, and the more meditative exercises there are to bring one in touch with the physical counterparts of subtle subjective experience. Their interplay is a significant characteristic of esoteric Tibetan practice.

Performing a ritual, one is seated in a specific posture, back straight, hands arranged with one palm over the other, thumbs touching each other or the base of the ring finger, shoulders even, mouth relaxed, the neck extended and curved "like a swan's." In most Buddhist traditions, the session begins with some form of breathing practice, understood also as a purification, that helps to stabilize and calm the mind. There are also methods of exercise or yoga that train the entire body in movements coordinated with specific visualizations or breathing.[44] In these and other ways, Tibetan practice recognizes that meditation affects bodily experience. However, it does not articulate the problem, especially well known among Westerners who spend their lives reading, of how to be "in the body" or "physically grounded." In a life spent in the rugged Tibetan highlands, striding a mantle of earth whose thickness is five times what it is elsewhere on the planet, being in the body is not an issue.

But we are in the West. And some feminists emphasize that it is a woman's special way of being in her body that shows the path to her female nature. Hélène Cixous, for example, emphasizes the centrality of bodily experience: "Censor the body, and you censor breath and speech at the same time." Cixous' work is interesting in this context because she suggests a merging of the oral and the literal, the physical and the mental. She does so in a way that uniquely expresses mind/body perplexities at the present moment in the Western history of speech and writing: "Text: my body—shot through with streams of song; . . . body (body? bodies?) no more describable than god, the soul, or the Other; that part of you that leaves a space between yourself and urges you to inscribe in language your woman's style."[45]

Cixous, like the traditional Buddhist practitioner, is more focused on embodying a text than interpreting it. Looking at her body, Cixous sees a flowing connection, not a gulf, between female writing and female being. But this way of starting from the body is unknown and perhaps unnecessary in Tibetan culture. It is necessary in the West, particularly for women. The female body, as Cixous, Irigaray, Flax, and others observe, has *not* been written into Western culture. For Cixous, the solution is a new way of writing that implicitly blurs distinctions between the written and spoken word and, analogously, between mind and body. "Flight" for Cixous is a flight through and with sound and sight, body and mind. To manifest as a flying woman is in Cixous' world a "daring feat," a "great transgression," forcing oneself to become both woman and speaking subject. "Listen to a woman speak at a public gathering (if she hasn't painfully lost her wind). She doesn't 'speak,' she throws her trembling body forward; she lets go of herself, she flies."[46] Physical power is present, but not a dimension of a consciousness characterized by spaciousness. The flight of the dakini, by contrast, is a flight through just that spacious dimension of mind.

Cixous' work, like much of feminism, is directed at healing various kinds of internal divisions, especially those that separate women from their bodies, feelings, and female selves. Hers is an exemplary Western way of healing a breach that distinguishes much of Western from much of traditional Tibetan culture. Tibetan ritual in its native context does not so much heal the mind-body breach as assume its absence. From a Western perspective, that absence may look like a solution. To put this another way, Westerners are often attracted to Buddhist or other meditative practices out of a wish to be more at home with themselves, especially, perhaps, their gendered selves. Buddhism does not address this as an issue. Feminism does, and its partnership with Buddhist ideas and practices may bring a newly expanded form of feminist experience into being, transforming American Buddhism in the process.

I have proposed that the feminist essentialist-postmodern debate is in part a reflection on what kind of space subjectivity occupies. In the West, internal self-space is primarily a territory to be filled with something or to be owned by someone. In postmodern reflection, the construction of mind as always and primarily shaped by context crowds out any possibility of completeness or wholeness.

The dakini who is the Great Bliss Queen, on the other hand, flies mentally, physically, and nonconceptually through a nondualistic expanse. In that calm dimension, she reclaims the distance between subject and object, whereby she displays a realm of universally available experience. One enters into the experience of the dakini through sound and silence, through visual proliferation and empty space, and above all through engaging with the most revered norms of Buddhist culture.

We have observed that for all their personal independence, traditional Buddhist practitioners are culturally, socially, and linguistically embedded in ways Westerners are not. Western women continue to strengthen their identities as individuals even as they seek to further their connections with others. Even as a quasi-essentialist,

Cixous pays homage to particularity in ways that a traditional Asian would not.[47]

Among the most stimulating challenges for Western Buddhists is to find a way to integrate personal narratives and historical specificity into the nonconceptual universals considered the goals of much of Buddhist practice. In the midst of negotiating this delicate intersection of uniqueness and connectedness, it is crucial that an engagement with "traditions" such as those of Tibetan Buddhism does not tip the balance by obstructing personal creativity and inspiration. Conversely, particularity is crucial, but it is important not to get lost in one's particulars, or to overidentify with them. There is a middle way where meet the two narratives engaged throughout this book: how feminists and Buddhists can expand each others narrative horizons, and what Western women practicing in Buddhist traditions might gain and where they might exercise caution.

Yeshey Tsogyel herself is associated with an extensive narrative, and at the same time she has a dimension of subjectivity that is not simply the product, container, or display of that narrative. In her ritual context she is not a mask; she is not a role model. She is an expression of one's own capacity and potential. To meet her in this way means, for Western women, to possess and come to terms with their own story. It is also to recognize that, however fine or tragic our stories are, they cannot define us completely. There are other dimensions of embodied subjective experience.

Recognizing this can help feminists too narrowly defined by either essentialist or postmodern characterizations of selfhood. Both have their purpose, so long as they do not become the sole foundation for self-definition. But our stories must have the attention they deserve. As we have already discussed, persons formed by a culture like Tibet that does not localize feelings within the bodily boundaries, that finds life a ubiquitous expression of the cosmos, rather than localized only within visible beings, are less likely to become alienated from their own personal histories in meditative practice. Westerners who would engage with Buddhism must find a different way to connect with themselves. I believe it is possible to discover one's own particularity and to move *with* that, not from it, into a dimension of experience less governed by particularity. It is also possible, and very necessary in the twentieth-century West, to entertain many particulars of identity and be neither constricted by any one of them nor disoriented by their multiplicity. In this way, too, if one is a practitioner, one's personal narrative need not be erased as one manifests as a Great Bliss Queen.

The practices of chanting, calm, and concentration all assume that the subject has depth as well as breadth, motion as well as ideas, and that these qualities provide personal coherence and power. They reveal a subjective realm that is in effect *terra nullius*, "space without a master," as late nineteenth-century European laws described lands inhabited by indigenous peoples.[48] Any place not subject to heroic mastery, in this view, either does not exist or is not worth discussing. Western feminism, like Western thought in general, has also regarded subjectivity in this way, as either governed by words (or images or feelings) or unclaimable. Yet unrestricted space, knowable but unalterable, is the realm of what Buddhists call the unconditioned. It is also the realm of the collateral coherence of mindfulness, the unbreachable state of equanimity that nonetheless recognizes others as harmful or helpful, the emptiness united with appearance, the symbols understood as empty, and the clarity of innate awareness that is not impeded by thoughts and feelings. In this domain some of the most important insights of contemporary theory can be enlivened and embodied. They can be brought deep into the vortex of mind-body experience rather than remaining solely in the province of the intellectual, the political, and the literary. Subjectivity is not just its contents.

CHAPTER 8

Inconclusion

> "The difference between mad people and sane people,"
> Brave Orchid explained to the children, "is that sane
> people have variety when they talk-story. Mad people have
> only one story that they talk over and over."
>
> Maxine Hong Kingston, *The Woman Warrior*

Western constructs of identity are filled with multiplicities that easily become polarized. Oppositions such as unity and multiplicity, self and other, reason and emotion, essence and construction, which fuel the debate between essentialist and postmodern forms of feminism, are from a Buddhist perspective false. Buddhist traditions offer a different configuration that can be useful both to feminist theory and to Western women looking for ways to reconsider their understanding of identity. But this does not mean Buddhist ideas can simply be plucked from their native context and set down in a new one.

Buddhist traditions are famous for their ability both to change the cultures they visit and to be altered by them. Yet when Buddhist thought and practices moved to Southeast Asia, or to China and then Korea and Japan, or to Tibet, they were part of a larger process of cultural exchange that extended over centuries. Never until today has such a wealth and variety of Buddhist resources—texts, practices, and living teachers—been made available in so short a period of time to populations who are at the same time so ignorant of the cultures from which these traditions have come.

Many Westerners who take Buddhism to heart do so in a spirit of great enthusiastic familiarity, as if the concepts on which Buddhist thought and practice are built are easily translatable. But modern constructions of personhood are unique; they did not occur in the cultures that gave rise to Buddhism. The Japanese girl unable to name her favorite color—not trained in playing the individual's game of personal choices—reminds us of these differences. Women, and men as well, need a story that has room for multiple incoherencies and incongruities. This room is available through focused and attentive presence, and thus through the interconnected dimensions of a subject not rooted only in language and an object not governed only by particularity.

In the absence of the embedded connections known in traditional cultures, bridges to other persons in the modern West need to be crafted one by one. Keen attention and a sense that one's identity is not wholly limited to the particulars of one's life—that one is open to others on a variety of levels—can assist this. In a highly individuated society, maintaining relationships is both of greater importance and greater difficulty than in a traditional one. For this very reason, profound human connection has an important place in Western spiritual development. Human connection grounds spirituality and expresses it, and maintaining such connection is as profound a challenge to accomplish as any advanced meditative state. Moreover, such connections require individuation, independence, and openness, and these qualities are greatly enhanced by acknowledging a dimension of subjective experience that is not entirely dominated by the special stories one exchanges in the process of relationship. Like a spiritual balm that soothes a whole range of problems, the subjective dimension of mindfulness, for example, helps guard against the loss of self in relationship, and at the same time softens the overly hard boundaries that construct oppositional posturings of self and other. Both of these elements, self-protection and satisfying connection, are crucial for women cultivating strength, independence, and connection in their own particular evolution of Western self-constructions.

Because personal and emotional expressions are vital to Western-ers in ways they are not for traditional Buddhists, it is a challenge to incorporate them into a conversation with Buddhist ideas and prac-tices. Subjective states such as mindfulness can facilitate both inde-pendent personal strength and alert connection to others, a combi-nation that may be the special configuration of women's individuality in the West.

How can a Westerner engaged either intellectually or through practice with a tradition that emphasizes attributes seen as univer-sal—the collateral coherence of mindfulness, the experience of emp-tiness, the innate awareness in everyone's mind—come to terms with the particularities, personal stories, and the variety of specific feel-ings and emotions that are part of Western identities? Above all, where does one place and how does one honor the personal narrative, including its personal pain, that is at the heart of the Western sense of personhood? This is a more complicated challenge for women than for men, because women are only now coming to recognize the value and gendered uniqueness of their own personal narratives, and have only recently begun to reclaim the stories of women who came before them. Buddhism's stated goal of freeing its adherents from all suffer-ing must not stand in the way of acknowledging that pain, learning from it, and connecting with others on the basis of shared anguish or injustice. Buddhist theory and practice in the West must take account of the need for individuality, personal stories, and clear connected-ness and support the expression of these. Western men by and large don't need more separation, and women, for whom the nature of con-nectedness is often troubled, do not necessarily wish to replicate he-roic male models of autonomy.

For Western students of Buddhism, it may therefore be helpful to initiate workshops or retreats where traditional practice is combined with interpersonal practice, for example, in developing the ability to speak without entirely obscuring or forgetting the unlanguaged dimension of oneself and others, in being sensitive to other persons within this experience, and in allowing other persons to see one struggle toward these goals. This process, like any carried through with deep clarity and focus, fosters joy, an expression of a natural internal ambience. Unlike usual forms of pleasure, this joy has little or nothing to do with what presents to one's senses. It originates inside, yet also emerges outside. It welcomes others, but does not depend on them, or anything else construed as external. Like the smile of the Great Bliss Queen, this is not a gladness about any particular thing. It is simply part of one's own experience of the focused dimension of mindfulness and concentration.

An encouragement to explore the silent dimension of mindfulness as a way to play with issues of selfhood is a major potential contribution of Buddhism to feminism. Even a description of the stages of that process is new to feminism. The poetic diction of essentialists is inspiring but gives little direction in this regard; similarly, when constructionists and postmodernists open up the possibility of new gender ideologies, they do not articulate methods by which women can experience them. Though language is, as they emphasize, deeply formative of experience and power relations, to conceive of the mind only as an arena to be taken over by feelings, language, and concepts denies a space in the mind that can be one's own. Buddhist orientations express that the mind is not just ideas; it is also a vehicle for physically grounded experience. This suggests that knowledge need not be measured always by domination, capturing, or completion. Silent knowing yields to being, including being in the body. This is a form of self-containment and autonomy useful to women in strengthening independence and, because of the openness to others it makes possible, connectedness as well.

If the greatest challenge in traditional Tibetan culture is an independence that does not rupture embeddedness, for modern Westerners the greatest challenge is to achieve a deep connectedness that does not undermine individual questing and creativity. By their own descriptions, modern Westerners are often either fractured and isolated individuals or overly dependent ones. Although neither of these traits characterize traditional Tibetans, Buddhist discussions of subjectivity can be understood to address them. Descriptions of mindfulness suggest that even an acute awareness of one's constitutive multiplicities and contradictions need not impede the collateral coherence of being physically and mentally centered. Women and men in the West do act with mental clarity, intensity, and focus in the midst of social or personal chaos, but few feminists or other Western philosophers have a name for this kind of practice or a method to strengthen it.[1]

One of the effects of mindfulness and other meditation practice is a calm that is not just the absence of worry or looking away from problems. Such calm both causes and results from going deeper into mind and body, becoming more deeply connected with the unlanguaged areas of mind and the more subtle energies of the body. In this way mindfulness and other practices expand the dimensions of selfhood. Mindfulness can also be profoundly disturbing, especially in initial periods of intense training, but finally one learns not to identify utterly with the agitation. That is, one can both experience it and be in some sense gathered in the face of it. Mindfulness is thus a way to combine the strength of essentialist depth with constructionist and postmodern breadth, fluidity, and particularity.

The discussions of concentration, compassion, selflessness, and the imagery and ritual of the Great Bliss Queen all suggest various compatibilities important for reshaping the essentialist-postmodern conversation in feminism. Empowered compassion, which also incorporates the dynamic of mindfulness, describes an identity that is energized and enlarged by its connection with others, partly because compassion does not take one "out" of oneself, but expresses the fluid complementarity between deliberate thought and spontaneous response. Compassion is the interactive expression of a kinesthetic sense of fluidity often associated with mindfulness and concentration. Feminist and other Western understandings of interpersonal dynamics can bring this training into play with the modern and largely individualistic sense of personhood.

Training in compassion gives women and men an opportunity to choose and shape values that have often been thrust upon women. What Buddhism offers is the suggestion that the same kind of mind need not handle all these different agendas of listening, individuating, and connecting. The mind has various dimensions. Because of the mind's multidimensionality, the distance between subject and object, self and other, and one's own internal voices can be bridged.

To this end, there are two advantages offered by the Buddhist categories of the nonconceptual, the unconditioned, and the primordially pure or empty. They facilitate discussion of certain types of experiences that can arise in meditation—the sense, for example, of a subjectivity that retains its collateral clarity and cohesiveness regardless of the flux of ordinary thoughts and events. More significant for most women is that to take these categories seriously in theories of self and subjectivity is to offer an alternative to the implication in contemporary feminist theory that mind is a surface that can be consumed, a material that can be fractured. Mindfulness suggests the possibility of a mind and identity sustained by its own collateral dynamism, a state that neither excludes others nor depends on them in the usual epistemological, psychological, or social terms.

Further, if the mind is experienced or understood as a kind of open sphere of infinite dimensions, then no single quality or emotion, nor any combination of these, can completely fill or occupy it. None can own or define it completely. Thus, intense feeling can be present without consuming one's identity. This is very important. Pain, for example, requires a great deal of attention, but it need not be construed as the whole of one's being. Similarly, happiness, however intensely felt, need not overwhelm awareness that pain always exists somewhere, in someone. The two experiences do not cancel each other out.

In the late stages of completing this book, I attended the first-ever Conference of Western Buddhist teachers. More than one hundred and twenty women and men came from all over the country, representing a variety of Theravada, Zen, and Tibetan Buddhist practice traditions. In terms of personal clarity, energy, and vision, it was an extremely distinguished group, with a number of women especially luminous among them.

At the same time, this was a group involved in a deep struggle: how to honor the traditional Asian context from which we learned so much and still be true to our modern, Western selves. Part of the struggle was also to deal with the pain of having in some sense cast away our own selves in order to become immersed in a "foreign" tradition that fascinated us. Some, especially but by no means exclusively women, had in addition experienced real abuse by teachers. There was a moment of enormous collective pain and tears, and in my own case a resurrection of many past griefs as well—deaths, losses, furies that, encouraged by such a supportive environment, seemed to mix into one powerful stream that welled up with considerable force. Several people spoke with eloquent simplicity of their specific griefs, and the entire atmosphere was flush with shared feeling.

A woman suggested we chant together. The sound *ah* was part of that chant, and as soon as I sounded it, my whole relationship to the grief I felt so powerfully was transformed. The sadness was still present, but not consuming. The sound, and my familiarity with it as a practice, provided a way to hold the grief as well as a connection with a part of my self not colored by it. (I believe, however, this can work only with grief that has actually been acknowledged and is there to be held.) One can feel intensely, and still somehow still be at peace.

Writing about this now brings me back to the gaze of Ani Mu Tso, almost unnerving in its gentle openness. The usual barriers met in someone's glance were absent; she seemed immediately available at the level of the entirely uncontrived, someone who could accept deeply into her spirit whatever came her way. Within a presence and strength of a mind that knows itself to be unconsumable there is nothing to fear.

It is of course an enormous challenge to live as if one were fearlessly available to experience whatever life presents. But there are many possible and interesting applications of this challenge. Is it possible not to feel overwhelmed in a life filled with an enormous diversity of choices, relationships, responsibilities, and cultures? Is it possible to take in new and strange ideas without dismissing them, but making best possible use of the fresh vistas they suggest?

Is it helpful to find that despite the deep impact of diversity on one's identity, there is a space of the self free from this fracturing, a space from which to proclaim what changes must be made? Can one also, from this deeper dimension, find a space to be free from others' constructions, and furthermore, from the limiting or prejudicial projections one throws onto others? Can one use this dimension to maintain a broader vision of the wider good of community, of the world itself, to open up the narrow focus of concern on self or family and act accordingly?

These questions take on particular importance when I am confronted with records of the bloodbath in Bosnia, for example, the suffering of the persecuted masses in Rwanda, the plight of the Vietnamese and Cambodians in recent decades, the horrors of the Cultural Revolution in China, and the Gulag that stretches between China and what was once an independent Tibet. Despite many differences, these records all tell the same story: wanton cruelty born of

a potent mix of prejudice and narrow ideology. The European Holocaust is also part of my family story, and watching films or documen-
taries about it—most recently *Schindler's List*—I try to see if I am able,
even for a moment, to hold that horror close and still retain some
sense of peace with it. I cannot do so for very long, but for the moments
when I can, it has seemed possible to encompass the suffering of the
whole more clearly. That is, being galvanized by one particular mur-
der or torture does not block out the larger dimensions and wider details of the situation—not only what happened in Germany, but the
ongoing suffering and danger of which the Holocaust is a part, a vir-
ulent strain of human history that may never be overcome but against
which one must always be on guard.

When I am reminded of persons languishing in refugee camps, of
native peoples throughout the New World robbed of their land and
ways of life, of political prisoners tortured in Colombia, Chile, China,
Romania, or Tibet, reflections on subjectivity can seem embarrass-
ingly trivial. And yet not. Because it seems very clear to me that in order to raise up a force against these violations, people must unite
against injustice across lines of nation, race, and culture. I believe it is
important to spread the understanding—in whatever cultural, religious, or philosophical terms are most effective—that there is a dimension through which persons can connect precisely because this
dimension is free from the particularities that otherwise define us.

A person who acknowledges this dimension of herself will not be
free of all distress. But distress will be much less likely to cut to the
quick, to the core of her identity, destroying the rest of her. This makes
the response of denial less seductive. The Buddhist understanding of
subjective dimensions and their corollaries opens up possibilities
now shrouded by contemporary Western reflections on self and subjectivity. Buddhist traditions describe and their practices access dimensions of experience and theory with which Western women can
meaningfully converse and from which they can draw strength.

A conversation is never static; it does not repeat itself, but continually produces new feelings and ideas, as well as new silences, among which each person must find her way. Dialogue is key to the processes of growth across cultures and between persons of the same culture, and this includes interior dialogue by which a single person constructs experience and understanding. The conversation between Buddhists and feminists helps the feminist project of uncovering cultural assumptions relevant to the status and experience of women; these same cultural assumptions regarding self and subjectivity are crucial for Buddhist practitioners in the West to recognize as well.

Feminist perspectives in general and its postmodern theories in particular seek a new way of experiencing self and world. The Buddhist practices and theories discussed throughout this book can provide creative impetus for these new sensibilities. I am not suggesting that Buddhist principles or practices be adopted wholesale by modern feminists or anyone else. I am, however, suggesting that the basic categories on which these practices and theories are premised can be helpful to contemporary women and to feminist theory. "Essentialist" subjective stability by no means precludes a "constructivist" perspective. If the mind is understood as allied with the body, and if mind and body are united by the currents of life itself—neither entirely physical nor entirely mental—then those currents can be navigated to experience something essential about being alive. Nor is this experience in any way contradicted by a multiplicity of ideas, stories, and histories of race, class, gender, and personal style. When the mind is understood as an open expanse, there is always room for something more. When mind explicitly retains its open, unlanguaged dimension in the face of such variety, the dynamic of collateral coherence is uninterrupted.

The Great Bliss Queen herself holds and expresses infinite multiplicities, and at the same time offers a dynamic of coherence. Her mandala suggests a world not constrained by boundaries, rich with inhabitants and images, yet not subject to the fragmentation modern Westerners associate with "real life." The spacious sky through which she flies is a sphere of limitless potential and variety, suggesting that the unique features and disparities of personal stories can be a cause of celebration, for coherence lies not in a unifying narrative, but in the dynamic of clarified attention. Keen and focused attention inevitably reveals that variety makes the only kind of whole that can be one.

NOTES

Preface

1. The term "Indo-Tibetan," though somewhat controversial in the field of Buddhist Studies, reflects well the situation of Geluk traditions, which self-consciously tried to revitalize and incorporate the Indian Buddhist texts they took as central to their scholarly and meditative endeavors.

2. This "importance" was constructed on the one hand by my comparative wealth and the possibility I would donate to the welfare of my host institution, and on the other by the fact that, as a translator, I could help extend the Tibetan tradition, fragile in exile, to the West. Furthermore, as an interested Westerner, I was evidence of the broad applicability and value of the teachings the Tibetans had treasured for so long. None of this, however, undermines the fact that, by and large, the teachers who gave so extensively of their time and expertise did so out of human kindness, and in response to their own training, which mandated that they should teach those who wanted to learn. In exile, that mandate had extended to those very foreigners who would have been prohibited from coming to Tibet when it was free.

3. For stories and perspectives of specific women active in Western Buddhist communities, see *Meetings with Remarkable Women* by Lenore Friedman (Boston: Shambhala Press, 1987), and Sandy Boucher, *Turning the Wheel: American Women Creating the New Buddhism* (1988; reprint, Boston: Beacon Press, 1993).

4. This point was inspired by an observation by Ken McLeod at "The Art of Teaching" conference of Western meditation teachers, Green Gulch Zen Center, Marin, Calif., September 9, 1993. For a description and critique of feminists' appropriation of the language of individualism, see

Elizabeth Fox-Genovese, *Feminism without Illusions* (Chapel Hill: University of North Carolina Press, 1991).

5. Judith V. Jordan, "Empathy and Self-Boundaries," in *Women's Growth in Connection: Writings from the Stone Center* (New York: Guilford Press, 1991).

6. Reported by Harvey B. Aronson from a workshop conducted by Kim Insoo Berg in Houston, Texas, Spring 1993.

7. I. B. Horner's *Women under Primitive Buddhism* (New York: E. P. Dutton, 1930) focused on India and was a pioneering work in this area; four decades later early Buddhist attitudes toward women were thematized by Alan Sponberg, "Attitudes toward Women and the Feminine in Early Buddhism," in *Buddhism, Sexuality, and Gender*, ed. José Cabezón (Albany: SUNY Press, 1992), pp. 3–36. Diana Paul's *Women in Buddhism* (Berkeley: Asian Humanities Press, 1979) examines images of women in Indian and Chinese Buddhist texts. More recently, stories of highly regarded Tibetan women have been chronicled in Tsultrim Allione's *Women of Wisdom* (London: Routledge and Kegan Paul, 1984), and the hagiography of Tibet's most renowned woman of enlightenment is available in two translations, Keith Dowman's *Sky Dancer: The Secret Life and Songs of the Lady Yeshey Tsogyel* (London: Routledge and Kegan Paul, 1984), and Tarthang Tulku's *Mother of Knowledge: The Enlightenment of Ye shes mtsho rgyal* (Berkeley: Dharma Publishing, 1983). Barbara Aziz examined Tibetan family life and women's role in it in *Tibetan Frontier Families: Reflections of Three Generations from Dingri* (Durham, N.C.: Carolina Academic Press, 1978), and China Galland has written a creative and insightful reflection on her own tandem Buddhist and Christian journeys in *Longing for Darkness: Tara and the Black Madonna* (New York: Viking Press, 1990). Rita Gross has published numerous articles broadly relating Buddhism and feminism: these are listed in the bibliography of her *Buddhism after Patriarchy* (Albany: SUNY Press, 1993), which appeared as I was in the penultimate stage of completing this manuscript. In this ambitious work, she considers the

present and potential relationship between North American women and Buddhism, working above all to retrieve through historical research what is useful for contemporary women. Also appearing just as this book goes to press is Miranda Shaw's *Passionate Enlightenment: Women in Tantric Buddhism* (Princeton: Princeton University Press, 1994).

1. Introduction

1. Dudjom Rinboche, *Ri chos bsab bya nyams len dmar khrid kho bder brjod pa grub pa'i bcud len* (Tibetan and English, private printing); English translation by John Reynolds under the title *The Alchemy of Realization* (Kathmandu: Simhanda Publications, 1978). I offer my own translation here, as elsewhere in this book except when specific attribution is given.

2. Ann Snitow, "A Gender Diary," in *Conflicts in Feminism*, ed. Maryanne Hirsch and Evelyn Fox Keller (New York: Routledge, 1990), pp. 9–43. Other manifestations of this divide, according to Snitow, are the debates between radical and cultural feminists, essentialists and social constructionists, cultural feminists and poststructuralists, motherists and feminists, and the proponents of equality versus proponents of difference between genders. Her article is a subtle reflection on the interrelationships among and within these pairings. (Thanks to Susan Lurie for suggesting this book to me at just the right moment.) See also Catharine R. Stimpson, "The New Scholarship about Women: The State of the Art," *Annals of Scholarship* 1, no. 2 (1980): 2–14 (discussed by Snitow, p. 14). The writers Stimpson discusses reveal the wide variety of thematics to which this tension can attach itself.

3. Jean Martin Charcot in *The Standard Edition of the Complete Psychological Works of Sigmund Freud*, trans. and ed. James Strachey (1893; London: Hogarth Press, 1962); cited in Peggy Papp, *The Process of Change* (New York: Guilford Press, 1983), p. 1.

4. See the ground-breaking article by Marcel Mauss, collected with several excellent essays that take this topic as a point of departure in Mi-

chael Carrithers, Steven Collins, and Steven Lukes, eds., *The Category of the Person* (Cambridge: Cambridge University Press, 1985).

5. Jane Flax, "Postmodernism and Gender Relations in Feminist Theory," *Signs* 12, no. 4 (Summer 1987): 624. In particular see pp. 622–23 n. 1 for a representative example of feminist deconstructivist theories. For a reflection on whether feminist postmodernists do themselves a disservice by focusing too much on the Enlightenment and a defense of the need for rationality and objectivity, see Sabina Lovibond, "Feminism and Postmodernism," in *Postmodernism: A Reader*, ed. Thomas Docherty (New York: Columbia University Press, 1993).

6. For an exemplary discussion of the perils and promise of such an idea, see Marilyn Massey, *Feminine Soul: The Fate of an Ideal* (Boston: Beacon Press, 1986), especially pp. 26–29.

7. Mary Daly, *Pure Lust: Elemental Feminist Philosophy* (Boston: Beacon Press, 1984), p. 175, also writes, "When Muses re-membering enter the rhythms of a Tidal Memory we experience a connectedness with the cosmos that had been broken." Luce Irigaray, in *This Sex Which Is Not One*, trans. Catherine Porter with Carolyn Burke (Ithaca: Cornell University Press, 1985), writes "Woman has sex organs more or less everywhere" (p. 28) or "Woman never speaks the same way. What she emits is flowing, fluctuating. *Blurring*. And she is not listened to, unless proper meaning (meaning of the proper) is lost" (p. 112). Such highly charged abstractions are typical of her work. Nevertheless, like other essentialists, Daly and Irigaray often seem insufficiently aware of the differences between women. Both writers imply that some form of woman-nature does exist, ready to be discovered. Daly recommends an "unforgetting," which leads to "recalling our first questions, our native powers." See Daly, *Pure Lust*, pp. 85, 89. Daly might well argue that to engage in this process of discovery is, paradoxically, to enact Simone de Beauvoir's famous dictum "One is not born, but rather becomes a woman" (*The Second Sex*, trans. and ed. H. M. Parshley [New York: Vintage Books, 1974], p. 249). See also Naomi Schor, "This Essentialism Which Is Not One:

Coming to Grips with Irigaray," in *Differences* 1, no. 2 (1989): 41. But Beauvoir and other critics of cultural feminism say that by claiming a universal or "natural" female essence, the role of culture and of individual particularity is unsuitably discounted.

8. Luce Irigaray, *Speculum of the Other Woman*, trans. Gillian C. Gill (Ithaca: Cornell University Press, 1985), p. 230.

9. Luce Irigaray, *Passions élémentaires* (Paris: Minuit, 1985), p. 18, quoted and discussed by Schor, "This Essentialism," p. 49.

10. Alice Echols includes Susan Griffin, Kathleen Barry, Janice Raymond, Florence Rush, Susan Brownmiller, and Robin Morgan among cultural feminist writers. For important bibliographical references on this form of feminist discourse, see Linda Alcoff, "Cultural Feminism versus Post-Structuralism: The Identity Crisis in Feminist Theory," *Signs* 13, no. 3 (Spring 1988): 410, n. 15. Alcoff's article, along with Jane Flax's "Postmodernism and Gender Relations" and Naomi Schor's "This Essentialism," has been critical to my analyses on this and following pages. I am grateful to the Feminist Faculty Reading Group at Rice University and especially to Jane Gallop for bringing Schor's work to my attention.

11. Contemporary feminism, of the past ten years at least, argues that "essentialist" goals are delusions; they are not the solutions to women's oppression but part of the process of constructing that oppression. See Diana Fuss, *Essentially Speaking* (London: Routledge and Kegan Paul, 1989).

12. Daryl McGowan Tress identifies six trends within postmodern theory in "Comment on Jane Flax's 'Postmodernism and Gender Relations in Feminist Theory,'" *Signs* 14, no. 11 (Autumn 1988): 197–98.

13. Teresa de Lauretis, *Alice Doesn't* (Bloomington: Indiana University Press, 1984), p. 182. For de Lauretis' main sources for her interpretation of Lacan, Eco, and Peirce see Alcoff, "Identity Crisis," p. 424 n. 45; see also Butler, *Gender Trouble*, p. 145. For Butler's more recent reflections

on constructedness and agency, see *Bodies that Matter* (New York: Routledge, 1993).

14. Hélène Cixous is an important exception here: she is concerned with both body and language; her work is unique for its conflation of them.

15. For an exemplary introduction to "deconstruction" and its context, see Jonathan Culler, *On Deconstruction* (Ithaca: Cornell University Press, 1982), especially pp. 94 ff. See also Jacques Derrida, *Positions*, trans. Alan Bass (Chicago: University of Chicago Press, 1981), pp. 27 ff.; and *Of Grammatology*, trans. Gayatri Spivak (Baltimore: Johns Hopkins University Press, 1976), pp. 166 ff.

16. There are nonetheless some theorists such as Paul Smith calling for a reassessment of essentialism's political efficacy. See Smith's *Discerning the Subject* (Minneapolis: University of Minnesota Press, 1988), p. 144. See also Fuss's discussion of this in connection with Irigaray in *Essentially Speaking*, pp. 70 ff. On the lighter side, a Christmas 1993 radio ad for perfume bridged the gap between these positions by claiming its scent was for "the individualist in every woman."

17. Linda Alcoff, "Identity Crisis," p. 412, observes that minority voices in the West are particularly sensitive to the dangers of essentialism, and for this reason African-American, Hispanic and Chicana, and other women of color overwhelmingly reject essentialist conceptions of gender. See, for example, Gloria Anzaldua, *Borderlands La Frontera: The New Mestiza* (San Francisco: Spinster/Aunt Lute, 1987) and the writings of Alice Walker, Audre Lorde, and Cherrie Moraga. Angela Valenzuela has pointed out in conversation the complex position of minority persons, on the one hand, needing to define themselves in opposition to a majority, and at the same time objecting to having an identity solely defined by that context.

18. Paul Ricoeur, in colloquium with Harvard Divinity School faculty, Boston, Mass., Fall 1983.

19. For recent summaries of significant feminist-postmodernist interactions, see Butler, *Gender Trouble*; Jane Flax, *Thinking Fragments: Psy-*

choanalysis, Feminism, and Postmodernism in the Contemporary West (Berkeley: University of California Press, 1990); Linda J. Nicholson, ed., *Feminism/Postmodernism* (New York: Routledge, 1990); and Chris Weedon, *Feminist Practice and Poststructuralist Theory* (Oxford: Basil Blackwell, 1987).

20. Some, like Teresa de Lauretis, stress that feminist theory is about a difference that characterizes feminist conceptions of women and the world. A related postmodern move is to emphasize that no circumstance or self is unitary, but a multiplicity of processes that can never be totalized or captured. See "Upping the Anti (sic) in Feminist Theory," in Hirsch and Keller, *Conflicts in Feminism*, pp. 255 ff. See also de Lauretis's *Alice Doesn't*, and Alcoff's "Identity Crisis."

21. See Schor, "This Essentialism," and Alcoff, "Identity Crisis." An analogous debate between "works" and "grace" has long occupied Christian theology in the West. (Thanks to my student Paula Cazamias for this observation.) Indeed, ever since Plato argued that truth could not be known but only remembered "discovery" analogues have been present in Western philosophy. My concern here, of course, is with particular Buddhist permutations of this theme.

22. Fuss, *Essentially Speaking*, p. 4; de Lauretis, "Upping the Anti (sic) in Feminist Theory," p. 267. As Fuss observes, the notion of "where I stand," that is, an understanding of one's own subject position is essential to social constructionist theories (p. 29). For her excellent and detailed articulation of this point, which I read only after completing this book, see especially the Introduction and chapter 1 of *Essentially Speaking*. The polarization between essentialist and postmodern perspectives is analogous to, yet quite different in focus from, the "two extremes" in Buddhism, permanence and annihilation.

23. "Patriarchy" is a foundational term in Western feminism, referring to the suppression of women by men in cultures around the world. Even though from this perspective Buddhism, too, is a patriarchal religion, it is very different in structure from the Jewish and Christian contexts from

which most Western feminist theory has developed. I avoid the term "patriarchy" here since it implies distinctly Jewish and Christian views of "the fathers." I use instead what seem to me less culture-bound and more specifically descriptive (if less familiar) terms such as "oppositional" and "male-dominant."

24. Despite the important analogies between feminist essentialist and Buddhist discovery orientations, there is an important structural difference between them. Feminists today do not necessarily valorize what they "discover" about the female, whereas Buddhists seek to discover qualities valuable in the quest for enlightenment. This difference acknowledged, what I want to emphasize is the different relationships to experience—good or bad—suggested by these strategies.

25. Jonathan Z. Smith, *Imagining Religion: From Babylon to Jonestown* (Chicago: University of Chicago Press, 1982), p. xiii. Here Smith paraphrases and then cites Victor Shklovsky, "Art as Technique," in *Russian Formalist Criticism: Four Essays*, ed. L. T. Lemon and M. J. Reis (Lincoln: University of Nebraska Press, 1965), especially pp. 13–22. My goal is not so much to map Buddhist and feminist positions onto each other, although we may occasionally attempt this for a specific purpose, nor simply to play them off against each other, but to see how each shapes its own mode of inquiry.

26. Translation of these texts has been the focal endeavor of Western scholars of Buddhism since 1836, when Brian Hodgeson, working as an officer of the East Indian company in Calcutta and Kathmandu, sent eighty-eight Sanskrit Buddhist texts to the Société Asiatique in Paris, from where Eugene Burnouf obtained and began to translate them. Burnouf set the standard for Buddhology for decades: "Not only did he study many Sanskrit Buddhist ms. but also Avestan and Pehlevi texts, and translated the Bhāgavata Purāṇa. In connection with Pāli studies he undertook the study of Sinhalese, Burmese, and Siamese translations and commentaries. Moreover, he did not neglect modern Indo-Aryan lan-

guages such as Bengali, Marathi, and Gujarati. For most of these languages he had to compile his own dictionary. All this was done without neglecting his duties as Professor at the College de France and often in poor health." This description is de Jong's, another hero in the same mold. See J. W. de Jong, "A Brief History of Buddhist Studies in Europe and America," *Eastern Buddhist* 7, no. 1 (May 1974), p. 73.

27. For a compelling critique of Said's *Orientalism* and a discussion of how institutions shape the knowledge one can have of another culture, see Robert Young, *White Mythologies: Writing History and the West* (London: Routledge, 1990), especially chapter 7, "Disorienting Orientalism."

28. Among those who have published major works that go well beyond textual study are Robert E. Buswell, *The Zen Monastic Experience: Buddhist Practice in Contemporary Korea* (Princeton: Princeton University Press, 1992); Bernard Faure, *Chan Insights and Oversights: An Epistemological Critique of the Chan Tradition* (Princeton: Princeton University Press, 1993), and *The Rhetoric of Immediacy: A Cultural Critique of Zen Buddhism* (Princeton: Princeton University Press, 1991); and Raoul Birnbaum, *The Healing Buddha* (Boston: Shambhala Press, 1989); as well as forthcoming books by Janet Gyatso and Donald S. Lopez.

29. H. Stuart Hughes, *Consciousness and Society: The Reorientation of European Social Thought* (New York: Knopf, 1961); cited by David Keightley, *Sources of Shang History* (Berkeley: University of California Press, 1978), p. 154.

30. Jigmay Lingpa ('Jigs-med-gling-pa, 1729–98), *kLong-chen-nying-tik* (n.p., n.d.), *AUM* 356:1–4; quoted by Dro-drup-chen III, in *Rig 'dzin yum ka bde chen rygal mo'i sgrub gzhung gi zin bris bde chen lam gzang gsal ba'i gron ma* (Notes on the basic text for emulating the Mother Knowledge Bearer, the Great Bliss Queen: A lamp clarifying the Good Path of Great Bliss), in volume 5 of the *Collected Works of Do-drup-chen* (Gantok, 1975), 470.1.

31. Steven D. Goodman, trans., "Ocean Woman Who Already Knows," *Alcheringa: Ethnopoetics* 3, no. 2 (1977): 42–44. The story of Yeshey Tsogyel's birth is from Do-drup-chen III, *Rig'dzin yum ka*, 471.5.

32. Keith Dowman, trans., *Sky Dancer: The Secret Life and Songs of the Lady Yeshey Tsogyel* (London: Routledge and Kegan Paul, 1984), p. 16.

33. Ibid., 110. The early history of Bön is much contested among scholars. See especially Per Kværne, "A Bönpo *bstan-rtsis* from 1804," in *Indo-Tibetan Studies: Papers in Honor and Appreciation of Prof. David Snellgrove*, ed. Tadeusz Skorupski, Buddhica Britannica Series, Continua II, (Tring, U.K., 1990), pp. 151–69. See also Ariane MacDonald, "Une lecture des Pelliot tibétain, 1286, 1287, 1038, 1047, et 1290: Essai sur la formation et l'emploi des mythes politiques dans la religion royale de Sroṅ-bcan-sgam-po," in *Études tibétaines dediée à la memoire de Marcelle Lalou* (Paris, 1971), pp. 190–389; R. A. Stein, "Tibetica Antiqua," *BE-FEO* 1983, 1984, and 1985; Anne-Marie Blondeau, "Le lHa'dre bka'thaṅ," in *Études tibétaines dediée à la memoire de Marcele Lalou*; and Erik Haarh, *The Yarluṅ Dynasty* (Copenhagen: G. E. C. Gad's Forlag, 1969).

34. Do-drup-chen III, *Rig 'dzin yum ka*, 474.2 ff.

35. For example, in the *Very Essence of the Great Expanse*, a major liturgical lineage within Nyingma.

36. Do-drup-chen III, *Rig 'dzin yum ka*, 471.5.

37. Her enjoyment body (*saṃbhogakāya longs sku*) is one of the three dimensions or bodies of enlightened persons.

38. Ngawang Denzin Dorje, *Ra tig/kLong chen snying gi thig le'i mkha' 'gro bde chen rgyal mo'i grub gzhung gi 'grel pa rgyud don snang ba* (Commentary on the practice for emulating the Sky Woman, the Great Bliss Queen, from the "Very Essence of the Great Expanse" tradition of Longchen Rabjam) (New Delhi: Sonam Topgay Kazi, 1972), 474.4.

39. Many of these guises link her with important male Buddhist figures. For example, as Tara she is said to have been born from a tear shed by the

male embodiment of compassion, Avalokiteshvara, and the historical Yeshey Tsogyel is famous as the consort of Guru Rinboche and for preserving and exemplifying his teachings. As Sarasvati she is paired with Vajrasattva and as Vajravārāhi with Shamvara.

40. Ngawang Dendzin Dorje, *Ra tig*, 50.2 ff.

41. What I have called the developmental and discovery (or sculpturing and gardening) orientations within Buddhism are more classically known as the gradual and sudden approaches.

42. A prime modern example of sectarianism is featured in the *Sphere of the Middle Way* (*Dbu ma chos dbyings/Dbu ma chos kyi dbyings rnam par 'byed pa'i grel pa smra ba ngan pa'i tsang tshang tshing 'joms ar byed pa'i bstan bcos gnam lcags me chad*) (n.p., n.d.), where the twentieth-century Geluk scholar Ngawang Chos-grub attacks Long-chen-ba, arguing that the Great Completeness (*rDzogs-chen*) lacks an ability to present the view (4.4) or establish valid cognition (*pramāṇa, tshad ma*), 19 ff.

Standing in contrast are scholars like Kensur Ngawang Lekden, my very first teacher, whom I met and shared a communal house with in Wisconsin in 1971. Ngawang Lekden was abbot emeritus of the prestigious Tantric College of Lower Lhasa until the Chinese Cultural Revolution, and by virtue of his position and training in line for the famous Throne of Tsong-kha-pa, one of the highest positions in the Geluk hierarchy. After his death, I learned from his close student Jeffrey Hopkins that he had quietly studied Nyingma with the great master Dudjom Rinboche. Khetsun Sangpo Rinboche, author of a thirteen-volume series on Tibetan history and culture, and currently head of the Nyingma Wishfulfilling Center in Kathmandu, was my earliest and most frequent Nyingma teacher. Khetsun Rinboche spent several years at Gomang College of Drebung University. Lama Gompo Tsayden, whose retreats I attended in California in the early 1980s, headed a Nyingma monastery in Amdo, a province of eastern Tibet since annexed by the People's Republic of China. It maintained particularly close ties with a major nearby

Geluk college. The Dalai Lama, head of the Geluk hierarchy, has taken a personal interest in Nyingma, especially in the Great Completeness. Namkhai Norbu Rinboche, whose retreat seminars I have frequently attended since the early 1980s, trained in the Sakgya tradition, and is a major contemporary Dzog-chen master who draws from both Nyingma and Bön sources. Finally, in 1991 I met and began to work with Tenzin Wangyal Rinboche, a Geshe in the Bön tradition trained by a Geluk- (Drebung-) educated Geshe in logic and philosophy.

43. This commentary was brought to my attention by Lama Gompo Tsayden; located and xeroxed with the help of his close student Helen MacEwan (a.k.a. Chos-dbyings-dpal-mo). A few years later I received another commentary on Yeshey Tsogyel written by Lama Gompo from Amdo, addressed to Helen and partly motivated, according to one of his students, by my interest in the Great Bliss Queen.

44. In the last several years the Sakgya teacher Jetsun Kusho-la (Mrs. R. W. Luding) has come to live and occasionally teach in the United States. I have recently learned of a few other strong women teachers in Tibet and Nepal, especially from the Nyingma tradition, and am making efforts to meet them and, possibly, invite them to this country.

45. Two of them are well known in the area of women and Buddhism: Tsultrim Allione (who was instrumental in arranging both visits) and Janet Gyatso. Also included were Michele Martin who as acquisitions editor helped SUNY Press to become a major publisher of Buddhist works and is now doing important translation work, and Tsultrim's nineteen-year-old daughter Aloka, who with a wisdom beyond her years suggested we lay aside the many detailed questions we were rehearsing and simply show our appreciation for a young teacher who was, during the visit in general, greatly overshadowed by her famous uncle.

46. I found myself on the unexpectedly painful cusp of this issue when this book was accepted by two exemplary publishers: Beacon, with a wide reputation in women's studies and religion, and a top university press

with a wide reputation in Asian scholarship. This made me aware of many of the untoward assumptions academic and nonacademic communities have about each other.

47. For an argument that Yeshey Tsogyel is a role model for American women, see Rita M. Gross, "Yeshe Tsogyel: Enlightened Consort, Great Teacher, Female Role Model," in *Feminine Ground: Essays on Women in Tibet*, ed. Janice Willis (Ithaca: Snow Lion, 1989). I am more cautious than Professor Gross in domesticating Yeshey Tsogyel as a twentieth-century role model. In addition to the cultural complexities of doing so, I note Caroline Walker Bynum's observation that "women's myths and rituals tend to explore a state of being." I believe the ritual of the Great Bliss Queen does just that. What is interesting in the Tibetan context is that rituals based on male figures have this emphasis as well. See *Gender and Religion*, ed. Caroline Bynum, Stevan Harrel, Paula Richman (Boston: Beacon Press, 1986), p. 13.

48. Carol Christ, "Why Women Need the Goddess," in *Womanspirit Rising*, ed. Judith Plaskow and Carol Christ (San Francisco: Harper and Row, 1979), pp. 273–86. A vibrant literature has grown up among contemporary European and American women, much of it implying vague essentialist notions of "the feminine." For critical reflection on goddess movements, see Rosemary Ruether, *Gaia and God: An Ecofeminist Ecology of Earth Healing* (San Francisco: Harper, 1992), chap. 6; Janet Biehl, *Rethinking Ecofeminist Politics* (Boston: South End Press, 1991); and Charlene Spretnak, *The Politics of Women's Spirituality: Essays on the Rise of Spiritual Power within the Feminist Movement* (New York: Anchor/Doubleday, 1982).

49. This is a position that may be about to gain more currency than it has had in European and North American thinking. Reading a chapter of this book in manuscript, Kathryn Milun pointed out to me the work of Giorgio Agamben, *Enfance et l'histoire: Dépérissement de l'experience et origine de l'histoire* (Paris: Éditions Payot, 1978), which suggests that the nonlinguistic dimension is something persons of all genders and cul-

tures share at infancy, that the term "infant" in fact derives from "in phones" meaning "without language," and that this memory and experience of being without language lingers all our lives.

2. Persons

1. For a biographical study of one such figure, and discussion of the genre of biography in Tibet in general, see Janet Gyatso's forthcoming *Dancing Moons and Dakini Talk: The Secret Autobiographies of Jigmay Lingba*.

2. Roy F. Baumeister, *Identity: Cultural Change and the Struggle for Self* (New York: Oxford University Press, 1986), p. 41; see also Alasdair MacIntyre, *After Virtue* (Notre Dame, Ind.: University of Notre Dame Press, 1981), p. 56.

3. Peter Abbs, "The Development of Autobiography in Western Culture: From Augustine to Rousseau" (Ph.D. diss., University of Sussex, 1986), p. 133. Raymond Williams also makes use of these and related examples in *Keywords: A Vocabulary of Culture and Society* (1976; reprint, London: Fontana, Flamingo Edition, 1983), pp. 161–62.

4. Abbs, "Autobiography in Western Culture," pp. 130–32.

5. Ibid., p. 129; quoted in Anthony Storr, *Solitude: A Return to the Self* (New York: Free Press, 1988), p. 79. See also Baumeister, *Identity*, p. 40.

6. Abbs, "Autobiography in Western Culture," pp. 131–32; cited in Storr, *Solitude*, pp. 79–80. Baumeister dates the term "consciousness" to 1690; the point is the same. He further notes that in German the pattern and dates were approximately the same as English, and in French the pattern occurred slightly later (*Identity*, p. 40).

7. Baumeister, *Identity*, p. 39. Strong feelings are even today popularly taken to be "givens," although, among others, Michelle Rosaldo, *Knowledge and Passion: Ilongot Notions of Self and Social Life* (New York: Cambridge University Press, 1980); James Clifford and George Marcus, eds., *Writing Culture: the Poetics and Politics of Ethnography* (Berkeley: University of California Press, 1986); and Catherine Lutz, *Unnatural Emo-*

tions: Everyday Sentiments on a Micronesian Atoll and Their Challenge to Western Theory (Chicago: University of Chicago Press, 1988) have done crucial work in revealing emotion as a cultural process. This discussion follows their lead.

8. Abbs, "Autobiography in Western Culture," p. 131, notes that on the continent at this time a variety of moves indicated the emergence of distinctive selves: Descartes' cogitating ego, Rousseau's celebration of his own uniqueness, Montaigne's affirmations of his idiosyncratic self; also, much earlier, in Germany and then in Holland, the self-portraits of Rembrandt and Dürer.

9. Baumeister, *Identity*, p. 39; R. Altick, *Lives and Letters: A History of Literary Biography in England and America* (New York: Knopf, 1965), pp. 191–93.

10. I quote Domna C. Stanton, "Autogynography: Is the Subject Different," in *The Female Autobiography*, ed. Domna C. Stanton (New York: New York Literary Forum, 1984), p. 11. See also Sidonie Smith, "Who's Talking/Who's Talking Back? The Subject of Personal Narrative," *Signs* 18, no. 2 (Winter 1993): 392–407; Abbs, "Autobiography in Western Culture," p. 132.

11. Mark Taylor writes of Madonna: "As one studies the masks she wears, images she fabricates, and personas she assumes, it becomes clear that we do not really know who Madonna is or even what she looks like. Thoroughly postmodern, Madonna is *image all the way down*. She is nothing but her masks and yet no mask represents her. This is not to imply that the true Madonna lies hidden behind her myriad masks. Madonna makes no such mistake, for she realizes that the real itself has become a simulacrum" (*Nots* [Chicago: University of Chicago Press, 1993], p. 205). But Madonna pays fierce attention to her masks, and the dynamic of attention should not be overlooked.

12. Storr, *Solitude*, p. 169, quotation from *Italian Painters of the Renaissance* (New York: Phaidon Publishers, 1952). The schooling of modern Westerners is also quite different from traditional purposes of schooling

such as the preservation of ancient wisdom in Tibet, or the beginning of a lifelong commitment to a guild or monastery in medieval Europe. See Randolph Franklin Lumpp, "Culture, Religion, and the Presence of the Word: A Study of the Thought of Walter Jackson Ong" (Ph.D. dissertation, University of Ottawa, 1976).

13. Augustine (*creatura non potest creare*) and Tasso cited by Williams, *Keywords*, p. 82.

14. Orality was of course also an important component in early Judaism and Christianity, and even today one is exhorted not to study the Torah alone. Moreover, mystical Judaism, the Kabala, stresses that interpreters of the Torah are cocreators of the moral universe. (Thanks to Michael Fischer on these points.) However, here as throughout I am contrasting traditional Buddhism primarily with contemporary and mainstream forms of Jewish and Christian religiosity.

15. Walter Ong, *Orality and Literacy: The Technologizing of the Word* (London: Methuen, 1983), pp. 130 ff. With its rise, Ong has also noted, "the old communal oral world had split up into privately claimed free-holdings" (p. 131). Ong further observes that "when in the past few decades doctrines of intertextuality arose to counteract the isolationist aesthetics of a romantic print culture they came as a kind of shock . . . because modern writers, agonizingly aware of literary history and of the *de facto* intertextuality of their own works, are concerned that they may be producing nothing really new or fresh at all" (pp. 133–34).

16. Charles Taylor, *Sources of the Self: The Making of the Modern Identity* (Cambridge: Harvard University Press, 1989), p. 34.

17. I draw in this paragraph on research reported by Linda Bell in "Song without Words: Listening to Japanese Families," *Networker*, March/April 1989, and on conversations with Professor Bell about her work.

18. See Gayatri Chakravorty Spivak, "Can the Subaltern Speak?" in *Marxism and the Interpretation of Culture*, ed. Cary Nelson and Lawrence Grossberg (Urbana: University of Illinois Press, 1988), especially pp. 291–92.

19. Elizabeth Fox-Genovese, *Feminism without Illusions* (Chapel Hill: University of North Carolina Press, 1991), p. 175.

20. Nancy Hartsock, "Rethinking Modernism: Minority vs. Majority Theories," *Cultural Critique* 7 (1987): 186–206; paraphrased and discussed by Di Stephano in "Dilemmas of Difference," in *Feminism/Postmodernism*, ed. Linda J. Nicholson (New York: Routledge, 1990), pp. 63–82.

21. Fox-Genovese, *Feminism without Illusions*, pp. 7 ff. Fox-Genovese argues that individualism rightly includes the idea of social obligation and socially responsible freedom.

22. Irvin D. Yalom, *Existential Psychotherapy* (New York: Basic Books, 1980). Thanks to Harvey Aronson for introducing me to this aspect of Yalom's work.

23. Ernst Becker, *The Denial of Death* (New York: Macmillan, 1973), pp. 5, 190.

24. Annie Leclerc in *New French Feminisms*, ed. Elaine Marks and Isabelle de Courtivron (New York: Schocken Books, 1980), pp. 82–83. See also the discussion of heroism and the heroic ego in Catherine Keller, *From a Broken Web* (Boston: Beacon Press, 1986), esp. chap. 2.

25. Gail Machlis, from her drawing of two women talking with three children at their knees, in "Quality Time," *Houston Chronicle*, Sunday, June 13, 1993.

26. Mary Daly, *Pure Lust: Elemental Feminist Philosophy* (Boston: Beacon Press, 1984). Daly's chapter 1 rightly explores the dominance of death metaphors in Western culture but thereby sacrifices the point that death must be faced.

27. Thanks to Marie-Pierre Stein for this observation.

28. Betty Friedan's path-making *Fountain of Age* (New York: Simon and Schuster, 1993) came out just as this book was going to press.

29. Simone de Beauvoir, *The Second Sex*, trans. and ed. H. M. Parshley (New York: Vintage Books, 1974), p. 72. Discussed by Rosemarie Tong in

Feminist Thought (Boulder: Westview Press, 1989), p. 205; also by Sherry Ortner, "Is Woman to Nature as Man Is to Culture?" in *Woman, Culture, and Society*, ed. Michelle Rosaldo and Louise Lamphere (Stanford: Stanford University Press, 1981), pp. 67–87. Becker even goes so far as to say that "killing is a symbolic solution of a biological limitation; it results from the fusion of the biological level (animal anxiety) with the symbolic one (death fear) in the human animal" (*The Denial of Death*, p. 99).

30. Jane Flax, *Thinking Fragments: Psychoanalysis, Feminism, and Postmodernism in the Contemporary West* (Berkeley: University of California Press, 1990), p. 161.

31. Adrienne Rich's famous use of this phrase, quoted and discussed in this context by Flax (ibid., p. 156).

32. Cited and discussed by Flax (ibid., p. 108).

33. Irvin D. Yalom argues powerfully in *Existential Psychotherapy* that a child's ability to deal early in life with the fear and reality of death is an important psychological milestone. He does not, however, make any connections with gender constructions and this issue.

34. Interview of Maxine Hong Kingston conducted by Kay Bonetti; discussed in King-Kok Cheung, "The Woman Warrior versus the Chinaman Pacific," in *Conflicts in Feminism*, ed. Marianne Hirsch and Evelyn Fox Keller (New York: Routledge, 1990), p. 243. Maxine Hong Kingston, *The Woman Warrior: Tales of a Girlhood among Ghosts* (New York: Knopf, 1976).

35. Becker, *Denial of Death*, pp. 171, 172. Descartes has been called the originator of this aspect of individualism, because his affirmation of the relationship between thinking and being requires that each person creates the conceptual architecture of his own life; similarly, Montaigne can be seen as the originator of the search for personal originality. Both philosophers posit a turning inward, however, a looking to the resources located only within oneself. See also Charles Taylor, *Sources of the Self*, pp. 177 ff., 193 ff.

36. Stan Royal Mumford, *Himalayan Dialogue: Tibetan Lamas and Gurung Shamans in Nepal* (Madison: University of Wisconsin Press, 1989). Thanks to Elizabeth Napper for mentioning this book to me at an especially apt moment. Mumford is working with Tibetan peoples in Nepal, and while I cannot say that their particular types of ritual performance or the specific relationships between shamanic and Buddhist groups that have arisen in Nepal replicate those in Tibet, from my own experience with Tibetans (many of whom had had little contact with Westerners when I first met them), I do believe Mumford has captured the general dynamics of a dialogue that is applicable in Tibet. However, the layers of ritual should not be neatly aligned with Buddhist and pre-Buddhist (e.g., Bön) elements of Tibetan culture to the extent that Mumford suggests. David Snellgrove notes the term Bön is often erroneously identified with pre-Buddhist Tibetan beliefs that were never referred to as Bön while they still represented the official religion of Tibet. Snellgrove, *Indo-Tibetan Buddhism* (Boston: Shambhala Press, 1987), vol. 2, p. 389.

37. See, for example, discussion of "ordinary" or "separate" persons below. Although much of traditional Tibetan culture has been changed forever, especially in central Tibet, there are places throughout the area where traditional ways linger, as they do among many Tibetan communities in India and Nepal. For this reason, and as a sign of hope, I use the present tense in describing Tibetan culture.

38. Nancy Levine, "The Theory of *Rü* Kinship, Descent, and Status in a Tibetan Society," in *Asian Highland Societies in Anthropological Perspective*, ed. Christoph von Fürer Haimendorf (New Delhi: Sterling Publishers, 1981), pp. 55–57, 63.

39. We cannot claim to be utterly bereft of some sense of cosmic connectedness ourselves. As I was revising this paragraph, I noticed a hum in the back of my head, a song from *West Side Story* suggesting that the universe does respond to human emotion: "Tonight . . . I'll see my love tonight, and for us, *stars will stop where they are*." A more edifying in-

stance of such connectedness in western culture is the "pathetic fallacy," a trope in which one sees human feelings reflected in nature.

40. Sherry Ortner also notes that, at least according to popular perception, village lamas are regarded as constantly "on call for the religious needs of the people. . . . A monk, on the other hand, does nothing but seek his own personal salvation; he does not respond to the needs of the people" (*Sherpas through Their Rituals* [Cambridge: Cambridge University Press, 1978], p. 136). In this sense, the lamas are seen as having a more embedded relationship with their society than the monks. In the area in which Ortner worked, most if not all of the "lamas" would have been Nyingma, the order of Tibetan Buddhism that has most in common with the Bön traditions. The tension we are referring to thus gets played out among the Buddhist schools, which differ considerably in the emphasis they place on the monastic life as a model of spiritual practice. It also gets played out between the shamanistic and philosophical elements of Tibetan religion, and between contemporary Bön and Buddhism as Mumford suggests. Mumford reframes conclusions drawn by Ortner in her work with Sherpas during the 1960s when he observes that what she calls a (Buddhist) lamaist ideology "tends to isolate individual identity from the matrix of social ties, while shamanic identity remains embedded in the world of relations, even accepting spirit penetrations into the self" (*Himalayan Dialogue*, p. 7).

41. André Bareau, "La notion de personne dans le boudhisme indien," in *Problèmes de la personne* (Paris: Mouton, 1973), pp. 88–89 (thanks to Bernard Faure for drawing my attention to this text). Whether or not these terms are always associated with these meanings, it is clear that Indian and Tibetan Buddhist philosophies do understand persons in these two senses.

42. This observation developed in conversation with Janet Gyatso.

43. A classic detailing of this cosmology is found in Longchen Rabjam, *Tshig don mdzod* (Treasury of meaning) (Gantok, Sikkim: Sherab Gy-

altsen and Khentse Labrang Palace Monastery, 1983). A classic example of the speaking cosmos is the *Kun byed rygal po* (Superb maker of everything), reprinted from Sde-sge edition in *gSung Thor-bu*, vol. 2 (Paro, Bhutan: Dilgo Khyantsey Rinboche, 1982). This is one of the seventeen ancient tantras of the old transmission (Nyingma) attributed to Samantabhadra. Eva Dargyey seeks to equate Samantabhadra with a Creator deity, a most controversial position. See her "The Concept of a 'Creator God' in Tantric Buddhism," *Journal of the International Association of Buddhist Studies* 8, no. 1 (1985): 31–47. See also her translation *The Sovereign All-Creating Mind* (Albany: SUNY Press, 1992). Long-chen-ba's commentary on this tantra has been translated by Kennard Lipman and Merill Petersen, under the guidance of Namkhai Norbu Rinboche, as *You Are the Eyes of the World* (Novato, Cal.: Lotsawa Press, 1987).

44. The cause and effect process of karma means that causality is not limited to material processes. For example, as Kensur Yeshey Tupden explains, if a farmer reaps a good harvest, this results not only from the physical work and seeds of the previous year, which are its direct causes, but also from the indirect causes of that farmer's past actions. See chapter 4 in Anne Klein, trans. and ed., *Path to the Middle, Oral Mādhyamika Philosophy in Tibet: The Spoken Scholarship of Kensur Yeshey Tupden* (Albany: SUNY Press, 1994).

45. Similarly, in the West "the ancient, oral world knew few 'explorers,' though it did know many itinerants, travelers, voyagers, adventurers, and pilgrims" (Ong, *Orality and Literacy*, p. 73).

46. Jack Goody and Ian Watt, "The Consequences of Literacy," in *Literacy in Traditional Societies*, ed. J. R. Goody (Cambridge: Cambridge University Press, 1968), pp. 57 ff. The authors further observe that in "literate society, merely by having no system of elimination, [a] 'structural amnesia' prevents the individual from participating fully in the total cultural tradition to anything like the extent possible in non-literate society."

47. Gam-po-pa, *Dam chos yid bzhin gyi nor bu thar pa rin po che'i rgyan*, translated by Herbert Guenther as *Jewel Ornament of Liberation* (1959; reprint, Boulder: Prajña Press, 1981), p. 38.

48. Ibid., p. 39. In discussing the same topic based on the *Kun bzang bla ma'i zhal lung* (Sacred word of Lama Gun Sang), Khetsun Sangpo said one should listen "like a deer listening to a guitar. It becomes so enthralled that a hunter can easily approach from behind. . . . [Moreover, when hearing, thinking about, or meditating on the doctrine,] you should be like a dumb person tasting something. His mind is so concentrated that he pays attention only to the taste." *Tantric Practice in Nyingma* (1982; reprint, Ithaca: Snow Lion, 1986), p. 33.

49. Keith Dowman, trans., *Sky Dancer: The Secret Life and Songs of the Lady Yeshey Tsogyel* (London: Routledge and Kegan Paul, 1984), p. 121.

50. Do-drup-chen III, *Rig 'dzin yum ka* (Notes on the basic text for emulating the Mother Knowledge Bearer) (Gantok, 1975), 473. 4 ff.

51. The various genres of oral performance associated with textual study and ritual practices are described in the Introduction to Klein, *Path to the Middle*.

52. Denma Lochö Rinboche, University of Virginia, Spring 1978.

53. In Yung Drung Bön's Southern Treasure, for example, the first four strata of the ninefold system, known as the "four causal vehicles" (*rgyu yi theg pa*), elaborate numerous rituals, among which that of "ransom" or "social retrieval" (*bla blu*) seems most to resemble what I know of this scholar's ritual.

54. Even today, Indian men and women will gather to touch the body of a dead tiger. They lay a hand on its body and then on themselves, to get its power. For a full account of the practice of preventing hail, including the complete list of "antidotes," see "Preventing Hail on the Tibetan Plateau: Tantric Practice and Ritual Protection" with Khetsun Sangpo Rinboche, in *Buddhism in Translation*, ed. Donald S. Lopez, Jr. (Princeton: Princeton University Press, forthcoming).

55. Taylor, *Sources of the Self*, pp. 190–91.

56. Thanks to Meredith Skura, a fellow member of the Rice Center for Cultural Studies Seminar, 1989–1991, who inadvertently reminded me of this comment by expressing her own amazement at it a week later. In this case, my own familiarity with Tibetan world views did me a disservice; the comment had not made much of an impression on me.

57. Hell beings, hungry ghosts, animals, humans, gods, and demi-gods are the six classic states of rebirth.

58. According to Arthur Anthony Macdonell, *A Practical Sanskrit Dictionary* (1954; reprint, London: Oxford University Press, 1965), and Vamam Shivram Apte, *The Practical Sanskrit-English Dictionary* (1965; reprint, Delhi: Motilal Banarsidass, 1975); Franklin Edgerton, *Buddhist Hybrid Sanskrit Grammar and Dictionary* (New Haven: Yale University Press, 1953; reprint, Delhi: Motilal Banarsidass, 1972), does not discuss this term.

59. Macdonell, *Sanskrit Dictionary*, p. 165; Apte, *Sanskrit-English Dictionary*, p. 624. *Puru* is, I believe, related to the Pāli *posa*, "to be fed or nourished." See T. W. Rhys-Davids and William Stede, eds., *Pāli-English Dictionary* (London: Pāli Text Society, 1972), p. 475. Of course, this is what men—the prototypical people—are, from the female viewpoint. It is only when the food is of an exalted sort, such as the nectar of the dharma that Yeshey Tsogyel received in our example above, that its provider is said to be male. Fittingly, therefore, a *posika* (also derived from *posa*) is a nurse or female attendant. On *purī*, Steven Collins gives a thorough discussion of the assimilation in Pali Buddhist texts of the meanings of "person" and "house"—and, of course, a town is composed of numerous houses. See *Selfless Persons: Imagery and Thought in Theravada Buddhism* (Cambridge: Cambridge University Press, 1982), pp. 166 ff.

60. Apte, *Sanskrit-English Dictionary*, p. 625, cites Ms. 5. 250; 5. 123, 6. 76; 4.56. The Pali terms *pursa*, *pussa*, *possa*, and *posa* also appear to be derived from this root; Macdonell, *Sanskrit Dictionary*, p. 165, cites *Saṃyutta Nikāya*, I.61 (although *posya* as an adjective is said to be related

with *poṣya*, gerund of *poseti*, from *pus*. (Rhys-Davids and Stede, *Pāli-English Dictionary*, p. 475). *Purīṣam* means feces, excrement, ordure; *purītat* refers to a particular intestine near the heart, or to entrails in general.

61. *Zag* was originally a Jain term, referring to actual physical outflows of karmic material.

62. *Bod rgya tshig mdzod chen mo* (The great treasury of Tibetan words) (Chengdu: Mi rigs dpe skyan Khang, 1984), vol. 1, p. 342.

63. *Puruṣa* is also translated by the colloquial term *mi*, "human," and therefore primarily signifies male humans. Like most Tibetan words, however, and unlike Sanskrit, the word *mi* carries neither a masculine nor a feminine ending.

64. Gam-po-pa, *Dam chos yid bzhin*, in Guenther, tr., *Jewel Ornament of Liberation*, p. 17.

65. Rhys-Davids and Stede, *Pāli-English Dictionary*, p. 466. In the *Lam rim* literature, "creatures" is the term of choice when persons are described in terms of their potential for the path. "Ordinary creature" is used to distinguish those who have not developed nonconceptual wisdom from those who have. To be ordinary is to be temporarily separate from one's potential.

66. Feminist analysis has not always been balanced regarding the situation of women since the Chinese takeover. For example, Julia Kristeva returned in the early 1970s from a trip to China impressed with the "effort being made to give women an active role not only in the home but on all levels of political and social activity" (in Marks and de Courtivron, *New French Feminisms*, pp. 139–40). She mentions not one word about the Cultural Revolution, in which many millions of Chinese died, nor anything about the world's largest gulag with millions imprisoned in Tibet's annexed provinces or the cultural genocide in which nuns even more than monks are singled out for special forms of torture and women are, in some cases, forced to have late-term abortions. Women's situation

is the legitimate focus of feminism but it cannot be treated in isolation. *That* would be a most unfortunate outcome of an essentialist response.

67. The discussion that follows is condensed and adapted from my "Primordial Purity and Everyday Life," in *Immaculate and Powerful: The Female in Sacred Image and Social Reality*, ed. Atkinson, Buchanan, and Miles (Boston: Beacon Press, 1986).

68. For a discussion of the origins of the nomads, see R. A. Stein, *Tibetan Civilization* (Stanford: Stanford University Press, 1972), pp. 109–12. See also the detailed study based on travels among Tibetan nomads in 1951 in Namkhai Norbu, *Byang 'brog gi lam yig* (A journey into the culture of Tibetan nomads) (Arcidosso, Italy: Shang-Shung Editions, 1983); also Charles A. Sherring, *Western Tibet and the Indian Borderland* (1916; reprint, Delhi: Cosmo Publications, 1974), p. 329.

69. William Woodville Rockhill, *The Land of the Lamas* (1891; reprint, New Delhi: Asian Publication Services, 1975), p. 230.

70. Tseten Dolkar, *Girl from Tibet* (Chicago: Loyola University Press, 1971), p. 8.

71. Geshe Rabten mentioned the Geluk bias in apologetic tones when it came up in a Tsong-kha-pa text we were reading. He said that it was a matter of its being more dangerous for women to stay alone in the kind of solitary places recommended for meditation (Upper McLeod Ganj, Dharamsala, Spring 1972). Pema Wangyal Rinboche commented on women's superiority in tantric practice in discussing Yeshey Tsogyel's biography in New York in 1977; I have heard second-hand reports of other Nyingma lamas saying the same thing.

72. There were exceptions to this. The Nu-wang tribe in eastern Tibet, which was a political enterprise of sufficient luster to establish an embassy noted in Chinese Sui dynasty accounts of 586 C.E., was ruled by women until 742 C.E., when a man was elected. Subsequently this district was absorbed by Lhasa. The female sovereign house had several hundred female attendants; the men had nothing to do with government, their activities being limited to battles and cultivating the land.

See Sherring, *Western Tibet*, p. 338. There are also indications that as the "public sector" develops a presence in the larger cities of Tibet, women's work roles are more arduous and of lower status than men's. Barbara Aziz cites the case of Palaceview, a hotel in Lhasa, where men and women are equally vociferous at meetings and socially equal as well, but only women clean the toilets, wash dishes, or take night shifts, and all for lower pay than the male workers. No man would agree to do housework. See Barbara Aziz, "Moving towards a Sociology of Tibet," in Janice D. Willis, *Feminine Ground: Essays on Women in Tibet* (Ithaca: Snow Lion, 1989). Aziz (p. 92) also cites James F. Fisher, *Trans-Himalayan Traders: Economy, Society, and Culture in Northwest Nepal* (Berkeley: University of California Press, 1980), pp. 75–79, for evidence that Tibetan peoples at least sometimes equated woman's work with polluting work.

73. This linguistic stratification was not widespread in eastern Tibet, where it was regarded, at best humorously, as an affectation. Similarly, in central Tibet, even a hungry guest was obliged to refuse food until the host had expended considerable energy in exhortation. Several times one or another Tibetan guest has said over dinner, "I am not from Lhasa; when I say I don't want any more, you can believe it."

74. Thanks to Michele Martin on the use of *chung ma*.

75. *Bud* means "expel" and *med* is a negative. See Sarat Chandra Das, *Tibetan-English Dictionary* (Calcutta, 1969; Compact edition, Kyoto, 1977), p. 872. See also Robert Poczik and Lobsang Tenzin Rikha, *English-Tibetan Dictionary*, 4th ed. (Dharamsala: Council for Tibetan Education, 1986), p. 267. It is not clear how *lus phra ma* came to have this meaning; *phra ma* itself means slander.

76. All terms are from *Bod rgya tshig mdzod chen mo*, vol. 2, p. 1834.

77. For a discussion of several modern-day Tibetan nuns, see Janice D. Willis, "Tibetan *Ani's*: The Nun's Life in Tibet," and Karma Lekshe Tsomo, "Tibetan Nuns and Nunneries," both in Willis, *Feminine Ground*.

78. Namkai Norbu gives this term as *ga ma* (*Byang 'brog gi lam yig*, pp. 188–89). According to Tulku Thondup, a Nyingma lama from a nomadic family of the Golok area in Tibet, the term *go-ga-ma*, synonymous with the above, has wide usage.

79. Norbu, *Byang 'brog gi lam yig*, p. 189.

80. For a fascinating account of a historic consultation with Tibet's most famous oracle, see the Dalai Lama's *Freedom in Exile* (New York: HarperCollins, 1990), pp. 49–57, 212–17. See also Sir Charles Bell, *The People of Tibet* (Oxford: Clarendon Press, 1928), p. 169.

81. Bell, *The People of Tibet*, pp. 192–94. For an autobiographical account of marriage arrangements in one of Tibet's most powerful noble families, see Rinchen Dolma Taring, *Daughter of Tibet* (London: Camelot Press, 1970), especially pp. 66–104.

82. Norbu, *Byang 'brog gi lam yig*, p. 225. For a good general discussion of Tibetan families, see Stein, *Tibetan Civilization*, pp. 94–109. For a focus on marriage customs among Tibetans on the Nepal border, see Barbara Aziz, *Tibetan Frontier Families: Reflections of Three Generations from Dingri* (Durham, N.C.: Carolina Academic Press, 1978), pp. 134–85.

83. Norbu, *Byang 'brog gi lam yig*, pp. 190–91.

84. Alan Winnington, *Tibet: Record of a Journey* (London: Lawrence and Wishart, 1957), p. 101; Bell, *The People of Tibet*, p. 179.

85. Thanks to Tulku Thondup for the explanation of the Yogurt Vow. See also Bell, *The People of Tibet*, p. 202. Some anthropologists would consider a ritual such as this to be indicative of generic auspiciousness, without the kind of gender significance I suggest. See, for example, the work of Frederique Marglin, *Wives of the God-King: The Rituals of the Devadasis of Puri* (Delhi/New York: Oxford University Press, 1985).

86. For a particularly dramatic case of a woman who moved out of her family to devote her life to meditation, see Tsultrim Allione, *Women of Wisdom* (London: Routledge and Kegan Paul, 1984), pp. 236–57, a con-

densed version of the story of Ayu Khandro as told to Namkhai Norbu Rinboche.

87. I am less certain about whether women were more likely than men to have a female figure as a personal deity (*yi dam*). My guess is this was so; no data exists that could verify or deny this.

88. The debates on substantial and reverse phenomena (*rdzas chos ldog chos*) can be found in the Geluk *Bsdus drva tshad ma'i gzhung don 'byed pa'i bsdus grva'i rnam bzhag rigs lam 'phrul gyi sde mig* (Collected topics) by Pur-bu-jok (Buxa, 1965). The story of the nuns is from Geshe Gendun Lodrö, Charlottesville, Va., 1979. On the subject of women teachers, see Rita Gross, *Buddhism after Patriarchy* (Albany: SUNY Press, 1993), p. 87.

89. The only Buddhist movement in the West to successfully attract women and men of color is the Japanese Soka Gakkai movement, of which Tina Turner is perhaps the most prominent Western adherent. Only now are other communities actively seeking to become more racially and economically integrated.

90. Quoted in Sandy Boucher, *Turning the Wheel: American Women Creating the New Buddhism* (1988; reprint, Boston: Beacon Press, 1993), p. 49. Another aspect of Buddhism's appeal in the West has arguably been its optimistic views of what is humanly possible. The Theravada, Tibetan, Pure Land, Soka Gakkai, Zen, and other Tibetan forms of Buddhism, which have been among the most well received in this country, promise the possibility of superior mental states or even enlightenment in this lifetime. Such emphasis on personal achievement maps well onto a capitalistic mentality, even as it appears to offer spiritual respite from materialistic goals.

3. Mindfulness and Subjectivity

1. See, for example, *Anguttara Nikāya*, I.10, the Theravada locus classicus regarding the mind's purity; see also definitions of mind in Elizabeth Napper, *Mind in Tibetan Buddhism* (Ithaca: Snow Lion, 1980).

2. This is especially true in the Geluk Consequentialist (*Prāsaṅgika*) school, which regards the errors it seeks to correct as not only mental or conceptual but as pervading sensory perception as well. Moreover, sensory perception can, at least in Buddhist theory, operate *without* conceptual overlay. For a discussion of Buddhism's claim to deal with a level of error more primal than language, see Elizabeth Napper, *Dependent Arising and Emptiness* (Boston: Wisdom Publications, 1989), pp. 92 ff.

3. Buddhaghosa, *The Path of Purification*, translation of *Visuddhimagga* by Bhikkhu Nyanamoli (Berkeley: Shambhala Press, 1976), 14.141.

4. Padma Garbo (Padma-dkar-po) makes this point in his *'Phag rgya chen po'i man ngag gi bshad byar rgyal ba'i gan mdzod*, fol. 88. For further discussion of this term, see Herbert Guenther, trans., *Jewel Ornament of Liberation* (1959; reprint, Boulder: Prajña Press, 1981), p. 229. See also Collett Cox, "Mindfulness and Memory: The Scope of *Smṛti* from Early Buddhism to the Sarvāstivādin Abhidharma," in *In the Mirror of Memory: Reflections on Mindfulness and Remembrance in Indian and Tibetan Buddhism*, ed. Janet Gyatso (Albany: SUNY Press, 1992), pp. 67 ff.

5. Khetsun Sangpo has observed, "The factor of mindfulness not deteriorating is clarity, while there is clarity, mindfulness is not deteriorating" (Discussion, Houston, Texas, March 1991). However, he observes, "it does not follow that when there is mindfulness there will be clarity, because one can have a dull mindfulness which lacks clarity." The general function of knowing, separate from any specific mental operations, is performed by the main mind (*citta, sems*) (Denma Lochö Rinboche, oral commentary on the Four Stabilizations of Mindfulness practice, UMA, Boonesville, Va., 1978).

6. Mind is defined as "that which is clear and knowing." The agent of its nondistracted clarity is mindfulness. In more developed states of calm, this is also associated with the "factor of subjective clarity" (*drang cha*), intensity (Tibetan *ngar*). See Geshe Gedun Lodrö, *Walking through*

Walls: A Tibetan Presentation of Calming Meditation, trans. Jeffrey Hopkins, ed. Anne C. Klein and Leah J. Zahler (Ithaca: Snow Lion, 1992), pp. 166 ff.

7. "One who is clever shows the scalpel stroke on it by means of a balanced effort" (Buddhaghosa, *Path of Purification*, 4.68. Mindfulness, which participates in both insight and concentration, moderates their respective tendencies toward "agitation" or "excitement" (*auddhataya, rgod pa*) and "idleness" or "laxity" (*laya, bying pa*) (ibid., 4.49).

8. From Khetsun Sangpo, *Tantric Practice in Nyingma* (1982; reprint, Ithaca: Snow Lion, 1986), p. 39. This tale appears in the *Sacred Word of Lama Kun Sang (Kun bSang blam'i zhal lung)* by Ba-drul Rinboche (dPa-sprul 'Jigs-med-chos-kyi-dbang-po, b. 1808) (Rum-theg: Karma'i chos-sgar, 1968).

9. Ledi Sayadaw, *The Requisites of Enlightenment*, translation of *Bodhipakkhiya-Dipani* by Sein Nyo Tun (Kandy, Ceylon [Sri Lanka]: Buddhist Publication Society, 1971), pp. 30–31. In contrast, with mindfulness, "there is no occasion when the attention becomes released from its object on account of the instability of thought" (pp. 28–29).

10. *Sammohavinodanī*, 168, quoted and discussed in Piaydassa Thera, *The Buddha's Ancient Path* (Kandy, Ceylon [Sri Lanka]: Buddhist Publication Society, 1974), p. 178.

11. Geshe-la was commenting on Shantideva's *Guide to the Bodhisattva's Way of Life* in a class at the Library of Tibetan Works and Archives, Dharamsala, India, Summer of 1972. This work can be read in a translation by Stephen Batchelor (London: Tharpa Publications, 1979).

12. Professor Donald S. Lopez made a similar point at the Conference on World Buddhism in Ann Arbor, Michigan, Summer 1987. I was also told, for example, that Ven. U Bha Khin, former accountant general of Burma as well as a teacher of Theravada meditation, taught meditation to his entire staff. Apparently his office ran very smoothly (related by S. N. Goenka, Bodhgaya, India, January 1972).

13. *Satipaṭṭhāna Sutta* (The foundations of mindfulness sutra), translated and introduced by Nyanaponika Thera in *The Heart of Buddhist Meditation* (1962; reprint York Beach, Maine: Samuel Weiser, 1984), p. 135. The text, translated into Tibetan as *Dran pa gnyer bzhag gzhi*, is not usually part of Tibetan scholarly or meditative training, but Lochö Rinboche, a high-ranking master in the Geluk order, selected it as a basis for mediation instruction he gave during his 1978 visit to the University of Virginia.

Sri Satya Narain Goenka has been instrumental in bringing Theravada practice to new Buddhist practitioners in India and the United States. He teaches yearly in Shelburne Falls, Massachusetts, and at his center in Dallas, Texas. Theravada meditation is also taught at the Insight Meditation Center in Barre, Massachusetts, where both women and men teach and administrate the center. The Theravada school has been particularly successful in training Western meditation teachers, among them, Jack Kornfield, Joseph Goldstein, Ruth Dennison, Sharon Salzburg, and Jacqueline Schwartz Mandell. Jacqueline, a former Theravada nun, is now in the interesting position of being both the mother of twin girls and an authorized meditation teacher in one of the most monastic and male-oriented of Buddhist traditions.

Ledi Sayadaw defines "foundations of mindfulness (*sattipaṭṭhāna*) as follows: *Bhusam titthati'ti paṭṭhānaṃ sati eva paṭṭhānaṃ satipaṭṭāna,* "What is firmly established is a 'foundation,' mindfulness itself is such a foundation" so that "there is no occasion when the attention becomes released from its object on account of the instability of thought" (*The Requisites of Enlightenment*, pp. 28–29). For further discussion of mindfulness by modern Theravadins, see Walpola Rahula, *What the Buddha Taught* (New York: Grove Press, 1980).

14. Buddhaghosa, *Path of Purification*, 21.27.

15. "Having seen the dissolution of that object, one contemplates the dissolution of the consciousness that had that as its object" (ibid., 21.23). More technically, Buddhaghosa speaks of the "knowledge of appearance

as terror" (21.29 ff.). Eventually, however, terror subsides and yields to bliss and peace.

16. Gregory Bateson, *Mind and Nature: A Necessary Unity* (New York: Dutton, 1979), p. 108. I discuss this example in relation to the function of higher states of concentration in "Mental Concentration and the Unconditioned: A Buddhist Case for Unmediated Experience," in *The Buddhist Path*, ed. Robert Buswell and Robert Gimello (Honolulu: University of Hawaii Press, 1991).

17. This point is echoed but less emphasized in Tibetan discussions; see Napper, *Mind in Tibetan Buddhism*, pp. 35–39. For a discussion of the characteristics of mind associated with *any* wholesome consciousness, including simple mindfulness, see Angarika Govinda, *The Psychological Attitude of Early Buddhist Philosophy* (London: Rider, 1969), pp. 120–21. The classic Theravada source for this is Buddhaghosa's *Path of Purification*. For a discussion of these issues according to Sarvastivāda, an Indian Buddhist philosophical system contemporary with Theravada, see Cox, "Mindfulness and Memory."

18. The practice of mindfulness can, however, have considerable psychological impact: "Mindfulness protects the mind from lapsing into the agitation that sometimes comes through faith, energy or understanding, and from lapsing into idleness that sometimes comes due to concentration. So it is as desirable in all instances as a seasoning of salt in all sauces" (adapted from Buddhaghosa, *Path of Purification*, 4.49).

19. Pali *pīti*, Skt. *prīti*, Tib. *dga ba*. The Tibetan term is usually translated "joy," but in the Theravada context, "pleasurable interest" is more to the point. This is one of a cluster of nineteen mental factors associated with every wholesome consciousness. Discussed in Govinda, *Early Buddhist Philosophy*. This state is in some ways analogous to what Donald Hall describes as the "absorbedness" that comes from craft discipline. See his *Life Work* (Boston: Beacon Press, 1993).

20. Meditations on impermanence and death are described in Khetsun Sangpo's *Tantric Practice in Nyingma* and Glenn Mullin's *Death and Dying: The Tibetan Tradition*. For an overview of the significance of death, especially in the Tibetan tradition, see Anne Klein, "Buddhism," in *Encounters with Eternity: Religious Views of Death and Life after Death*, ed. Christopher Jay Johnson and Marsha G. McGee (New York: Philosophical Library, 1986).

21. *Bod rgya tshig mdzod chen mo* (Great treasury of Tibetan words) (Chengdu: Mi rigs dpe skyan khang, 1984), p. 907.

22. For a detailed account of the stages of developing concentration according to Tibetan Geluk, see Rinboche et al., *Meditative States* (London: Wisdom Publications, 1983).

23. Paul Griffiths, *On Being Mindless: Buddhist Meditation and the Mind-Body Problem* (La Salle, Ill.: Open Court, 1986), is an important exception here. See also Robert K. C. Forman, ed., *The Problem of Pure Consciousness* (New York: Oxford University Press, 1990).

24. The dissolution of the distance between subject and object is discussed in detail in Klein, "Mental Concentration and the Unconditioned."

25. For a concise discussion of the development of calm abiding, see Jeffrey Hopkins, *Meditation on Emptiness* (London: Wisdom Publications, 1983), pp. 80–90. The most detailed English discussion of calm abiding in the Tibetan tradition is *Walking through Walls* by Geshe Gedun Lodrö. We can compare this developed awareness, for example, with Hegel's self-consciousness, which in revealed religion is "aware of itself in pictorial objectification, not as yet as self-consciousness" (*Phenomenology of Spirit*, trans. A. V. Miller with analysis and foreword by J. N. Findlay (Oxford: Clarendon Press, 1977), p. 589. Further, if we accept Domna Stanton's statement that in Hegel "the knowing subject called 'consciousness of self' . . . emerges as a unity and passes through one transcendent act of cognition after another" ("Language and Revolu-

tion: The Franco American Dis-connection," in *The Future of Difference*, ed. Hester Eisenstein and Alice Jardine [Boston: G. K. Hall, 1980], p. 74), we can note that Buddhist sources do not describe the knowing subject as a unity; rather, awareness itself reveals the arising and ceasing of one moment of consciousness followed by another.

26. See Charles Taylor, *Sources of the Self: The Making of the Modern Identity* (Cambridge: Harvard University Press, 1989), pp. 185 ff.

27. This internal energy, however, does not fit into the usual categories by which contemporary feminists consider the extent to which thought or consciousness is affected by bodily experience. See Jane Flax, *Thinking Fragments: Psychoanalysis, Feminism, and Postmodernism in the Contemporary West* (Berkeley: University of California Press, 1990), p. 62. Consider also Kristeva and Cixous' emphasis on the body, especially Kristeva's alignment of feminine and masculine uses of language with feminine and masculine libidinal energy. See Chris Weedon, *Feminist Practice and Poststructuralist Theory* (Oxford: Basil Blackwell, 1987), pp. 70 ff.

28. Buddhaghosa, *Path of Purification*, 18.33.

29. Innate awareness is also literally the "factor of knowing" (*mkhyan cha*) of the Buddha nature (*thathāgathagarba, bde bzhin gshegs pa'i snying po*).

30. This type of awareness is known as *dran rig* (from discussion with Khetsun Sangpo Rinboche, Houston, Texas, March 1991. See also M. Kapstein, "The Amnesiac Monarch," in Gyatso, *Mirror of Memory*.

31. This is a quality of natural nondistraction (*ma yengs byed mkhyen*) (from discussion with Khetsun Sangpo Rinboche, Houston, Texas, March 1991).

32. Quoted by Khetsun Sangpo Rinboche in *Tantric Practice in Nyingma*, p. 40. For a biography of Ma-ji-lab-drön see Tsultrim Allione, *Women of Wisdom* (London: Routledge and Kegan Paul, 1984). See also

Janet Gyatso, "The Development of the *Gcod* Tradition," in *Soundings in Tibetan Civilization*, ed. M. Kapstein and B. Aziz (Delhi: Manohar, 1985), pp. 320–41.

33. Khetsun Sangpo Rinboche's oral commentary on Do-drup-chen's *rDzogs chen thor bu* (Various topics on the Great Completeness), Bodhanath, Nepal, Spring 1980. Do-drup-chen uses the term "stringent mindfulness" (*'jur dran*) in the *rDzogs chen thor bu*, in volume 5 of the *Collected Works of Do-drup-chen* (Gantok, 1975), 182.5.

34. From the *Kun bzang bde ba'i lung* (Scripture of the Blissful Samantabhadra), a Bön Dzog-chen text quoted in Li-shu-stag-ring, *gTan tshigs gal mdo rid pa'i tshad ma* (Authenticity of innate awareness) (Delhi: Tenzin Namdak, Tibetan Bön Monastic Centre, 1972), 101.2.

35. Mipham refers to this capacity as the Great Unconditioned in *bDe gshegs snying bo'i stong thun chen mo seng ge'i nga ro* (The lion's roar of the Great Accordance between emptiness and the Tathagatha essence) (Delhi: Ngagyur Nyingma Sungrab, 1976), vol. 62.

36. The *Letter to a Friend* is referred to in the poem as *Shes pa'i springs yig*.

37. Oral gloss by Khetsun Sangpo, referring to those who look to Padmasambhava for primary inspiration and validation.

38. This unpublished poem was written January 28, 1991, shortly after Khetsun Sangpo arrived in Charlottesville, Virginia. He said, "This is a little like calling the lama, which was something I did just before my [1989] operation. In this poem, I am calling upon myself for action" (From discussion March 1991, Houston, Texas).

39. For two very different ways of problematizing "experience" as a category, see for example, Sheila Devaney, "The Limits of the Appeal to Women's Experience," in *Shaping New Vision* (Ann Arbor: UMI Research Press, 1987), and Alice Jardine, "The Demise of Experience: Fiction as Stranger than Truth?" in *Postmodernism: A Reader*, ed. Thomas Docherty (New York: Columbia University Press, 1993).

40. Linda Alcoff, "Cultural Feminism versus Post-Structuralism: The Identity Crisis in Feminist Theory," *Signs* 13, no. 3 (Spring 1988): 433. Chris Weedon and Teresa de Lauretis also understand subjectivity to emerge in response to the coordinates of a woman's lived experience. See Weedon, *Feminist Practice*, and de Lauretis, ed., *Feminist Studies/Critical Studies* (Bloomington: Indiana University Press, 1984).

41. Mary Daly, *Pure Lust: Elemental Feminist Philosophy* (Boston: Beacon Press, 1984), pp. 143, 175.

42. For descriptions of such situations, see, for example, Alice Miller, *The Drama of the Gifted Child* (New York: Basic Books, 1981).

43. Mary Daly scathingly satirizes Christian ascetics, whom she sees as emblematic of patriarchal religiosity, for denying who they are to become something else, and finding glory in that. This is the essence of what she calls sado-ritual. See *Pure Lust*, pp. 36–38.

44. Judith Plaskow, *Sex, Sin, and Grace: Women's Experience and the Theologies of Reinhold Niebuhr and Paul Tillich* (Washington, D.C.: University Press of America, 1980), p. 68.

45. Susan Griffin, "The Way of All Ideology," *Signs* 7, no. 3 (Spring 1982): 641–60. In the literature on calm abiding, "mindfulness" is distinguished from the function of introspection (*samprajanaya, shes bzhin*). See Jeffrey Hopkins, *Meditation on Emptiness* (London: Wisdom Publications, 1983), pp. 74–76. Shantideva makes the classic Mahayana distinction between mindfulness and introspection in *Bodhisattvacāryāvatāra*, the latter one notices whether faults such as laxity or excitement are present. See Stephen Batchelor's translation, *Guide to the Bodhisattva's Way of Life*, chap. 4. See also Cox, "Mindfulness and Memory."

46. Thich Nhat Hanh, *The Practice of Mindfulness in Psychotherapy*, audiocassette A103, available from Sounds True, 1825 Pear Street, Dept. Fc3 Boulder, Colo. 80302.

47. *Dhammapāda*, p. 157; quoted by Piyadassa Thera in *The Buddha's Ancient Path*.

48. Daly, *Pure Lust*, pp. xii, 89; Valerie Saiving, "The Human Situation: A Feminine View," in *Womanspirit Rising*, ed. Judith Plaskow and Carol Christ (San Francisco: Harper and Row, 1979), p. 37.

49. Doris Lessing, *The Four-Gated City* (New York: Bantam Books, 1969), pp. 36–38.

50. Ven. Henepola Gunaratana, *Sati: Mindfulness in Plain English*, California Buddhist Dhamma Dana Series No. 3 (Concord, Calif., n.d.), pp. 3 and 4. The author is a traditional monk with many years' experience in the United States. Strictly speaking, Buddhist language uses terms like "bare attention" or "nondiscrimination" to indicate that the processes of judgment are halted. This therefore translates emotionally as "self-acceptance." In a similar vein, being kind to oneself is something that American women teachers of Buddhism tend to stress.

51. Nyanaponika Thera, *Heart of Buddhist Meditation*, pp. 114–15.

52. This idea was developed in conversation with Courtney Thompson, Stanford, Calif., November 1985.

53. As reported by a participant in this discussion with the Dalai Lama. See also Plaskow and Christ, *Womanspirit Rising*, p. 37.

54. The image of a self that emerges through dialogue is suggested in different ways in the work of, for example, Cixous, Bakhtin, and Griffin and among psychologists such as Fairbairn, Gilligan, Guntrip, Melanie Klein, Kohut, Winnicott, and the Stone Center researchers at Wellesley.

55. As Susan Griffin elegantly puts it: "The self is irrevocably split so that it does not recognize its other half" and "the denied self [is] projected onto the other" ("The Way of All Ideology," p. 643 and 644).

56. This attention is also the goal of the person *in* analysis. A kind of mental silence allows the analyst to listen closely to the analysand, and the analysand to be aware of what is coming to her own consciousness. (Thanks to Meredith Skura for this observation in the course of a seminar sponsored by the Rice Center for Cultural Studies, Fall 1990). See also Flax, *Thinking Fragments*, p. 217, with reference to Richard Rorty, "Freud and Moral Reflection," in *Pragmatism's Freud: The Moral Dis-*

position of Psychoanalysis, ed. Joseph H. Smith and William Kerrigan (Baltimore: Johns Hopkins University Press, 1986).

57. See Jacques Derrida, "How to Avoid Speaking: Denials," in *Derrida and Negation Theology*, trans. Ken Frieden (Albany: SUNY Press, 1974), especially pp. 74–142.

58. See Gayatri Chakravorty Spivak, "Can the Subaltern Speak?" in *Marxism and the Interpretation of Culture*, ed. Carey Nelson and Lawrence Grossberg (Urbana: University of Illinois Press, 1988), especially pp. 293 ff. Because "silence" is such a dangerous issue for women, it is very important to note that the issues Spivak poses are quite different from ours.

59. For an introduction to Theravada discussions of mindfulness, see NyanaponikaThera, *Heart of Buddhist Meditation*; for an introduction and overview of Tibetan Buddhism see Hopkins, *The Tantric Distinction*; and for an introduction to the Great Completeness see Namkhai Norbu, *Dzogchen: The Self-Perfected State* (London: Arkana Books, 1989), or Tenzin Wangyal, *The Wonders of the Natural Mind* (Barrytown, N.Y.: Station Hill Press, 1993).

60. See Robert F. Thurman, trans., *The Holy Teaching of Vimalakīrti: A Mahāyāna Scripture* (University Park: Pennsylvania State University Press, 1976), pp. 24 and 77, for the silences of Shariputra and Vimalakirti. The Bodhisattva of wisdom, Manjushri, praises Vimalakirti for demonstrating "the entrance into the nonduality . . . here there is no use for syllables, sounds, and ideas."

61. See, for example, Jonathan Culler, *On Deconstruction* (Ithaca: Cornell University Press, 1982), p. 92 ff; and Jacques Derrida, *Of Grammatology*, trans. Gayatri Spivak (Baltimore: Johns Hopkins University Press, 1976), p. 12 ff., also pp. 7–8, 20, and 158–59. Indeed, both "presence" and "absence" derive from the same Latin root (*American Heritage Dictionary* (1973), p. 1515. For an accessible discussion of this aspect of presence, see Culler again, p. 105.

62. Indeed, a synonym for a nonconceptual mind is a "complete engager" (*viddhi-pravṛtti, sgrub 'jug*) because it is considered to engage every aspect of its object. In this sense it is fully present to the aspects of the object that present themselves to consciousness. Discussed in Napper, *Mind in Tibetan Buddhism* (where it is translated as "collective engager"). For a detailed discussion of the idea that sense consciousnesses "take on the aspect" of the objects they know, see Anne Klein, *Knowledge and Liberation: Buddhist Epistemology in Support of Transformative Religious Experience* (Ithaca: Snow Lion, 1986), chap. 3.

63. Hélène Cixous and Catherine Clement, *The Newly Born Woman*, trans. Betsy Wing (Minneapolis: University of Minnesota Press, 1986), p. 87. Yet this is also a cause of concern. How can an endless body shape identity? Without strong identity, how does one avoid being colonized by a limited set of ideals or roles?

64. Derrida discusses this under the rubric of two well-known topics: supplementation and *différance*. See Jacques Derrida, "Différance," in *Margins of Philosophy*, trans. Alan Bass (Chicago: University of Chicago Press, 1981).

65. Daly, *Pure Lust*, p. 85; Luce Irigaray in *New French Feminisms*, ed. Elaine Marks and Isabelle de Courtivron (New York: Schocken Books, 1980), p. 101; Cixous and Clement, *The Newly Born Woman*, p. 88. It has been argued that Irigaray's "two lips" are a metaphor; Diana Fuss describes the relation between body and language in Irigaray's work as *metonymic*, arguably Irigaray's favorite trope. See Fuss, *Essentially Speaking* (London: Routledge, 1989), pp. 62 ff.

66. See Jane Flax, "Remembering the Selves: Is the Repressed Gendered?" *Michigan Quarterly Review* 26, no. 1 (1986): 92–107.

67. Namkhai Norbu Rinboche, Cazedero, Calif., Summer 1986; see also Wangyal, *Wonders of the Natural Mind*.

68. Roland Barthes, *S/Z*, trans. Richard Miller (New York: Hill and Wang, 1974), pp. 13–16. Barthes' understanding of "rereading" is brilliantly expanded by Barbara Johnson, *The Critical Difference: Essays in*

the Contemporary Rhetoric of Reading (Baltimore: Johns Hopkins University Press, 1980), pp. 3–12.

4. Gain or Drain?

1. I am not aware of a clear historical basis for the claim that the Seven Unfoldings originated with the Buddha. Candrakirti was an early systemizer of the Middle Way philosophy that goes hand in hand with this perspective on compassion. For discussion of the dates of Nagarjuna and Candrakirti, see David Ruegg, *The Literature of the Madhyamaka School of Philosophy in India* (Wiesbaden: Harrassowitz, 1981), pp. 2–4 and 71.

2. For a highly accessible discussion of this practice, Kensur Lekden in Jeffrey Hopkins, trans. *Compassion in Tibetan Buddhism* (Ithaca: Snow Lion, 1980). For an equally readable and broader discussion, see Natalie Maxwell, "Compassion: The Chief Cause of Bodhisattvas" (Ph.D. dissertation, University of Wisconsin, Madison, 1975).

3. Haribhadra, p. 20, 1.14: *śunyākaruṇāgarbham bodhicittamutpādhya*. Because of multivalent meanings of the Sanskrit term *garbha* (womb, nature, essence, source), this could also be translated as "having taken up the mind of enlightenment which has the *essence* (etc.) of emptiness and compassion."

4. Tsong-kha-pa, *Lam rim chen mo* (Great exposition of the Stages of the Path) (P6001, vol. 152), 570.6 ff.; translated by Elizabeth Napper in *Dependent Arising and Emptiness* (London: Wisdom Publications, 1989), p. 176. This equanimity is one of the "four immeasurables" common to Theravada and Mahayana: love, compassion, sympathetic joy, and equanimity. For discussion of Tsong-kha-pa's use of the term, see Maxwell, "Compassion," p. 128 ff.

5. Tsong-kha-pa, *Lam rim*, 570.6 ff; quoted in Maxwell, "Compassion," p. 128.

6. Tsong-kha-pa, *Lam rim*, 571.2 and 573.2 ff; quoted in Maxwell, "Compassion," p. 134.

7. Geluk teachers in the United States have included Geshe Wangyel (1900–83), founder of the Tibetan Buddhist Learning Center (1958), which continues to run educational programs in Washington, New Jersey; Geshe Lhundup Sopa, founder of Deer Park outside Madison, Wisconsin, and currently teaching at the University of Wisconsin; Geshe Ngawang Gelek in Ann Arbor, Michigan; Geshe Tshultrim Gyeltsen, founder of the Thupten Thargyey Ling Center in Los Angeles, with a branch center in Houston; Geshe Jambel Thandö of the Jefferson Tibet Society in Charlottesville, Virginia; Geshe Tharchen in Howell, New Jersey, and Tupten Sopa and Tupten Yeshe, founders of various centers, especially Vajrapani near Santa Cruz, California. The newest major Geluk center in North America is the Namgyel Institute, located in Ithaca, New York, where reside monks from the Dalai Lama's monastery. Teachers connected with the Buddhist Great Completeness tradition in the United States include Chögyal Namkhai Norbu Rinboche, founding inspiration of the Dzog Chen Community, with major U.S. centers in Conway, Massachusetts, and Berkeley, California; Lama Tharchin Rinboche, whose Vajrayana Foundation is centered in Santa Cruz, California; Khenchen Palden Sherab Rinboche and his brother, Kenpo Tsewang Dongyal Rinboche, whose main base is upstate New York and whose Padmasambhava Centers are located in Florida and Tennessee; Chadud Tulku, in Portland, Oregon. The only representative of the Bön Great Completeness tradition in this country is Tenzin Wangyal Rinboche, whose Ligmincha Institute is located in Charlottesville, Virginia, where his teacher Lobön Tenzin Namdak occasionally visits. Recently I have been invited to speak at this center, at the Tibetan Buddhist Learning Center in New Jersey, and at the Namgyal Institute. As this book goes to press, two Western teachers strongly connected with the Buddhist Dzog-chen traditions, Tsultrim Allione and Lama Surya Das (Jeff Miller), are taking up residence in southern Colorado and Cambridge, Massachusetts, respectively. This list includes only centers or teachers with whom I am personally acquainted; it is by no means complete. For current updates on developments in a variety of locations

and communities see the *Snow Lion Newsletter* (Ithaca: Snow Lion Publications).

8. The example of traveling in a plane was used by Geshe Rabten in teaching the Seven Unfoldings in Dharamsala, India, Spring and Summer 1972.

9. The purpose of such training is to strengthen a capacity for equanimity; it is not an indication one should put up with abusive behavior, much less seek it out. One could, in principle, reach out and push the harmer away with equanimity, just as one can distinguish between friends and enemies yet remain internally balanced. But this requires some training (Geshe Rabten, oral commentary, Dharamsala, Summer 1971).

10. Buddhaghosa, *The Path of Purification* (Berkeley: Shambhala, 1976), 9.41 (vol. 1, pp. 332–33).

11. This focus on the mother seems to be a Tibetan contribution. In India, all relatives are included. Jan Nattier, "Eke Bolugsan: A Note on the Colophon to the Bolor Erike," *Acta Orientalia* (Budapest) 44 (1990): 395–408.

12. The first phrase is from Gam-po-pa, *Dam choz yid bzhin*, translated by Herbert Guenther, *Jewel Ornament of Liberation* (1959; reprint Boulder: Prajña Press, 1981), p. 93; the second, from an oral teaching by Geshe Rabten, Dharamsala, India, Fall 1972.

13. As the late Kensur Ngawang Ledken, abbot emeritus of the Tantric College of Lower Lhasa, told it: "Shariputra . . . generated an altruistic aspiration to highest enlightenment for the sake of all sentient beings. . . . A demon came near him while he was cultivating compassion in meditation. . . . he approached Shariputra and said 'I am making offerings and need a human hand. Please give me one of your hands.' [Shariputra] gave it to him." Shariputra, however, only comes to regret this gift; he had lacked sufficient awareness to know that his gift was out of proportion to his actual capacity to give at that time (see Hopkins, *Compassion in Tibetan Buddhism*, pp. 53–54).

14. For further detail on this practice, see Maxwell, "Compassion," or Lekden in Hopkins, *Compassion in Tibetan Buddhism*.

15. Shantideva, *Bodhisattvacāryāvatāra*, 8: 95–96. See Stephen Batchelor, trans., *A Guide to the Bodhisattva's Way of Life* (London: Tharpa Publications, 1979). For further discussion see Gyatso, *Meaningful to Behold*, p. 235 ff.

16. Lati Rinboche, Charlottesville, Virginia, April 1977.

17. See Gyatso, *Meaningful to Behold*, pp. 236–39, and Tsong-kha-pa, *Lam rim*, 594.6 ff., quoting Shantideva's *bsLab bdu*, discussed in Maxwell, "Compassion," p. 160.

18. Gyel-tsap, *sPyod 'jug rnam bshad* (Port of entry to the Bodhisattvas) (Sarnath, India: Pleasure of Elegant Sayings Press, 1973), pp. 181–82. Gyel-tsap's line of thought does not follow the rules of formal logic; rather, he is putting a sympathetic construction on a set of otherwise unrelated observations.

19. Shantideva, *Bodhisattvacāryāvatāra*, 8.111, in Batchelor, *Guide to the Bodhisattva's Way of Life*, p. 117. Bracketed inserts from Gyel-tsap, *sPyod 'jug rnam bshad*, p. 186.

20. Jonathan Culler, *On Deconstruction* (Ithaca: Cornell University Press, 1982), p. 86.

21. Jane Flax, *Thinking Fragments: Psychoanalysis, Feminism, and Postmodernism in the Contemporary West* (Berkeley: University of California Press, 1990), p. 181; Carol Gilligan, "Do the Social Sciences Have an Adequate Theory of Moral Development?" in *Social Sciences as Moral Inquiry*, ed. N. Haan et. al. (New York: Columbia University Press, 1982), pp. 41–45. Discussed by Joan Tronto, "Women and Caring: What Can Feminists Learn about Morality from Caring?" in *Gender/Body/Knowledge: Feminist Reconstructions of Being and Knowing*, ed. Alison N. Jagger and Susan N. Brodo (New Brunswick: Rutgers University Press, 1989), p. 180.

22. See for example Marilyn Massey's discussion of Rich, Kristeva, and Irigaray in *Feminine Soul: The Fate of an Ideal* (Boston: Beacon Press, 1986).

23. Susan Griffin, "The Way of All Ideology," *Signs* 7, no. 3 (Spring 1982): 643.

24. See Carol Gilligan, "Remapping the Moral Domain: New Images of Self in Relationship," in *Reconstructing Individualism*, ed. Thomas C. Heller, Morton Sosna, David E. Welberry (Stanford: Stanford University Press, 1986), pp. 237–52.

25. This dichotomy is also being questioned in the West in a variety of ways. See, for example, Lawrence Blum, *Friendship, Altruism, and Morality* (London: Routledge and Kegan Paul, 1980).

26. Flax, *Thinking Fragments*, p. 219. Catherine Keller, *From a Broken Web: Separation, Sexism, and Self* (Boston: Beacon Press, 1986), p. 178. See also her entire chapter 4 ("The Selves of Psyche," pp. 155–215) for a careful examination of "relational" forms of selfhood.

27. Ann Snitow, "A Gender Diary," in *Conflicts in Feminism*, ed. Maryann Hirsch and Evelyn Fox Keller (New York: Routledge, 1990).

28. Barbara Johnson, *A World of Difference* (Baltimore: Johns Hopkins University Press, 1987), p. 190. I follow her here in citing the Thoreau passage from *Walden* (New York: Signet, 1960), p. 66.

29. See Flax, *Thinking Fragments*, pp. 192, 194.

30. Ibid., p. 194. See also Melanie Klein, "The Importance of Symbol-Formation in the Development of the Ego," in *Love, Guilt, and Reparation* (New York: Delta, 1975). I agree with Flax's main point here, that there may be "far more radical ways to 'displace philosophy' than internal critiques or theories of writing."

31. Emily Martin, *The Woman in the Body: A Cultural Analysis of Reproduction* (1987; reprint, Boston: Beacon Press, 1992), p. 163.

32. Ibid., p. 164.

33. Sigmund Freud, *Civilization and Its Discontents* (New York: W.W. Norton), p. 19; quoted and discussed by Flax, *Thinking Fragments*, p. 80.

Nancy Chodorow, *Feminism and Psychoanalytic Theory* (New Haven: Yale University Press, 1989), p. 109, also suggests that Freud's inability to focus on the pre-Oedipal years and the relationship of mother to child prevented him from a full understanding of the nature of gender identification.

34. I would like to see a study that explores men's and women's attitudes toward death and another that investigates the reasons they have for writing. I suspect these attitudes, shaped by strong cultural forces, will break sharply along lines of gender. In writing, fears of mortality are likely at play, though to the extent that one writes not so much to "make a mark" as to discover and express one's deepest observations, the dynamic is different.

35. Discussed by Flax, *Thinking Fragments*, p. 128.

36. Chodorow, *Feminism and Psychoanalytic Theory*, p. 104.

37. *Madhyamakāvatāra/dbU ma la 'jug pa*, 1.c–ff, adapted from translation by Hopkins, *Compassion in Tibetan Buddhism*, p. 102. See also Rabten, *Echoes of Voidness*, trans. and ed. Stephen Batchelor (London: Wisdom Publications, 1983).

38. Conversation with Susan Lurie, September 11, 1992.

39. Quotation from Carol Gilligan, *In a Different Voice* (Cambridge: Harvard University Press, 1982), p. 30. See also Carol Gilligan, Nona Plessner Lyons, and Trudy J. Hammer, eds., *Making Connections: The Relational Worlds of Adolescent Girls at Emma Willard School* (Cambridge: Harvard University Press, 1990). Gilligan's work has inspired much debate; see, for example, texts cited in Snitow, "A Gender Diary," p. 40 n. 30. Gilligan's later work, however, and much of current psychological theory by women, suggests a social as well as moral preference for a relational and caring network, in contrast to the more popular ideals of autonomous individualism.

40. See Blum, *Friendship*, especially p. 2 ff. Blum's work argues against those who interpret Kant as rendering the world of feeling irrelevant to ethical behavior. Others who have questioned the dominant Kantian

form of morality include Alasdair MacIntyre and Stanley Hauerwas, eds., *Revisions: Changing Perspectives in Moral Philosophy* (Notre Dame, Ind.: University of Notre Dame Press, 1983); John Kekes, "Moral Sensitivity," *Philosophy* 59 (1984): 3–19; and Peter Winch, *Ethics and Action* (London: Routledge and Kegan Paul, 1972). See also Tronto, "Women and Caring."

41. Robert C. Solomon, *The Passions: The Myth and Nature of Human Emotion* (New York: Doubleday, 1977), p. 10. Chris Weedon, *Feminist Practice and Poststructuralist Theory* (Oxford: Basil Blackwell, 1987), points out that radical feminists such as Mary Daly and Susan Griffin link Western rationality with "male power and control over women and nature" (pp. 6–7) and that Cixous and Kristeva both argue, in different ways, that there are feminine modes of language that cannot be contained by the rational (what Kristeva calls "thetic") structure of the symbolic order (pp. 69 ff.).

42. Joan Cocks, "Wordless Emotions: Some Critical Reflections on Radical Feminism," *Politics and Society* 13, no. 1 (1984), cited in Rosemary Tong, *Feminist Thought* (Boulder: Westview Press, 1989), p. 131.

43. On Blum, see note 40 above. As Kathleen Wallace observes, others also attempt to avoid this opposition (e.g., Sousa and Habermas), but judgment itself tends to remain a function of "reason" ("Reconstructing Judgment: Emotion and Moral Judgment," *Hypatia* 8, no. 3 (Summer 1993): 77 n. 3.

44. Cocks, "Wordless Emotions," p. 38. Cocks traces three historical events associated with this shift: the rise of positive science, the rise of capitalism, and the rise of the technocratic state. Quoted and discussed by Tong, *Feminist Thought*, pp. 131–34. Claims that thought could be used to cultivate specific attitudes were in fact made by nineteenth-century women in North America. See Jane Tompkins's discussion of domestic fiction in *Sensational Designs: The Cultural Work of American Fiction, 1790–1860* (New York: Oxford University Press, 1985). Women

during this period understood that they did not automatically feel love for their husbands or families, and there was a great deal of talk about cultivating feelings appropriate to the "cult of domesticity." This goal is largely antithetical to modern feminist perspectives, but such cultivation was part of a broader vision that saw the real center of power to be in the home. Some may have seen it as the power of the powerless, but many nineteenth-century women saw it as a source of great strength, power, and influence. (Thanks to my colleague Elizabeth Long for helping me make this connection.)

For an elaboration of the claim that emotional structures are identical with, not opposed to, intellectual structures, see Solomon, *The Passions*. For a feminist proposal that emotions are necessary, not inimical, to the construction of knowledge and are themselves socially constructed, see Alison M. Jagger, "Love and Knowledge: Emotion in Feminist Epistemology," in *Gender/Body/Knowledge*, ed. Alison Jagger and Susan Brodo (New Brunswick: Rutgers University Press, 1989), pp. 145–71.

45. See Christine Di Stefano's discussion of feminine rationalism and antirationalism in "Dilemmas of Difference," in *Feminism/Postmodernism*, ed. Linda Nicholson (New York: Routledge, 1990), p. 66. Here she discusses three strategies in which debates about gender differences are embedded and that relate contemporary Western feminism with the Enlightenment legacy of humanistic rationalism: (1) feminist rationalism, which critiques sexism on the ground that it is irrational; (2) feminist antirationalism, which reconceives the meaning of "rational" in order to take account of women's traditional activities; and (3) feminist postrationalism, which argues for a thorough break with the rationalist paradigm. For further discussion of the relationship between women and rationalism, Di Stefano draws especially from Carol McMillan's *Women, Reason, and Nature: Some Philosophical Problems with Feminism* (Princeton: Princeton University Press, 1982); Genevieve Lloyd's *The Man of Reason: "Male" and "Female" in Western Philosophy* (Minneapolis: University of Minnesota Press, 1984); and Sandra Harding's

254 NOTES TO PAGES 113–15

The Science Question in Feminism (Ithaca: Cornell University Press, 1986).

46. A conversation with Professor Sidney Keith at the Jemez Bodhi Mandala Zen Center "Seminar on the Sutras," Summer 1991, helped focus this issue for me.

47. The Tibetan term for this most authentic feeling conception to be discarded is "innate conception [of an inherent] self" (*bdag 'dzin hlan skyes*). For a precise discussion of the gradual discarding of learned and innate errors in the sutra path, see Jeffrey Hopkins, *Meditation on Emptiness* (London: Wisdom Publications, 1983), pp. 91–109.

48. The term "conceptual" (*kalpanā/vitarka, rnam rtog*) covers a considerable range of mental experience. See Anne Klein, *Knowledge and Liberation: Buddhist Epistemology in Search of Transformative Religious Experience* (Ithaca: Snow Lion, 1986), chapters 4 and 9.

49. This is a classical definition of mind. For details on the relationship of conceptual to nonconceptual minds in Geluk, see ibid., especially the Introduction and final chapter. On the importance of concentration, see Klein, "Mental Concentration and the Unconditioned: A Buddhist Case for Unmediated Cognition," in *The Buddhist Path*, ed. Robert Buswell and Robert Gimello (Honolulu: University of Hawaii Press, 1991).

50. Mary Field Belenky, Blythe McVicker Clinchy, Nancy Rule Goldberger, and Jill Mattuck Tarule, *Women's Ways of Knowing: The Development of Self, Voice, and Mind* (New York: Basic Books, 1986).

51. This is Habermas's "ideal speech situation," which has been described by Jean Bethke Elshtain as "speech that simultaneously taps and touches our inner and outer worlds within a community of others with whom we share deeply felt, largely inarticulate, but daily renewed intersubjective reality" ("Feminist Discourse and Its Discontents: Language, Power, and Meaning," *Signs* 7 [1982]: 603–21). Discussed in Belenky et al., *Women's Ways of Knowing*, pp. 145–46. This understanding of "communication" could also be applied to the nineteenth-century North

American women who were cultivating their own styles of responsiveness to their families and environments. See note 44 above.

52. See Nona Plessner Lyons, "Two Perspectives: On Self, Relationships, and Morality," in *Mapping the Moral Domain*, ed. Carol Gilligan, Janie Victoria Ward, and Jill McLean Taylor with Betty Bardige (Cambridge: Harvard University Press, 1988), pp. 21–45; and in the same volume, Carol Gilligan's "Remapping the Moral Domain," p. 4. This is the kind of polysemia that contemporary theory relishes. It is also a way of noting that the variety of meanings constellated in a word will not be replicated in translation, as in Derrida's famous example of the Greek term *pharmakon*, used by Plato to mean both "remedy" and "poison." This multivalency cannot be translated into English, choices must be made. See Irene E. Harvey, *Derrida and the Economy of Différance* (Bloomington: Indiana University Press, 1986), p. 112. She is referring to Derrida's *Positions* (Chicago: University of Chicago Press, 1981), pp. 58–59; for a more detailed account of this issue, see Derrida's essay "La pharmacie de Platon," in *Phèdre/Platon* (Paris: Flammarion, 1989).

53. Gilligan, "Remapping the Moral Domain," p. 6.

54. Lyons, "Two Perspectives," p. 36.

55. This argument derived in conversation with Harvey Aronson. Whereas Buddhism is highly articulate about the causally and perceptually interdependent nature of things, it does not bring this observation to bear on interpersonal dynamics.

56. That the self is produced through relationship is a crucial development in recent psychoanalytic theory. Donald Winnicott, for example, understands identity to emerge through relationship with "objects," that is, with other persons, most notably the mother or primary caretaker. Jane Flax comments ironically on Winnicott's use of the impersonal term "object" to stand for the person with whom relationship is now being valued (*Thinking Fragments*, p. 123). Other prominent contemporary figures, for example, Alice Miller, Jean Baker Miller, Melanie Klein, Fairbairn, Guntrip, and Kohut, also emphasize in different ways

the relational aspect of selfhood. Daniel Stern's work with infants takes this a step further, indicating that infants do not merely receive parental affection but actively interact with parents and thus are co-creators of the parent-child relationship. See Daniel Stern, *The Interpersonal World of the Infant* (New York: Basic Books, 1985), especially chaps. 6 and 7.

57. Gilligan, "Remapping the Moral Domain," pp. 6, 7.

58. The "alter" aspect of "altruism" fades to the extent that a particular connection becomes the basis for action. For this reason I have eschewed a common translation of *bodhicitta* as "altruistic aspiration to enlightenment."

59. Gilligan, "Remapping the Moral Domain," p. 6.

60. See the description of the three types of temperament and the practices appropriate for them in Buddhaghosa, *Path of Purification*, 3.74–103.

61. Thanks to Marie-Pierre Stein for this observation. Buddhist traditions do not reflect on the social context for this effort or ask why it cannot be shared by men. Nor does Buddhism ask why actual women and mothers do not have the opportunities for education and meditation open to the monks who largely practice this technique.

62. In the 1970s, there were no children at Buddhist retreats, largely because the first generation of American Buddhists were only in their twenties and did not yet have children. Retreats that I have attended since at least the early 1980s, however, frequently feature child care and even age-appropriate programs for children. See Boucher, *Turning the Wheel*, chap. 7. See also Deborah Hopkinson, Michele Hill, and Eileen Kiera, eds., *Not Mixing Up Buddhism* (New York: White Pine Press, 1986), section 3, "Issues in Everyday Life," pp. 65–94.

5. Self

1. Tenzin Gyatso, His Holiness the Dalai Lama, *Kindness, Clarity, and Insight*, trans. and ed. Jeffrey Hopkins, with Elizabeth Napper (Ithaca: Snow Lion, 1984), p. 162.

2. For discussion of this process, see the Fifth Dalai Lama (Ngag-dbang-blo-bzang-rgya-mtsho, 1617–82), "Practice of Emptiness," in *The Sacred Word of Mañjuśrī: Instructions on the Stages of the Path to Enlightenment*, trans. Jeffrey Hopkins (Dharamsala, India: Library of Tibetan Works and Archives, 1974), pp. 11–12.

3. Ibid., p. 12.

4. Tsong-kha-pa, *Lam rim chen mo* (Great exposition of the Stages of the Path) (P6001, vol. 152); translated by Elizabeth Napper in *Dependent Arising and Emptiness* (London: Wisdom Publications, 1989), p. 176. See in particular her chapter "Misidentifying the Object of Negation," p. 176 ff.

5. For a detailed account of the sevenfold analysis by which this reflection proceeds, see Jeffrey Hopkins, *Meditation on Emptiness* (London: Wisdom Publications, 1983), pp. 47–51 and 175–96.

6. Fifth Dalai Lama, "Practice of Emptiness."

7. In terms of Western psychology, such students would be aware of the "vital importance of developing a sense of continuity, identity, and on-goingness in existence." See Jack Engler, "Therapeutic Aims in Psychotherapy and Meditation: Developmental Stages in the Representation of Self," *Journal of Transpersonal Psychology* 16, no. 1 (1984): 25.

8. Tsong-kha-pa, in the Perfection of Wisdom section of his *dbU ma dgongs pa rab gsal* (Illumination of the thought) (Sarnath: Pleasure of Elegant Sayings Press, 1973), 119.12 ff. Such a turn to nihilism is technically considered an "abandonment of emptiness." See Kensur Yeshey Thupden, oral commentary on *dbU ma dgongs pa rab gsal*, translated by Anne Klein in *Path to the Middle, Oral Mādhyamika Philosophy in Tibet: The Spoken Scholarship of Kensur Yeshey Tupden* (Albany: SUNY Press, 1994).

9. Harvey Aronson, "Guru Yoga—A Buddhist Meditative Visualization: Observations Based upon Psychoanalytic Object Relations Theory and Self Psychology," Paper in honor of Sersi Ma Bel delivered at the 1985 American Academy of Religion Annual Meeting, Anaheim, Calif.,

p. 44. The experience of emptiness can be contrasted with the idea that one is always somewhat apart from the self one understands. For Buddhists, to know emptiness is to know oneself most profoundly. This is quite different from saying "self-consciousness . . . necessarily involves consciousness of self as object. . . . [It] is impossible apart from self-objectification" (Mark Taylor, *Journeys to Selfhood: Hegel and Kierkegaard* [Berkeley: University of California Press, 1980], p. 186). For a brief description of errors encountered in the process of achieving emptiness, see Hopkins, *Meditation on Emptiness*, pp. 296–304.

10. In contrast, Theravada Buddhism maintains that there are ultimate particles known as *dhammas*, which cannot be further broken down, and Vaibhāṣika Buddhism maintains that there are partless particles that produce all aggregated phenomena. However, Mahayana polemics may attribute more "solidity" to these than is warranted.

11. From my own notes taken in Dharamsala, India, Summer 1971. English translation at that time was by Geshe Rabten's long-time student, Ven. Gonsar Rinboche, now teaching at Rabten Choeling (formerly Tharpa Choeling), the center founded by Geshe Rabten in Mt. Pelerin, Switzerland.

12. Conversation with Harvey Aronson, a psychotherapist and Buddhist Studies scholar who is currently developing his own theories about the psychological pitfalls of American Buddhist practitioners.

13. It will be interesting to see Asian women take up this matter, as the first international convention of Buddhist nuns recently made an important step toward doing. See Karma Lekshe Tsomo, ed., *Daughters of the Buddha* (Ithaca: Snow Lion, 1988). Also, partly inspired by Western social and political models, the present Dalai Lama has begun to articulate principles of government and international cooperation in line with Buddhist values and perspectives. See, for example, Tenzin Gyatso, His Holiness, the Dalai Lama, with D. Goleman et al., *Worlds in Harmony: Dialogues on Compassionate Action* (Berkeley: Parallax Press, 1992). Also the Dalai Lama's *A Policy of Kindness* (Ithaca: Snow Lion, 1990).

Some of the early Indian Buddhist kings, most notably Aśoka, as well as early Buddhist rulers in South Asia, did try to articulate social programs in consonance with Buddhist teachings of compassion for all.

14. Some Buddhist teachers, most notably Thich Naht Hahn, have effectively used dependent arising as a principle for cultivating both ecological and social awareness. The psychological dimension of dependent arising is a further step in this direction.

15. Ven. Gen Lam Rim-ba, Stanford University, Spring 1989.

16. Magliola and Huntington largely overlook this comparison by focusing primarily on emptiness (the reciprocal meaning of dependent arising) in relation to contemporary theory. See Robert Magliola, *Derrida on the Mend* (West Lafayette, Ind.: Purdue University Press, 1984), and Huntington, C. W., and Geshe Namgyal Wangchen, *The Emptiness of Emptiness* (Honolulu: University of Hawaii Press, 1989).

17. Somewhat similarly, Judith Butler notes that "there is no self that is prior to the convergence [of such forces] or who maintains integrity prior to its entrance into this conflicted cultural field" (*Gender Trouble: Feminism and the Subversion of Identity* [New York: Routledge, 1990], p. 145).

18. Teresa de Lauretis, *Alice Doesn't* (Bloomington: Indiana University Press, 1984), p. 182. For the main sources for her interpretation of Lacan, Eco, and Peirce, see Linda Alcoff, "Cultural Feminism versus Post-Structuralism," *Signs* 13, no. 3 (Spring 1988): 424 n. 45.

19. Jorge Luis Borges, *Labyrinths: Selected Stories and Other Writings* (New York: New Directions, 1964), p. 171.

20. Butler, *Gender Trouble*, p. 147.

21. See Napper, *Dependent Arising and Emptiness*, Introduction and passim.

22. This observation was made in conversation by Elizabeth Napper, Fall 1990.

23. For excellent discussions of this, see Jane Flax, "Mother-Daughter Relationships: Psychodynamics," in *The Future of Difference*, ed. Hester

Eisenstein and Alice Jardine (Boston: G. K. Hall, 1980), pp. 21 ff. See also Flax's observation that, given the repressive contexts that Western women are likely to encounter, feminism has a special interest in theories that construct self without taking account of the full complexity of subjectivity. ("Remembering the Selves: Is the Repressed Gendered?" *Michigan Quarterly Review* 26, no. 1 [1986]: 93). See also Gregory Bateson, *Steps toward an Ecology of Mind* (New York: Ballantine Books, 1972), pp. 313–14.

24. Descriptions of the Buddhist path lay out the type of mental perception associated with the gradual elimination of ontological error. This typifies the joining of epistemological and ontological concerns.

25. These terms mean quite different things in different systems; the "clarity" of the standard Geluk definition of mind as "that which is clear and knowing" is not to be confused, for example, with the clarity that is a natural quality of mind in the Great Completeness. (See Tenzin Gyatso, "Union of the Old and New Schools," in *Kindness, Clarity, and Insight*.) However, for our purposes the principle is the same: mind is not ideas only, nor separate from bodily energies.

26. These are characteristics classically associated with calm abiding, the minimal level of concentration required for actual insight into the unconditioned emptiness. See Geshe Gedun Lodrö, *Walking through Walls: A Tibetan Presentation of Calming Meditation* (Ithaca: Snow Lion, 1992), p. 166. Calm abiding is acquired developmentally, culminating in the "nine states" (*gnas dgu*). Facility with mindfulness, "the power of mindfulness," is said to be completed at the fourth of these states.

27. The minimal type of concentration required by this point is known as calm abiding (*śamatha, zhi gnas*).

28. Saussure recognized the arbitrary relation between word and referent, or signifier and signified, yet considered this arbitrary relation to take place in a complete, totalizing linguistic system. Derrida, in his critical responses to the work of Saussure, points to the lack of any totalizing linguistic context, social structure, or ultimate essence that can serve as

a foundation for purpose, meaning, or identity. And indeed Derrida is partly reacting against Hegel's idea of an absolute subject, or absolute spirit.

29. Also important for Derrida, but less so for our discussion, is the way that writing supplements speech. This is possible because speech itself, like writing, operates through *différance* and is never complete in itself. In this Derrida takes issue with Rousseau's statement that "languages are made to be spoken . . . writing serves only as a supplement to speech." Derrida's point is that speech is not a different species from writing; it too is capable of being amplified, supplemented. See Jacques Derrida, *Positions*, trans. Alan Bass (Chicago: University of Chicago Press, 1984), pp. 25 ff.

30. Butler, *Gender Trouble*, p. 143, also pp. 45–52. See also Juliet Mitchell's Introduction to *Feminine Sexuality: Jacques Lacan and the Ecole Freudienne*, ed. Juliet Mitchell and Jacqueline Rose (New York: W.W. Norton, 1985). See also Maureen A. Mahoney and Barbara Yngvesson, "Subjectivity and Resistance," *Signs* 18, no. 1 (Autumn 1992): 44–73. For Derrida, Lacan, Butler, de Lauretis, and Mitchell, language is intrinsic to selfhood. See Jonathan Culler, *On Deconstruction* (Ithaca: Cornell University Press, 1982), pp. 123–24. For example, Culler observes that Wittgenstein's suggestion that one cannot say "bububu" and mean "if it does not rain I shall go for a walk" has, paradoxically, made it possible to do just that.

31. In this way, subjective silence occupies a position distinct from either of the post-Enlightenment narratives that, according to Lyotard, have dominated the modern West: Enlightenment narrative (exemplified by Kant) and the narrative of the Spirit (exemplified by Hegel). Their claim of "completeness" is all the more telling in that the Indian-based Buddhist epistemologies understand words to divide one from what they represent. In addition, language and conceptuality produce minds that only partially engage their objects, whereas nonconceptual perception, including that brought about through deep concentration, is full and com-

plete. See Anne Klein, *Knowledge and Liberation: Buddhist Epistemology in Support of Transformative Religious Experience* (Ithaca: Snow Lion, 1986).

32. My colleague Philip Wood observes, "Perhaps what distinguishes the philosophy and ethos of the modern West from traditional societies and their thought-forms such as Buddhism, is that the West is incapable of conceiving a world based simultaneously on something like *différance* and an absolute unconditioned other to that world." I agree, with the exception that Buddhism, and much of Hinduism, actually finds the unconditioned to be part of that world, not unqualifiedly other to it. As K. N. Nayak writes, "We are now located in the fading dominance of the *exclusive* frames in the world. The ideological pendulum can now swing *only* toward the growth of the *inclusive* frame with a simultaneous decline and eclipse into dormancy but not complete extinction of the *exclusive*" (*Cultural Relativity: A Unified Theory of Knowledge* [New Haven: Saddharma Prakashana, 1982], p. 33).

33. Flax, *Thinking Fragments*, p. 213 ff. This exclusion, as Flax observes, does not arise owing to the logic of language, but through a failure of gendered analysis (pp. 214–15).

6. Nondualism and the Great Bliss Queen

1. For an account of nondualisms in Buddhism, Vedanta, and Taoism, see David Loy, *Nonduality: A Study in Comparative Philosophy* (New Haven: Yale University Press, 1988).

2. The Great Completeness monastery was founded in 1685 by Pema Rig-zin (1625–87). See *Crystal Mirror* (Emeryville, Calif.: Dharma Publishing), vol. 5, p. 283. The Do-drup-chen monastery's use of Geluk scholarship is reported by Tulku Thondup, a close associate of the present incarnation of Do-drup-chen. The works of Jam-yang-shay-ba, Tsong-kha-pa, and Gyel-tsap were studied there. (Jam-yang-shay-ba's own monastery, still functioning in what was formerly Amdo, Tibet, and is now part of Gansu Province, China, has long maintained warm rela-

tions with local Nyingma monasteries.) The Great Completeness monastery also included Geluk works until these were replaced by the writings of Khenpo Shen-ga (*gzhan phan chos kyi snang ba*, 1871–1927) and Mipham (1846–1912). This monastery also emphasized works by Longchen Rabjam and Pa-trul Rinboche. (Namkhai Norbu Rinboche confirms that Jam-yang-shay-ba was not studied there.) Tulku Thondup further reports study there of the Geluk scholar Jang-gya's *Identification of the Mother* (*A ma ngos 'dzin*), considered an expression of Great Completeness views, and Tsong-kha-pa's *Questions and Answers, an Excellent Medicinal Ambrosia* (*Zhu lan gdud rtsi sman mchog*), also considered a Great Completeness text and sometimes taken as evidence by Nyingmas that Tsong-kha-pa, the great founder of Geluk, in the end supported the Great Completeness perspective. Indeed, there are no known criticisms of it by him.

A closely related instance of Geluk-Nyingma synthesis is the work of Amdo-born Shab-gar-tshog-drug-rang-drol (Zhabs-dkar-tshogs-drug-rang-grol, 1781–1850). A student of Do-drup-chen III, he studied with four abbots of the Do-drup-chen monastery and debated with the most famous Nyingma scholar of the day, Mipham. See Steven D. Goodman, "The *kLong-chen-snying-thig*: An Eighteenth-Century Tibetan Revelation" (Ph.D. dissertation, Saskatoon, Saskatchewan, 1983), p. 155.

3. Jigmay Lingpa, *Long chen sNying thig rza pod* (The very essence of the Great Expanse), vols. *Om, Ah, Hum*; block prints reprinted under the auspices of Dingo Khentse Rinboche (Bhutan?, n.d.). The root text of this liturgy has been published as *The Queen of Great Bliss in the Long-chen-Nying-thig by Kun-khyen [the omniscient] Jigme Ling-pa*, trans. Tulku Thondup (Gantok: Do-drup-chen Rinboche, Sikkhim National Press, 1982). This corpus was inspired by the fourteenth-century scholar and meditation master Longchen Rabjam and codified in the late 1700s by the most famous scholar-practitioner of that era, the visionary Jigmay Lingpa ('Jigs-med-gling-pa, 1729–98). For a history of this lineage, see Steven D. Goodman, "Rig 'dzin 'Jigs-med-gling-pa and the kLong-

Chen sNying-Thig," in *Tibetan Buddhism: Visionary and Philosophical Explorations*, ed. Steven Goodman and Ronald M. Davidson (Albany: SUNY Press, 1992). See also Tulku Thondup, *The Tantric Tradition of the Nyingmapa* (Marion, Mass.: Buddhayana Foundation, 1984), and, for a carefully selected anthology of Long-chen-ba's writings, Thondup's *Buddha Mind*, ed. Harold Talbott (Ithaca: Snow Lion, 1989). See also Stephen Beyer, *The Cult of Tara* (Berkeley: University of California Press, 1978), p. 470.

4. Do-drup-chen III, in *Rig 'dzin yum ka bde chen rygal mo'i sgrub gzhung gi zin bris bde chen lam gzang gsal ba'i gron ma* (Notes on the basic text for emulating the Mother Knowledge Bearer, the Great Bliss Queen: A lamp clarifying the Good Path of Great Bliss) (Gantok, 1975), discusses a variety of wisdom figures with whom the Great Bliss Queen is identified, and then goes on to untangle various difficult points in the liturgy. The text by Abbot Ngawang Denzin Dorje is a much longer work (206 folios compared with 42) and is, to my knowledge, the only commentary to discuss the entire liturgy line by line. Another noteworthy text that discusses various points in the liturgy is Gön-chok-drön-may's *rJe bla mas gsungs pa'i yum ka'i zin bris kyi kha skong rig 'dzin shal lung* (Sacred word of the Well-Spoken Knowledge Bearer) (Gantok, 1977), reproduced from a collection of manuscripts from the library of Do-drup-chen.

5. In an earlier version of this chapter, I have referred to evolutionary nondualism as "developmental nondualism." I have not reconceived it here, but have given it another name so as to avoid confusion with the discovery/developmental dyad, which is different. While the nondualistic emphasis may seem to support Caroline Bynum's observation that "women's mode of using symbols seems given to the muting of opposition," it behooves us to observe again that men as much as women participate in this ritual, and that rituals centered on male deities also emphasize these nonoppositionalities. See Bynum's Introduction to *Gender and Religion*, ed. S. Harrell and P. Richman (Boston: Beacon Press, 1986), p. 13.

6. That is, between conventional truths (*saṃvṛti satya, kun rdzob bden pa*) and ultimate ones (*paramārtha-satya, don dam bden pa*). For more discussion of the Geluk assertion that these are objects rather than abstractions, see Jeffrey Hopkins, *Meditation on Emptiness* (London: Wisdom Publications, 1983), pp. 405 ff.

7. In the Geluk interpretation of Nagarjuna's statement that "samsara is nirvana," nirvana refers to natural nirvana, another name for emptiness. In other words, "samsara is nirvana" is not taken to mean that these qualities are utterly indistinguishable, but that they are never found apart. This, according to Geluk interpretations is one significant way to understand the famous statement from the *Heart Sutra* that "form is emptiness and emptiness is form." Form is qualified by and inseparable from emptiness, and emptiness inseparable from form, or whatever else it qualifies. This is their mutuality. This meaning of "natural nirvana" (*prakṛti-nivṛti, rang gzhin gyi myang ngan las 'das pa*) is mentioned in the opening lines of the *Unraveling of the Thought Sutra* (*Samdhinirmocana Sutra*). (Thanks to Jeffrey Hopkins on this point.)

8. More technically, the relationship between ultimate and conventional, or unconditioned and conditioned, is described by Tsong-kha-pa and others after him as "one entity but different for thought" (*ngo bo gcig ltog pa tha dad*, literally, "one entity but different isolates/opposites of the negative"). See Tsong-kha-pa, *Lam rim chen mo* (Great exposition of the Stages of the Path) (P6001, vol. 152), 176.5. For a technical discussion of "isolates" and their significance for cognitive processes as a major school of Buddhist epistemology understands them, see Anne Klein, *Knowledge and Liberation: Buddhist Epistemology in Support of Transformative Religious Experience* (Ithaca: Snow Lion, 1986). Only upon enlightenment can both conventional and ultimate be cognized directly and simultaneously. Therefore, there is no need for conventional phenomena—the things with which we in samsara are familiar—to disappear in the face of wisdom that knows the ultimate (*paramārtha, don dam pa*). This is a somewhat controversial point within Tibetan philosophical discourse,

but it is one of the distinguishing features of Geluk epistemology. Khet-sun Sangpo points out that this is also stated in Nyingma, though it is more characteristic of their lower vehicles than of the Great Complete-ness point of view.

9. Freud discusses this in *Mourning and Melancholia* (1917); SE 14:237–58 (on identification); also in *The Economic Problem of Masoch-ism* (1924), SE 19:155–70, and *Inhibitions, Symptoms, and Anxiety* (1926) SE 20:75–175. (Volume and pages are from *The Standard Edi-tion of the Complete Psychological Works of Sigmund Freud*, ed. James Strachey (London: Hogarth Press).

10. Nagarjuna, *Mādhyamikakārika* (Treatise on the Middle Way), 24.14 (P5224, vol. 95). See Hopkins's translation and discussion, *Medi-tation on Emptiness*, p. 438.

11. Some early Indian schools considered this to mean that each person carried a small embryonic Buddha inside. This latter claim is probably from the *Ratnakūṭa Sutra*. See Joe Wilson, "Chittamātra" (Ph.D. dis-sertation, University of Virginia, 1983).

12. That is, it is not to be read as a *tatpuruṣa* compound, as meaning "the womb of the Tathagatha."

13. Phyllis Trible, *God and the Rhetoric of Sexuality* (Philadelphia: For-tress Press, 1978), p. 35.

14. For a discussion of the "meaning" of such fluid mother-child bound-aries, see Linda M. G. Zerilli, "A Process without a Subject: Simone de Beauvoir and Julia Kristeva on Maternity," *Signs* 18, no. 1 (Autumn 1992): 111–35.

15. Jeffrey Hopkins, based on Jam-yang-shay-ba, in *Meditation on Emptiness*, p. 354.

16. Discussed extensively in Longchen Rabjam, *Tshig don mdzod* (Trea-sury of meaning) (Gantok: Sherab Gyaltsen and Khentse Labrang Pal-ace Monastery, 1983), 189.2 ff. For translation and discussion of this text, see David Germano, "Poetic Thought, the Intelligent Universe, and the

Mystery of the Self: The Tantric Synthesis of *rDzogs-chen* in Fourteenth-Century Tibet" (Ph.D. dissertation, University of Wisconsin, 1992).

17. For other symbolism and meanings associated with the dakini, see Janice D. Willis, "*Dākinī*: Some Comments on Its Nature and Meaning," in *Feminine Ground: Essays on Women in Tibet*, ed. Janice D. Willis (Ithaca: Snow Lion, 1989).

18. Sir Monier Williams, *A Sanskrit-English Dictionary* (Oxford: Clarendon Press, 1951), p. 430. Williams refers here to Panini (ref. 4.2, 51). I have not found any etymological analyses of this definition. A different etymology is cited by Adelheid Herrmann-Pfandt in *Ḍākiṇīs: Die Stellung und Symboli des Weiblichen im Tantrischen Buddhismus* (Bonn: Indica et Tibetica Verlag, 1992), p. 115. She notes that the *Cakrasamvara* tantra understands a dakini as *fliegen* and synonymous with *ākāśa -gāmini*, which means, literally, like the Tibetan, "a goer in space." Thanks to Richard Kohn for mentioning this book to me almost as soon as it was published.

19. See Diana Paul, *Women in Buddhism*, especially part 1 (Berkeley: Asian Humanities Press, 1979).

20. Mipham, *bDe gshegs snying po'i stong chen no seng ge'i nga ro* (The lion's roar of the Great Accordance between emptiness and the Tathagatha essence), Ngagyur Nyingma Sungrab, vol. 62 (Delhi, 1976), 564.4.

21. Khetsun Sangpo, *Tantric Practice in Nyingma* (1982; reprint, Ithaca: Snow Lion, 1986), p. 14. The term I here translate as "very essence" (following Steven D. Goodman) is *snying thig*, literally, "heart essence" or "essential heart."

22. Discussed by Longchen Rabjam in *Tshig don mdzod*, 183.5 ff. This text is one of the Seven Treasures central to this tradition of the Great Completeness. Longchen Rabjam (1308–63) is said to be the author of 263 works, 25 of which remain extant.

23. Ngawang Denzin Dorje, *Ra Tig* (Commentary on the practice for emulating the Sky Woman) (New Delhi: Sonam Topgay Kazi, 1972), 12.1.

24. Li-shu-stag-ring, *gTan tshigs gal mdo rig pa'i tshad ma* (Authenticity of innate awareness: A collection of essential reasonings) (Delhi: Tenzin Namdak, Tibetan Bön Monastic Centre, 1972), no. 73, 7.5, pp. 58.2 ff. and passim. The tenth-century *Authenticity* contained in the *Essential Collection*, or *kal mdo*, which is the oldest cyclic of Bön Great Completeness texts still in active use. My discussion of *thig le nyag gcig* is drawn from this text, which I am in the process of translating in collaboration with Tenzin Wangyal Rinboche.

25. Padmasambhava, *Yang dag gi gzang 'grel chen mo* (The great secret commentary of Heruka); cited by Ngawang Denzin Dorje in *Ra tig*, 12.3.

26. Paraphrase of Ngawang Denzin Dorje (*Ra tig*, 17.5–6) as discussed by Tulku Thondup.

27. Ibid., 12.1–2.

28. Ibid., 18.5–6, quote from the *Nyang ter* (discovered by Nyang Ral Nyima Özer, 1124–92).

29. Padmasambhava, *Yang dag gi gzang 'grel chen mo*, cited in ibid., 17.5.

30. Li-shu-stag-ring, *gTan tshigs gal mdo rig pa'i tshad ma*, 54.1.

31. I first heard this threefold description in 1983 in a lecture by Namkhai Norbu Rinboche, who has since then described it in *The Crystal and the Way of Light*, compiled and edited by John Shane (New York: Routledge and Kegan Paul, 1986), pp. 36 ff. This way of presenting the various traditions of practice is also found in the Yung Drung Bön tradition, and is discussed by Lobon Tenzin Namdak in *The Condensed Meaning of an Explanation of the Teachings of Yungdrung Bön* (Kathmandu: Bonpo Foundation, n.d.), pp. 9–14. See note 32.

32. This way of dividing practices into the paths of renunciation, transformation, and self-liberation stems from the Bön tradition's discussion of the nine vehicles of the Southern Treasure. The Dzog-chen master

Namkhai Norbu Rinboche mentions them briefly in *Dzogchen: The Self-Perfected State* (London: Arkana Books, 1989), pp. 14–16; they are also discussed in *Wonders of the Natural Mind* by Tenzin Wangyal Rinboche (Barrytown, N.Y.: Station Hill Press, 1993).

33. Tulku Thondup, Cambridge, Mass., Winter 1983.

34. Sangpo, *Tantric Practice in Nyingma*, p. 29.

35. Tenzin Gyatso, *Kindness, Clarity, and Insight*, p. 218.

36. Longchen Rabjam, *Tshig don mdzod*, 19.5–6.

37. The meaning is "destroyed" in that only one term can be operative; that is, if one is active, one is not passive.

38. Here I follow Toril Moi's discussion of Cixous' *La Jeune Née*, part of which is translated as "Sorties" in *New French Feminisms*, ed. Elaine Marks and Isabelle de Courtivron (New York: Schocken Books, 1980). See Moi, *Sexual/Textual Politics: Feminist Literary Theory* (London: Routledge, 1985), pp. 104–10.

7. Becoming the Great Bliss Queen

1. For this explanation I follow Lama Tharchin, Santa Cruz, Calif., Spring 1988, and Ngawang Denzin Dorje, *Ra tig* (Commentary on the practice for emulating the Sky Woman (New Delhi: Sonam Topgay Kazi, 1972). The contemporary teacher Lama Gompo Tsayden calls this the "ground of the effect"—the "primordial wisdom that is one's own status of immutable great bliss.

2. Quoted and commented on by Ngawang Denzin Dorje, *Ra tig*, 12.1; translation adapted from Tulku Thondup's translation of the liturgy, *The Queen of Great Bliss in the Long-chen-Nying-thig by Kun-Khyen Jigme Ling-pa* (Gantok: Sikkim National Press, 1982).

3. This self-arisen state is also the profound cast (*mdangs*) of one's own natural condition (*gnas lugs*).

4. Quoted in Ngawang Denzin Dorje, *Ra tig*, 15.6. This is a prayer to the female Protection Buddha Ekazati contained in the *Very Essence of the*

Great Expanse revealed tradition of Jigmay Lingpa. Ekazati is the female dimension of actuality (*chos sku*) known as Samantabhadri, who is also female. The third line of this prayer, *gang nas gyang khod gyi mtshan*, is not quoted in the *Ra tig* but appears in the *kLong chen snying gi thig le las bka' srung ma mkhon lcam dral*, p. 10. Tulku Thondup points out that while it is not unusual to identify female beings such as those indicated by MA and MO as primordial, it is uncommon for the Actuality Dimension to be identified as a Sky Woman.

5. This is a crucial element of Dzog-chen traditions.

6. Tenzin Gyatso, His Holiness the Dalai Lama, *Kindness, Clarity, and Insight*, trans. and ed. Jeffrey Hopkins with Elizabeth Napper (Ithaca: Snow Lion, 1984), p. 212, except I have rendered *rol ba/līla* as "play" where he uses "sport."

7. From the *Mañjuśrināmasaṃgiti* (Song of the name of Manjushri), cited in *Ra tig*, 37.3.

8. Khetsun Sangpo, *Tantric Practice in Nyingma* (1982; reprint, Ithaca: Snow Lion, 1986), pp. 28 ff.

9. Tenzin Gyatso, *Kindness, Clarity, and Insight*, p. 218 (substituting "Great Completeness" for "Great Perfection," as Jeffrey Hopkins himself does nowadays).

10. Nagawang Denzin Dorje, *Ra tig*, 36.5. More literally, the "actual basis" (*dngos gzhi*).

11. Paraphrase of statement by Jigmay Lingpa, quoted in ibid., 14.6–15.1.

12. This is most likely a quote from *Yon dan mrdzod* (Treasury of qualities) but I have not been able to locate it. The Sanskrit term *dharmakāya* (Tibetan: *chos sku*) is often translated as "truth body" or "body of the law"; I use the less substantive term "dimension of actuality" based on numerous Dzog-chen discussions of Namkhai Norbu Rinboche.

13. *sKye med rin po che'i mdzod Ratnasukośa* (Treasury of the precious birthlessness), Tohoku, 3839.

14. The same is true of music in general: "the meaning does not lurk elsewhere, but is *in* the sounding" (Don Ihde, *Listening and Voice: A Phenomenology of Sound* [Athens: Ohio University Press, 1976], p. 158).

15. This paragraph and other comments on orality in this chapter are adapted from my Introduction to *Path to the Middle, Oral Mādhyamika Philosophy in Tibet: The Spoken Scholarship of Kensur Yeshey Tupden* (Albany: SUNY Press, 1994).

16. Highly advanced practitioners can carry this experience into daily life, thus unifying the two "layers" and all they suggest.

17. These are the five colors associated with the five Buddha families and with the elements of which the womb-world is comprised.

18. Ngawang Denzin Dorje, *Ra tig*, 41.5 ff.

19. Ibid., 44.1. Ngawang Denzin Dorje's use of ninth-century scholars like Padmasambhava and Vimalamitra indicates that an association of the spherelike mansion of the mandala with the female womb is very ancient, though its use in the Buddhist context may have been expanded in Tibet.

20. The Star or Shield of David is most likely of non-Jewish origin. According to Gersham Scholem, it "began its career in larger Jewish circles not as a symbol of monotheism but as a magic talisman against evil spirits" (p. 266), and its usage is part of Jewish magical traditions known as the "practical Kabbalah," but it is not part of the Kabbalistic theosophy and symbolism (p. 263). Its first certain occurrence in a Jewish context is on the seal of one Joshua ben Asaiah [Joshua, son of Asia], which dates from about 600 B.C.E. Its next appearance, in which it contains a clearly indicated point at its center, is among ornamental motifs on a frieze that decorates the synagogue of Capernaum, second or third century B.C.E. The same frieze displays a *svāstika* right next to it (p. 260), indicating, perhaps, an initial connection between the six-pointed star and the *svāstika*, which both appear in the ritual we are now discussing. See "The Star of David: History of a Symbol," in Ger-

shom Scholem's *The Messianic Idea in Judaism* (New York: Schocken Books, 1971), pp. 257–81. (Thanks to Arnold Eisen for suggesting this reference.)

The *svāstika* is an ancient symbol in India and Tibet that has gained horrific associations only in the twentieth-century West. In Tibetan it is called *gyung drung*, which is etymologized, at least in the Bön tradition, as "changeless and ceaseless." In Sanskrit the term *svāstika* means "itself" (*sva*) "it is" (*asti*).

21. The *locus classicus*, Freud's discussion of the oceanic feeling, is in "Civilization and Its Discontents." See *The Standard Edition of the Complete Psychological Works of Sigmund Freud*, trans. and ed. James Strachey (London: Hogarth Press, 1961), 21:59–68.

For an outstanding account of Freud's developing interest and assessment of this, see William B. Parsons, "Psychoanalysis and Mysticism: The Freud-Rolland Correspondence" (Ph.D. Dissertation, University of Chicago, 1993). See also Henri Vermorel and Madeleine Vermorel, *Sigmund Freud et Romain Rolland Correspondance 1923–1936* (Paris: Presses Universitaires de France, 1993), especially chap. 9. (Thanks to my colleague Bill Parsons for this reference.)

22. For a major thematization of this distinction between Western religions and certain forms of Madhyamika and Zen, see Keiji Nishitani, *Religion and Nothingness* (Berkeley: University of California Press, 1982), especially pp. 95–129.

23. Ngawang Denzin Dorje, *Ra tig*, 49.5 ff.

24. Ibid., 46.6 ff. Her appearance to others is described as her "external clarity"; her own enlightenment is her "internal clarity."

25. Ibid., 47.4.

26. Ibid., 50.2 ff.

27. It would be interesting to consider in detail the relationship to this bliss of the *jouissance* discussed especially by French feminists such as Julia Kristeva and Luce Irigaray.

28. Ngawang Denzin Dorje, *Ra tig*, 46.3–4, 50.5 ff.

29. Ibid., 46.4.

30. "Excision" (*bCod*) is also the name for a meditative practice most appropriately translated as "excising (or cutting) attachment" but sometimes rendered as "exorcism." For a description of this rite, which involves the female Buddha Vajrayogini, who is iconographically similar to the Great Bliss Queen, see Khetsun Sangpo, *Tantric Practice in Nyingma* (Ithaca: Snow Lion, 1983), pp. 16–166. For a condensed biography of the female originator of this practice, see Tsultrim Allione, *Women of Wisdom* (London: Routledge and Kegan Paul, 1984), and Janet Gyatso, "Ma-ji-lap-dron," in *Soundings in Tibetan Civilization*, ed. M. Kapstein and B. Aziz (Delhi: Manohar, 1985).

31. The liturgy goes on to describe, and the commentary to explain in great detail, the symbolism of the ornaments on her head and person, and the positioning of her three eyes.

32. Jonathan Z. Smith, "The Bare Facts of Ritual," in *Imagining Religion: From Babylon to Jonestown* (Chicago: University of Chicago Press, 1982), p. 63.

33. This important observation was made by Paula Saunders in a seminar sponsored by the Rice Center for Cultural Studies, Fall 1991.

34. Catharine Bell, *Ritual Theory, Ritual Practice* (Oxford: Oxford University Press, 1992), p. 35.

35. Ibid., p. 19.

36. This is a most interesting idea that probably needs further documentation. Walter Ong discusses it, citing Carother. Here Ong is talking about what he calls "primary" oral cultures; Tibet would not fit this category, but its oral orientation is sufficiently strong that if Ong's insight is valid it should hold for Tibet. See Walter Ong, *Orality and Literacy: The Technologizing of the Word* (London: Methuen, 1982), p. 69; also J. C. Carother, "Culture, Psychiatry, and the Written Word," *Psychiatry* 22 (1959): 307–20.

37. I owe these insights on the importance of lineage especially to discussions with Harvey Aronson and Steven Goodman, who in turn have benefited from the unpublished anthropological research of Nina Egart.

38. See Charles Taylor, *Sources of the Self: The Making of the Modern Identity* (Cambridge: Harvard University Press, 1989), pp. 186–88.

39. "To visualize" is the usual but perhaps not altogether appropriate translation for *dmigs pa byed*, literally, "to take as a focus."

40. For detailed discussion and liturgy of Guru Yoga, see Sangpo, *Tantric Practice in Nyingma*, pp. 167–82.

41. Moi, *Sexual/Textual Politics*, p. 116.

42. Indeed, tantric initiation emphasizes that one is thereby being born into the family of the Buddhas. Guru devotion, including devotion to a figure such as the Great Bliss Queen, is thus a further refinement of this. For further discussion of the guru-disciple relationship in a Western context, see Michele Martin, "Bringing Up Dharma" (manuscript, 1994).

43. Dr. Barbara Aziz, an anthropologist who has spent twenty years doing fieldwork among Tibetans in Nepal and India, quoted by Katy Butler, "Encountering the Shadow in Buddhist America," *Common Boundary*, May/June 1990, p. 19.

44. The Yantra Yoga taught by Namkhai Norbu Rinboche and his students is to my knowledge the only exoteric form of these practices. Usually known in Tibet as *rdza rlung* (training of the channels and winds), they are among the most secret of Tibetan practices. For a clear, concise description of the types of consciousness associated with the stages of death, states the yogi emulates in advanced practices, see Jeffrey Hopkins, trans., *Death, the Intermediate State and Rebirth* (Ithaca: Snow Lion, 1979), especially the Preface.

45. Hélène Cixous, "Utopias," in *New French Feminisms*, ed. Elaine Marks and Isabelle de Courtivron (New York: Schocken Books, 1980), pp. 250, 252.

46. Ibid., p. 251.

47. "In woman, personal history blends together with the history of all women, as well as national and world history" (ibid., pp. 252–53).

48. Kathryn Milun, "The Agoraphobic's Maps of Modernity" (manuscript), pp. 9–10.

8. Inconclusion

1. James's "voluntary attention" is one possible name. José Cabezón has recently done research indicating the virtually limitless period of focused attention possible for those who have trained extensively in it. See *Buddhism, Sexuality, and Gender* (Albany: SUNY Press, 1992). Julie Henderson, in *The Lover Within* (Barrytown: Station Hill Press, 1990), sees an energetic fluidity of movement without "losing" oneself as a hallmark of health, and she gives exercises to help develop this centered fluidness.

GLOSSARY

Cross-referenced terms appear in bold type.

ASANGA. Sixth-century Indian Buddhist philosopher, regarded as part of the transmission lineage of the Seven Unfoldings.

ATISHA (Atīśa). Eleventh-century Indian Buddhist teacher, a major figure in the second transmission of Buddhism from India to Tibet.

BODHICITTA. A mind intent on achieving enlightenment for the sake of others.

BODHISATTVA. A person who has **bodhicitta**, and who has therefore vowed to seek enlightenment in order to be capable of leading all persons to their enlightenment.

BÖN. Major Tibetan religious tradition, which since the seventh century has been very much influenced by and influential upon Buddhism. Bön, like **Nyingma**, has its own **Great Completeness** traditions.

BUDDHAGHOSA. Fifth-century Indian-born formulator of **Theravada** doctrines, did his major work in Sri Lanka, author of *Path of Purification (Visuddhimagga)*.

BUDDHAHOOD. Complete enlightenment, freedom from both conceptual and sensory error regarding the nature of self and world.

CANDRAKIRTI. Seventh-century Indian Buddhist philosopher, famous for his development of the **Middle Way** school first systematized by **Nagarjuna**.

COGNITIVE NONDUALISM. Sense of subject and object as unseparated by image or distance.

COLLATERAL COHERENCE. A cohesiveness associated with mental clarity and stability; contrasted with **narrative coherence**.

CONSEQUENTIALIST (*Prāsaṅgika*). One of the two major **Middle Way** (*Mādhyamika*) schools of Buddhism, widely regarded in Tibet as the subtlest philosophical discussion of emptiness and ignorance.

DAKINI (rhymes with Fellini). See **Sky Woman**.

DEPENDENT ARISING. Any thing or person that exists in dependence on causes and conditions, or on its own parts (temporal or spatial), or in dependence on being designated by the mind that observes it. In the Indo-Tibetan **Consequentialist** schools of Buddhism, everything that exists is a dependent arising.

DEVELOPMENTAL BUDDHIST TRADITIONS. Styles of practice, for example, **Theravada** or **Geluk** sutra traditions, that emphasize the necessity of cultivating various qualities; coextensive with what some Buddhists refer to as "gradualist" forms of practice.

DISCOVERY BUDDHIST TRADITIONS. Styles of practice, for example, Zen and the **Great Completeness**, that emphasize that full realization is already present and awaits discovery; coextensive with what some Buddhist traditions refer to as "sudden" traditions.

DZOG-CHEN (*rDzogs-chen*). See **Great Completeness**.

EMANATION. The appearance in human form of an enlightened person.

EMPTINESS. The absence of **inherent existence** (according to **Geluk Consequentialists**).

EVOLUTIONARY NONDUALISM. The absence of any final boundary between ordinary persons and the state of Buddhahood, or enlightenment.

GELUK (RHYMES WITH "HEY LOOK"). "Yellow Hats," the most populous and politically powerful of the four orders of Tibetan Buddhism.

GREAT COMPLETENESS. Regarded as the highest practice by both **Nyingma** Buddhist and **Bön** practitioners.

INHERENT EXISTENCE. The existence of any thing or person *without* depending on causes, parts, or a mind that designates; the opposite of **dependent arising**. Nothing whatever exists in this manner; to conceive of things this way is thus a deeply ingrained error.

INNATE AWARENESS (*rig pa*). A mind's natural and clear awareness of itself, a state identified for **Great Completeness** practitioners so that they can discover it in the course of their training.

KARMA. "Action," refers to the relationship between an action of body, speech, or mind and its effect.

LONGCHEN RABJAM (*kLong-chen-rab-'byams*) or LONG-CHEN-BA. Fourteenth-century spiritual inspiration of the *Very Essence of the Great Expanse*, one of the main liturgical lineages of **Nyingma** and the tradition of the Great Bliss Queen liturgy.

MAHAYANA. The "Great Vehicle" Buddhist traditions, associated with the **Bodhisattva** vow, practiced today in Tibet, China, Korea, Japan, Vietnam.

MAITREYA. The Bodhisattva whose name means "love" and who, after the demise of Buddhist traditions, will incarnate as the Buddha who revives them.

MANDALA. In Tibetan ritual, a representation of the divine abode of an enlightened being.

MANJUSHRI (*Mañjuśrī*). A special kind of **Bodhisattva** who is the embodiment of all the wisdom of all enlightened Buddhas.

MANTRA. Sacred syllable used in recitation and other ritual practices.

MIDDLE WAY (*Mādhyamika*). A major **Mahayana** school of philosophy that expresses a principle to which virtually all Buddhist schools claim to adhere, namely, a path of moderation between philosophical extremes, especially the beliefs that persons are permanent or do not exist at all, or between behaviors such as severe asceticism and lavish luxury.

NAGARJUNA. Late tenth-century Indian Buddhist philosopher regarded as systematizer of **Middle Way** philosophy.

NARRATIVE COHERENCE. The kind of cohesiveness that can come from a story that is complete and conclusive, a cohesiveness that does not exist for postmodern sensibilities.

NIRVANA. Often synonymous with enlightenment and freedom from cyclic existence (**samsara**) and for this reason translated into Tibetan as "passage beyond suffering."

NYINGMA (rhymes with "Sing Ma"). Oldest school of Tibetan Buddhism, brought to Tibet from India in seventh century by Padmasambhava.

ONTOLOGICAL NONDUALISM. Indissoluable unity between conventional, conditioned phenomena and their ultimate or unconditioned nature of emptiness.

PADMASAMBHAVA. Consort and teacher of Yeshey Tsogyel, and a founding figure of Buddhist **Great Completeness** traditions in Tibet.

SAMANTABHADRA. The primordial Buddha, in some contexts also the primordially pure innate awareness of each individual.

SAMSARA. The round of birth and death.

SHANTIDEVA (Śhāntideva). Eighth-century Indian Buddhist scholar and poet, author of *Guide to the Bodhisattva's Way of Life* (*Bodhisattvacāryāvatāra*).

SINGLE SPHERE (*thig le nyag gcig*). A **Great Completeness** term referring to the whole of everything in all its diversity, as experienced by **innate awareness**.

SKY WOMAN (*ḍākinī*). Female muse of enlightenment, associated especially with the **Great Completeness** and other esoteric Buddhist practice lineages.

SUTRA. Scriptures said to have been spoken by the Buddha, but written down at least one or more centuries after his lifetime.

TANTRA. A diverse group of meditative techniques considered especially esoteric and effective, often working with physical posture and the body's energy currents or involving the experience of oneself as a particular enlightened being. The writings associated with these practices are also known as tantras.

THERAVADA. Early form of Indian Buddhism, practiced today in Burma, Cambodia, Laos, Thailand, and Sri Lanka.

TRACES. The residue of past actions or ideas and the harbingers of future ones.

TSONG-KHA-PA. Fourteenth-century master scholar and teacher of the first Dalai Lama, regarded as the founder of the **Geluk** order.

UNCONDITIONED. That which does not depend on causes or conditions for its existence, and which does not change in any way during the course of its existence. Space and **emptiness** are two prime examples of the unconditioned in most Buddhist traditions.

VAJRAVARAHI. A special "Enjoyment Body" form of Yeshey Tsogyel, the Great Bliss Queen, that can be seen only by highly developed spiritual practitioners.

Bibliography

Unless a translator's name is given, English renderings of Tibetan and Sanskrit titles do not indicate that the work exists in English. "P" or "Peking edition" refers to the Tibetan Tripiṭaka *(Tokyo-Kyoto: Tibetan Tripiṭaka Research Foundation, 1956).*

Abbs, Peter. "The Development of Autobiography in Western Culture: From Augustine to Rousseau." Ph.D. dissertation, University of Sussex, 1986.

Agamben, Giorgio. *Enfance et histoire: Dépérissement de l'experience et origine de l'histoire.* Paris: Éditions Payot, 1978.

Alcoff, Linda. "Cultural Feminism versus Post-Structuralism: The Identity Crisis in Feminist Theory." *Signs* 13, no. 3 (Spring 1988): 406–36.

Anzaldúa, Gloria. *Borderlands/La Frontera: The New Mestiza.* San Francisco: Spinsters/Aunt Lute, 1987.

Apte, Vaman Shivram. *The Practical Sanskrit-English Dictionary.* 1956. Reprint, Delhi: Motilal Banarsidass, 1975.

Aronson, Harvey. *Love and Sympathy in Theravāda Buddhism.* Delhi: Motilal Banarsidas, 1975.

Aziz, Barbara. *Tibetan Frontier Families: Reflections of Three Generations from Dingri.* Durham, N.C.: Carolina Academic Press, 1978.

Bakhtin, M.M. *Art and Answerability: Early Philosophical Essays.* Austin: University of Texas Press, 1990.

———*Problems of Dostoevsky's Poetics.* Edited and translated by Caryl Emerson, Introduction by Wayne C. Booth. Theory and History of Literature, vol. 8. Minneapolis: University of Minnesota Press, 1984.

———*The Dialogic Imagination.* Edited by Michael Holquist and translated by Caryl Emerson and Michael Holquist. Austin: University of Texas Press, 1981.

Bareau, André. "La notion de personne dans le bouddhisme indien." In *Problèmes de la personne*, ed. Ignace Meyerson. Paris: Mouton, La Haye, 1973.

Barthes, Roland. *S/Z*. Translated by Richard Miller. New York: Hill and Wang, 1974.

Batchelor, Stephen, trans. *A Guide to the Bodhisattva's Way of Life*. London: Tharpa Publications, 1979.

Bateson, Gregory. *Mind and Nature: A Necessary Unity*. New York: Dutton, 1979.

———*Steps toward an Ecology of Mind*. New York: Ballantine Books, 1972.

Becker, Ernst. *The Denial of Death*. New York: Macmillan, 1973.

Bell, Catherine. *Ritual Theory, Ritual Practice*. New York: Oxford University Press, 1992.

Bell, Sir Charles. *The People of Tibet*. Oxford: Clarendon Press, 1928.

Bell, Linda. "Song without Words: Listening to Japanese Families." *Networker*, March/April 1989.

Beyer, Stephen. *The Cult of Tara*. Berkeley: University of California Press, 1978.

Bielefeldt, Carl. *Dogen's Manuals of Zen Meditation*. Berkeley: University of California Press, 1978.

Blum, Lawrence A. *Friendship, Altruism, and Morality*. London: Routledge and Kegan Paul, 1980.

Borges, Jorge Luis. *Labyrinths: Selected Stories and Other Writings*. New York: New Directions, 1964.

Boucher, Sandy. *Turning the Wheel: American Women Creating the New Buddhism*. 1988. Reprint, Boston: Beacon Press, 1993.

Brodzki, Bella, and Celeste Schenck, eds. *Life/Lines: Theorizing Women's Autobiography*. Ithaca: Cornell University Press, 1988.

Buddhaghosa. *The Path of Purification*. Translation of *Visuddhimagga* by Bhikkhu Nyanamoli. Reprint, Berkeley: Shambhala Press, 1976.

Butler, Judith. *Bodies that Matter*. New York: Routledge, 1993.

———*Gender Trouble: Feminism and the Subversion of Identity*. New York: Routledge, 1990.

Butler, Katy. "Encountering the Shadow in Buddhist America." *Common Boundary*, May/June 1990.

Bynum, Caroline Walker, Stevan Harrell, and Paula Richman, eds. *Gender and Religion: On the Complexity of Symbols*. Boston: Beacon Press, 1986.

Cabezón, José Ignacio. *Buddhism, Sexuality, and Gender*. Albany: SUNY Press, 1992.

Candrakirti (7th Century). *dbU ma la 'jug pa'i bshad pa'/dbU ma la 'jug pa'i rang 'grel Madhyamakāvatārabhāṣya* (Commentary on the "Supplement of [Nagarjuna's] "Treatise on the Middle Way." Bhopal: Tibetan Publishing House, 1968. P5263, vol. 98.

Carother, J. C. "Culture, Psychiatry, and the Written Word." *Psychiatry* 22 (1959): 307–20.

Carrithers, Michael, Steven Collins, and Steven Lukes, eds. *The Category of the Person*. Cambridge: Cambridge University Press, 1985.

Chodorow, Nancy. *Feminism and Psychoanalytic Theory*. New Haven: Yale University Press, 1989.

Cixous, Hélène, and Catherine Clement. *The Newly Born Woman*. Translated by Betsy Wing. Minneapolis: University of Minnesota Press, 1986.

Clifford, James, and George Marcus, eds. *Writing Culture: The Poetics and Politics of Ethnography*. Berkeley: University of California Press, 1986.

Collins, Steven. *Selfless Persons: Imagery and Thought in Theravada Buddhism*. Cambridge: Cambridge University Press, 1982.

Culler, Jonathan. *On Deconstruction*. Ithaca: Cornell University Press, 1982.

Cutler, Joshua, trans. *The Path of Well-Being for Those Travelling to Omniscience: Essential Guide to the Stages of the Path to Enlightenment by the First Panchen Lama, Lo-sang Cho-gyi-gyal-tsen*. N.p., n.d.

Daly, Mary. *Pure Lust: Elemental Feminist Philosophy*. Boston: Beacon Press, 1984.

Dargyay, Eva K. Neumaier. "The Concept of a Creator God in Tantric Buddhism." *Journal of the International Association of Buddhist Studies* 8, no. 1 (1985): 31–47.

————, trans. *The Sovereign All-Creating Mind—the Motherly Buddha: A Translation of the Kun byed rgyal po'i mdo*. Albany: SUNY Press, 1992.

Davaney, Sheila Greeve. "The Limits of the Appeal to Women's Experience." In *Shaping New Vision*, ed. Clarissa Atkinson, Constance Buchanan, and Margaret Miles. Ann Arbor: UMI Research Press, 1987.

de Beauvoir, Simone. *The Second Sex*. Translated and edited by H. M. Parshley. New York: Vintage Books, 1974.

De Jong, J. W. "A Brief History of Buddhist Studies in Europe and America." *Eastern Buddhist* 7, no. 1 (May 1994).

De Lauretis, Teresa. "Upping the Anti (sic) in Feminist Theory." In *Conflicts in Feminism*, ed. Maryanne Hirsch and Evelyn Fox Keller. New York: Routledge, 1990.

————*Alice Doesn't*. Bloomington: Indiana University Press, 1984.

————, ed. *Feminist Studies/Critical Studies*. Bloomington: Indiana University Press, 1986.

Denma Ngawang Chos-grub. *dbU ma chos dbyings/dbU ma chos kyi dbyings rnam par 'byed pa'i 'grel pa smra ba ngan pa'i tsang tshang tshing 'joms par byed pa'i bstan bcos gnam lcags me chad* (Sphere of the Middle Way). N.p., n.d.

Derrida, Jacques. *Positions*. Translated by Alan Bass. Chicago: University of Chicago Press, 1981.

————"Différance." In *Margins of Philosophy*, trans. Alan Bass. Chicago: University of Chicago Press, 1982.

————"How to Avoid Speaking: Denials." In *Derrida and Negation Theology*, ed. Ken Frieden. Albany: SUNY Press, 1974.

Di Stephano, Christine. "Dilemmas of Difference: Feminism, Modernity, and Postmodernism." In *Feminism/Postmodernism*, ed. Linda J. Nicholson. New York: Routledge, 1990.

Docherty, Thomas, ed. *Postmodernism: A Reader*. New York: Columbia University Press, 1993.

Do-drup-chen III (Jig-may-den-ba-nyi-ma/'Jig-med-bstan-ba'i-nyi-ma, 1865–1926). *Rig 'dzin yum ka bde chen rgyal mo'i sgrub gzhung gi zin bris bde chen lam gzang gsal ba'i gron me* (Notes on the basic text for emulating the Mother Knowledge Bearer, the Great Bliss Queen: A lamp clarifying the Good Path of Great Bliss). In *The Collected Works of Do-drup-chen*, vol. 5. Gantok, 1975.

————*rDzogs chen thor bu* (Various topics on the Great Completeness). In *The Collected Works of Do-drup-chen*, vol. 5, pp. 179–200. Gantok, 1975.

Dolkar, Tseten. *Girl from Tibet*. Chicago: Loyola University Press, 1971.

Dowman, Keith, trans. *Sky Dancer: The Secret Life and Songs of the Lady Yeshey Tsogyel*. London: Routledge and Kegan Paul, 1984.

Du Bois, W. E. B. *The Souls of Black Folks*. Millwood, N.Y.: Kraus-Thomson, 1973.

Edgerton, Franklin. *Buddhist Hybrid Sanskrit Grammar and Dictionary*. New Haven: Yale University Press, 1973. Reprint, Delhi: Motilal Banarsidass, 1972.

Ekvall, Robert B. *Cultural Relations on the Kansu-Tibetan Border*. University of Chicago Publications in Anthropology, Occasional Papers, no. 1. Chicago: University of Chicago Press, 1939.

Engler, Jack. "Therapeutic Aims in Psychotherapy and Meditation: Developmental Stages in the Representation of Self." *Journal of Transpersonal Psychology* 16, no. 1 (1984): 25.

Felstiner, Mary Lowenthal. "Taking Her Life/History." In *Life/Lines: Theorizing Women's Autobiography*, ed. Bella Brodzki and Celeste Schenck. Ithaca: Cornell University Press, 1988.

Fifth Dalai Lama (Ngag-dbang-blo-bzang-rgya-mtsho, 1617–82). "Practice of Emptiness." From *The Sacred Word of Mañjuśrī: Instructions on the Stages of the Path to Enlightenment*, trans. Jeffrey Hopkins. Dharamsala: Library of Tibetan Works and Archives, 1974.

Fischer, Michael J., and Mehdi Abedi. *Debating Muslims*. Madison: University of Wisconsin Press, 1992.

Fisher, James F. *Trans-Himalayan Traders: Economy, Society, and Culture in Northwest Nepal*. Berkeley: University of California Press, 1980.

Flax, Jane. *Thinking Fragments: Psychoanalysis, Feminism, and Postmodernism in the Contemporary West*. University of California Press, 1990.

————"Postmodernism and Gender Relations in Feminist Theory." *Signs* 12, no. 4 (Summer 1987): 621–43.

————"Remembering the Selves: Is the Repressed Gendered?" *Michigan Quarterly Review* 26, no. 1 (1986): 92–110.

————"Reply to Tress." *Signs* 14, no. 1 (Autumn 1988): 201–3.

Forman, Robert K. C., ed. *The Problem of Pure Consciousness*. New York: Oxford University Press, 1990.

Fox-Genovese, Elizabeth. *Feminism without Illusions*. Chapel Hill: University of North Carolina Press, 1991.

Freud, Sigmund. *The Standard Edition of the Complete Psychological Works of Sigmund Freud*. Translated and edited by James Strachey. London: Hogarth Press, 1953.

————*Civilization and its Discontents*. London: Hogarth Press, 1953. Reprint, W. W. Norton, 1961.

Friedman, Lenore. *Meetings with Remarkable Women*. Boulder: Shambhala Press, 1987.

Fuss, Diana. *Essentially Speaking*. New York and London: Routledge, 1989.

Galland, China. *Longing for Darkness: Tara and the Black Madonna.* New York: Viking Press, 1990.

Gallop, Jane. *Reading Lacan.* Ithaca: Cornell University Press, 1985.

————*The Daughter's Seduction: Feminism and Psychoanalysis.* Ithaca: Cornell University Press, 1982.

Garner, Shirley Nelson, Claire Kahane, and Madelon Sprengnether, eds. *The (M)other Tongue.* Ithaca: Cornell University Press, 1985.

Gedun Lodrö, Geshe. *Walking through Walls: A Tibetan Presentation of Calming Meditation.* Translated by Jeffrey Hopkins, edited by Anne C. Klein and Leah J. Zahler. Ithaca: Snow Lion, 1992.

Gilligan, Carol. "Joining the Resistance: Psychology, Politics, Girls, and Women." In *The Female Body: Figures, Styles, Speculations.* Edited by Laurence Goldstein. Ann Arbor: University of Michigan Press, 1991.

————*In a Different Voice: Psychological Theory and Women's Development.* Cambridge: Harvard University Press, 1982.

Gilligan, Carol, Annie G. Rogers, and Lyn Mikel Brown. "Epilogue: Soundings into Development." In *Making Connections*, ed. Carol Gilligan, Nona Plessner Lyons, and Trudy J. Hanmer. Cambridge: Harvard University Press, 1990.

Gilligan, Carol, Nona Plessner Lyons, and Trudy J. Hanmer, eds. *Making Connections: The Relational Worlds of Adolescent Girls at Emma Willard School.* Cambridge: Harvard University Press, 1990.

Gilligan, Carol, Janie Victoria Ward, and Jill McLean with Betty Bardige, eds. *Mapping the Moral Domain.* Cambridge: Harvard University Press, 1988.

Gön-chok-drön-may (dKon-mchog-sgrong-me). *rJe bla mas gsungs pa'i yum ka'i zin bris kyi kha skong rig 'dzin shal lung* (Sacred word of the Well-Spoken Knowledge Bearer: A commentary on the Mother stated by the Venerable Lama). Reproduced from a collection of manuscripts from the library of Do-drup-chen. Gangtok, 1977.

Goodman, Steven D. "Rig'dzin 'Jigs-med gling-pa and the kLong-Chen sNying-Thig." In *Tibetan Buddhism: Reason and Revelation*, ed. Steven D. Goodman and Ronald M. Davidson. Albany: SUNY Press, 1992.

————"Ocean Woman Who Already Knows," by Khams-snyon Dharma-Senge. *Alcheringa: Ethnopoetics* 3, no. 2 (1977): 42–54.

Goody, J. R., ed. *Literacy in Traditional Societies*. London: Cambridge University Press, 1968.

Govinda, Angargika. *The Psychological Attitude of Early Buddhist Philosophy*. London: Rider, 1969.

Graham, William A. *Beyond the Written Word: Oral Aspects of Scripture in the History of Religion*. Cambridge: Cambridge University Press, 1987.

Griffiths, Paul J. *On Being Mindless: Buddhist Meditation and the Mind-Body Problem*. La Salle, Illinois: Open Court, 1988.

Gross, Rita M. *Buddhism after Patriarchy*. Albany: SUNY Press, 1993.

————"Yeshe Tsogyel: Enlightened Consort, Great Teacher, Female Role Model." In *Feminine Ground: Essays on Women in Tibet*, ed. Janice Willis. Ithaca: Snow Lion, 1989.

Grosz, Elizabeth. *Sexual Subversions: Three French Feminists*. Boston: Allen and Unwin, 1989.

Guenther, Herbert, trans. *Jewel Ornament of Liberation*, by sGam-po-pa. Boulder: Prajñā Press, 1981.

Gyatso, Geshey Kelsang. *Meaningful to Behold*. London: Wisdom Publications, 1980.

Gyatso, Janet. "The Development of the *Gcod* Tradition." In *Soundings in Tibetan Civilization*, ed. M. Kapstein and B. Aziz. Delhi: Manohar, 1985.

————, ed. *In the Mirror of Memory: Reflections on Mindfulness and Remembrance in Indian and Tibetan Buddhism*. SUNY Series in Buddhist Studies, M. Kapstein, ed. Albany: SUNY Press, 1992.

Gyatso, Tenzin, His Holiness the Dalai Lama. *Kindness, Clarity, and Insight*. Translated and edited by Jeffrey Hopkins, with Elizabeth Napper. Ithaca: Snow Lion, 1984.

————, with D. Goleman et al. *Worlds in Harmony: Dialogues on Compassionate Action*. Berkeley: Parallax Press, 1992.

Gyel-tsap (rGyal-tshab, 1364–1432). *sPyod 'jug rnam bshad rgyal sras 'jug ngogs* (Port of entry to the Bodhisattvas: An explanation of [Shantideva's] "Entering [the Bodhisattva] Deeds." Sarnath, India: Pleasure of Elegant Sayings Press, 1973.

Haarh, Erik. *The Yarluṅ Dynasty*. Copenhagen: G. E. D. Gad's Forlag, 1969.

Hanh, Thich Nhat. *Being Peace*. Berkeley: Parallax Press, 1987.

————*The Practice of Mindfulness in Psychotherapy*. Audiocassette A103. Sounds True, 1825 Pear Street, Dept. Fc3, Boulder, Colo. 80302.

Harvey, Irene E. *Derrida and the Economy of Différance*. Bloomington: Indiana University Press, 1986.

Heller, Thomas C., Morton Sosna, and David E. Welberry, eds. *Reconstructing Individualism*. Stanford: Stanford University Press, 1986.

Herrmann-Pfandt, Adelheid. *Ḍākiṇīs: Die Stellung und Symboli des Weiblichen im Tantrischen Buddhismus*. Bonn: Indica et Tibetica Verlag, 1992.

Hillesum, Etty. *An Interrupted Life: The Diaries of Etty Hillesum, 1941–1943*. New York: Washington Square Press, 1982.

Hirsch, Maryanne, and Evelyn Fox Keller, eds. *Conflicts in Feminism*. New York: Routledge, 1990.

Hopkins, Jeffrey. *Meditation on Emptiness*. London: Wisdom Publications, 1983.

Hopkinson, Deborah, Michele Hill, and Eileen Kiera, eds. *Not Mixing Up Buddhism*. New York: White Pine Press, 1986.

Horner, I. B. *Women under Primitive Buddhism*. New York: E. P. Dutton, 1930.

Huntington, C. W., and Geshé Namgyal Wangchen. *The Emptiness of Emptiness*. Honolulu: University of Hawaii Press, 1989.

Ihde, Don. *Listening and Voice: A Phenomenology of Sound*. Athens: Ohio University Press, 1976.

Irigaray, Luce. *Speculum of the Other Woman*. Translated by Gillian C. Gill. Ithaca: Cornell University Press, 1985.

————*This Sex Which Is Not One*. Translated by Catherine Porter with Carolyn Burke. Ithaca: Cornell University Press, 1985.

————"Luce Irigaray." In *New French Feminisms*, ed. Elaine Marks and Isabelle de Courtivron. New York: Schocken Books, 1980.

Jagger, Alison, and Susan R. Bordo. *Gender/Body/Knowledge: Feminist Reconstructions of Being and Knowing*. New Brunswick: Rutgers University Press, 1989.

Jardine, Alice. "The Demise of Experience: Fiction as Stranger than Truth?" In *Postmodernism: A Reader*, ed. Thomas Docherty. New York: Columbia University Press, 1993.

Jig-may-den-bay-nyi-ma. See Do-drup-chen III.

Jigmay Lingpa ('Jigs-med-gling-pa, 1729–98). *kLong chen sNying thig rza pod* (The very essence of the Great Expanse). *Om, Ah, Hum*. 3 vols. Block prints reprinted under the auspices of Dingo Khentse Rinboche. Bhutan(?), n.d.

Johnson, Barbara. *A World of Difference*. Baltimore: Johns Hopkins University Press, 1987.

————*The Critical Difference: Essays in the Contemporary Rhetoric of Reading*. Baltimore: Johns Hopkins University Press, 1980.

Jordan, Judith V. "Empathy and Self Boundaries." In *Women's Growth in Connection: Writings from the Stone Center*, ed. Judith Jordan et al. Guilford Press, 1991.

Jordan, Judith V., et al., eds. *Women's Growth in Connection: Writings from the Stone Center*. New York: Guilford Press, 1991.

Karmay, Samten. *The Great Perfection: A Philosophical and Meditative Teaching of Tibetan Buddhism*. Leiden: Brill, 1988.

Keller, Catherine. *From a Broken Web: Separation, Sexism, and Self.* Boston: Beacon Press, 1986.

Klein, Anne C. *Path to the Middle, Oral Mādhyamika Philosophy in Tibet: The Spoken Scholarship of Kensur Yeshey Tupden.* SUNY Series in Buddhist Studies, M. Kapstein, ed. Albany: SUNY Press, 1994.

————"Mental Concentration and the Unconditioned: A Buddhist Case for Unmediated Experience." In *The Buddhist Path,* ed. Robert Buswell and Robert Gimello. Honolulu: University of Hawaii Press, 1991.

————*Knowing, Naming, and Negation: A Sourcebook on Tibetan Sautrāntika.* Ithaca: Snow Lion, 1990.

————*Knowledge and Liberation: Buddhist Epistemology in Support of Transformative Religious Experience.* Ithaca: Snow Lion, 1986.

————"Primordial Purity and Everyday Life: Exalted Female Symbols and the Women of Tibet." In *Immaculate and Powerful: The Female in Sacred Image and Social Reality,* ed. Clarissa Atkinson, Constance Buchanan, and Margaret Miles. Boston: Beacon Press, 1985.

Kun byed rygal po (Superb maker of everything). Reprinted from sDesge edition in *gSung Thor-bu,* vol. 2. Paro, Bhutan: Dilgo Khyantsey Rinboche, 1982. [Attributed to Samantabhadra.]

Lessing, Doris. *The Four-Gated City.* New York: Bantam Books, 1969.

Levine, Nancy. "The Theory of *Rü:* Kinship, Descent, and Status in a Tibetan Society." In *Asian Highland Societies in Anthropological Perspective,* ed. Christopher von Fürer Haimendorf. New Delhi: Sterling Publishers, 1981.

Ling, Amy. "I'm Here." In *Feminisms,* ed. Robyn R. Warhol and Diane Price Herndl. New Brunswick: Rutgers University Press, 1992.

Lipman, Kennard, and Merrill Peterson, trans., under inspiration of Namkhai Norbu. *You Are the Eyes of the World.* Novato, Calif.: Lotsawa Press, 1987.

Li-shu-stag-ring. *gTan tshigs gal mdo rig pa'i tshad ma* (Authenticity of innate awareness: A collection of essential reasonings). Delhi: Tenzin Namdak, Tibetan Bön Monastic Centre, 1972. No. 73, 7.5, p. 54.1.

Longchen Rabjam (kLong-chen-rab-'byams/kLong-chen-pa Dri-med-'od-zer, 1308–63). *Byang chub kyi sems kun byed rgyal po'i don khrid rin chen sgru bo.*

————*Tshig don mdzod* (Treasury of meaning)/*bSang ba bla na med pa 'od gsal rdo rje snying po'i gnas gsum gsal bar byed pa'i tshig don rin po che'i mdzod* (Meaning of the words, a clear explanation of the three essential areas of the Vajra essence, the Clear Light of the Unexcelled Secret: A precious treasure). Reproduced from prints from the Sde-dge blocks belonging to Lopon Sonam Sangpo. Gantok: Sherab Gyaltsen and Khentse Labrang Palace Monastery, 1983.

Lovibond, Savina. "Feminism and Postmodernism." In *Postmodernism: A Reader*, ed. Thomas Docherty. New York: Columbia University Press, 1993.

Loy, David. *Nonduality: A Study in Comparative Philosophy*. New Haven: Yale University Press, 1988.

Lumpp, Randolph Franklin. "Culture, Religion, and the Presence of the Word: A Study of the Thought of Walter Jackson Ong." Ph.D. dissertation, University of Ottawa, 1976.

Lurie, Susan. "The 'Woman' (in) Question: Feminist Theory and Cultural Studies." *Discourse* 14, no. 3 (Summer 1992).

Lutz, Catherine A. *Unnatural Emotions: Everyday Sentiments on a Micronesian Atoll and Their Challenge to Western Theory*. Chicago: University of Chicago Press, 1988.

Macdonell, Arthur Anthony. *A Practical Sanskrit Dictionary*. 1954. Reprint, London: Oxford University Press, 1965.

MacIntyre, Alasdair. *After Virtue*. Notre Dame, Ind.: University of Notre Dame Press, 1981.

Magliola, Robert. *Derrida on the Mend*. West Lafayette, Ind.: Purdue University Press, 1984.

Mahoney, Maureen A., and Barbara Yngvesson. "Subjectivity and Resistance." *Signs* 18, no. 1 (Autumn 1992).

Marks, Elaine, and Isabelle de Courtivron, eds. *New French Feminisms*. New York: Schocken Books, 1980.

Martin, Emily. *The Woman in the Body: A Cultural Analysis of Reproduction*. 1987. Reprint, Boston: Beacon Press, 1992.

Massey, Marilyn. *Feminine Soul: The Fate of an Ideal*. Boston: Beacon Press, 1986.

Maxwell, Natalie. "Compassion: The Chief Cause of Bodhisattvas." Ph.D. dissertation, University of Wisconsin, Madison, 1975.

Meyerson, Ignace, ed. *Problèmes de la personne*. Paris: Mouton, La Haye, 1973.

Miller, Alice. *The Drama of the Gifted Child*. New York: Basic Books, 1981.

Mipham (Mi-pham, 1846–1912). *bDe gshegs snying po'i stong thun chen mo seng ge'i nga ro* (The lion's roar of the Great Accordance between emptiness and the Tathagatha essence). Ngagyur Nyingma Sungrab, vol. 62. Delhi, 1976.

Mitchell, Juliet, and Jaqueline Rose, eds. *Feminine Sexuality: Jaques Lacan and the École Freudienne*. New York: Norton, 1985.

Modleski, Tania. "Feminism and the Power of Interpretation: Some Critical Readings." In *Feminist Studies/Critical Studies*, ed. Teresa de Lauretis. Bloomington, Ind.: Indiana University Press, 1986.

Moi, Toril. *Sexual/Textual Politics: Feminist Literary Theory*. New Accents Series, ed. Terence Hawkes. London: Routledge, 1985.

Mumford, Stan Royal. *Himalayan Dialogue: Tibetan Lamas and Gurung Shamans in Nepal*. Madison: University of Wisconsin Press, 1989.

Namdak, Lopon Tenzin. *The Condensed Meaning of an Explanation of the Teachings of Yungdrung Bon*. Kathmandu: Bonpo Foundation, P.O. Box 4640, n.d.

Napper, Elizabeth. *Dependent Arising and Emptiness*. London: Wisdom Publications, 1989.

————*Mind in Tibetan Buddhism*. London: Rider, 1980. Reprint, Ithaca: Snow Lion, 1986.

Nattier, Jan. "Eke Bolugsan: A Note on the Colophon to the Bolor Erike." *Acta Orientalia* (Budapest) 44, no. 3 (1990): 395–408.

Nayak, K. N. *Cultural Relativity: A Unified Theory of Knowledge*. New Haven: Saddharma Prakashana, 1982.

Ngawang Denzin Dorje (Ngag-dbang-bstan-'dzin-rdo-rje, 18th century). *Ra tig/kLong chen snying gi thig le'i mkha' 'gro bde chen rgyal mo'i grub gzhung gi 'grel pa rgyud don snang ba* (Commentary on the practice for emulating the Sky Woman, the Great Bliss Queen, from the "Very Essence of the Great Expanse" tradition of Long-chen-rab-jam). New Delhi: Sonam Topgay Kazi, 1972.

Nicholson, Linda, ed. *Feminism/Postmodernism*. New York: Routledge, 1990.

Norbu, Namkhai. *Dzogchen: The Self-Perfected State*. London: Arkana Books, 1989.

————*The Crystal and the Way of Light*. Edited and compiled by John Shane. New York: Routledge and Kegan Paul, 1986.

————*Byang 'brog gi lam yig* (A journey into the culture of Tibetan nomads). Arcidosso, Italy: Shang Shung Editions, 1983.

Norris, Christopher. *Deconstruction Theory and Practice*. 1982. Reprint, London: Routledge, 1992.

Ong, Walter. *Orality and Literacy: The Technologizing of the Word*. London: Methuen, 1982.

————*Rhetoric, Romance, and Technology*. Ithaca: Cornell University Press, 1971.

————*The Presence of the Word*. New Haven: Yale University Press, 1967.

Ortner, Sherry C. "Is Female to Nature as Male Is to Culture?" In *Woman, Culture, and Society*, ed. Michelle Rosaldo and Louise Lamphere. Stanford: Stanford University Press, 1983.

————*Sherpas through Their Rituals*. Cambridge: Cambridge University Press, 1978.

Papp, Peggy. *The Process of Change*. 1979. Reprint, New York: Guilford Press, 1983.

Plaskow, Judith. *Sex, Sin, and Grace: Women's Experience in the Theologies of Reinhold Niebuhr and Paul Tillich*. Washington, D.C.: University Press of America, 1989.

————, and Carol Christ, eds. *Womanspirit Rising*. San Francisco: Harper and Row, 1979.

Pur-bu-jok (Phur-bu-lcog Byams-pa-rgya-mtsho, 1825–1901). *bsDus grva'i/tshad ma'i gzhung don 'byed pa'i bsdus grva'i rnam bzhag rigs lam 'phrul gyi sde mig* (Collected topics). Buxa, 1965.

Rabten, Geshe. *Echoes of Voidness*. Translated and edited by Stephen Batchelor. London: Wisdom Publications, 1983.

————*The Life and Teaching of Geshe Rabten: A Tibetan Lama's Search for Truth*. Translated by Alan B. Wallace. London: Allen and Unwin, 1980.

Rockhill, William Woodville. *The Land of the Lamas*. 1891. Reprint, New Delhi: Asian Publication Services, 1975.

Rosaldo, Michelle Z. *Knowledge and Passion: Ilongot Notions of Self and Social Life*. Cambridge: Cambridge University Press, 1980.

Rowell, Galen, and His Holiness the Dalai Lama. *My Tibet*. Berkeley: University of California Press, 1990.

Ruegg, David. *La Theorie du Tathāgathagarbha et du Gôtra*. Paris: École Française d'extrême Orient, 1969.

Saiving, Valerie. "The Human Situation: A Feminine View." In *Womanspirit Rising*, ed. Judith Plaskow and Carol Christ. San Francisco: Harper and Row, 1979.

Sangpo, Khetsun. *Tantric Practice in Nyingma*. 1982. Reprint, Ithaca: Snow Lion, 1986.

Sayadaw, Ven. Ledi. *The Requisites of Enlightenment*. Translation of

Bodhipakkhiya-Dipani by Sein Nyo Tun. Kandy, Ceylon [Sri Lanka]: Buddhist Publication Society, 1971.

Scholem, Gershom. *The Messianic Idea in Judaism.* New York: Schocken, 1971.

Schor, Naomi. "This Essentialism Which Is Not One: Coming to Grips with Irigaray." *Differences* 1, no. 2 (1989): 41.

Sherring, Charles A. *Western Tibet and the Indian Borderland.* 1916. Reprint, Delhi: Cosmo Publications, 1974.

Smart, Ninian. *Religion and the Western Mind.* Albany: SUNY Press, 1987.

Smith, Jonathan Z. *Imagining Religion: From Babylon to Jonestown.* Chicago: University of Chicago Press, 1982.

Smith, Paul. *Discerning the Subject.* Minneapolis: University of Minnesota Press, 1988.

Smith, Sidonie. "Who's Talking/Who's Talking Back? The Subject of Personal Narrative." *Signs* (Winter 1993).

Snitow, Ann. "A Gender Diary." In *Conflicts in Feminism*, ed. Maryanne Hirsch and Evelyn Fox Keller. New York: Routledge, 1990.

Solomon, Robert C. *The Passions: The Myth and Nature of Human Emotion.* New York: Doubleday, 1977.

Spivak, Gayatri Chakravorty. "Can the Subaltern Speak?" In *Marxism and the Interpretation of Culture*, ed. Cary Nelson and Lawrence Grossberg. Urbana: University of Illinois Press, 1988.

Sponberg, Alan. "Attitudes toward Women and the Feminine in Early Buddhism." In *Buddhism, Sexuality, and Gender*, ed. José Cabezón. Albany: SUNY Press, 1992.

Stanton, Domna C. "Autogynography: Is the Subject Different?" In *The Female Autograph*, ed. Domna C. Stanton. New York: New York Literary Forum, 1984.

———"Language and Revolution: The Franco-American Dis-connection." In *The Future of Difference*, ed. Hester Eisenstein and Alice Jardine. Boston, Mass.: G. K. Hall, 1980.

Stein, R. A. *Tibetan Civilization*. Stanford: Stanford University Press, 1972. Originally published as *La civilisation tibetaine* (Paris: Dunod Editeur, 1962).

Stern, Daniel N. *The Interpersonal World of the Infant*. New York: Basic Books, 1985.

Stimpson, Catharine R. "The New Scholarship about Women: The State of the Art." *Annals of Scholarship* 1, no. 2 (1980): 2–14.

Suleiman, Susan Rubin. "Writing and Motherhood." In *The (M)other Tongue*, ed. Shirley Nelson Garner, Claire Kahane, and Madelon Sprengnether. Ithaca: Cornell University Press, 1985.

Tarthang, Tulku, trans. *Mother of Knowledge: The Enlightenment of Ye shes tsho rygal*, by Nam-mkhai'i snying po (*Bod kyi jo-mo ye-shes mtsho-rgyal-gyi mdzad tshul rnam-par thar-pa gab-pa mngon byung rgyud-mangs dri-za'i glu phreng ba*). Edited by Jane Wilhelms, Deborah Black, and Leslie Bradburn. Berkeley: Dharma Publishing, 1983.

Taylor, Charles. *Sources of the Self: The Making of the Modern Identity*. Cambridge: Harvard University Press, 1989.

Taylor, Mark C. *Nots*. Chicago: University of Chicago Press, 1993.

Thera, Nyanaponika. *The Heart of Buddhist Meditation*. York Beach, Maine: Samuel Weiser, 1984.

Thera, Piyadassa. *The Buddha's Ancient Path*. Kandy, Ceylon [Sri Lanka]: Buddhist Publication Society, 1974.

Thera, Soma, trans. *The Way of Mindfulness: The Satipaṭṭhāna Sutta and Commentary*. Kandy, Ceylon [Sri Lanka]: Buddhist Publication Society, 1967.

Thondup, Tulku. *Buddha Mind: An Anthology of Longchen Rabjam's Writings on Dzogpa Chenpo*. Edited by Harold Talbott. Ithaca: Snow Lion, 1989.

————*The Origin of Buddhism in Tibet: The Tantric Tradition of the Nyingmapa.* Marian, Mass.: Buddhayana Foundation, 1984.

————, trans. *The Queen of Great Bliss in the Long-chen-Nying-thig by Kun-khyen* [the omniscient] *Jigme Ling-pa.* Gantok: Do-drup-chen Rinboche, Sikkhim National Press, 1982.

Thoreau, Henry David. *Walden.* New York: Signet, 1960.

Tong, Rosemarie. *Feminist Thought.* Boulder: Westview Press, 1989.

Tress, Daryl McGowan. "Comment on Jane Flax's 'Postmodernism and Gender Relations in Feminist Theory.'" *Signs* 14 (Autumn 1988).

Trible, Phyllis. *God and the Rhetoric of Sexuality.* Philadelphia: Fortress Press, 1978.

Tronto, Joan. "Women and Caring." In *Gender/Body/Knowledge: Feminist Reconstructions of Being and Knowing,* ed. Alison Jagger and Susan Bordo. New Brunswick: Rutgers University Press, 1989.

Tsayden, Lama Gompo (d. 1900). *Yum ka mtsho rgyal bde chen rgyal mo'i rdza ba'i sgrub pa bde chen dpal phreng gi tshig 'grel pad dgar phreng mdzes* (Emulating the quintessence of the Mother Yeshe Tsogyel, the Great Bliss Queen: A beautiful white lotus garland, commenting on the words of the Garland of the Splendid Great Bliss Queen). Privately printed.

Tsomo, Karma Lekshe. "Tibetan Nuns and Nunneries." In *Feminine Ground: Essays on Women in Tibet,* ed. Janice D. Willis. Ithaca: Snow Lion, 1989.

Tsong-kha-pa, *dbU ma la 'jug pa'i rgya cher bshad pa dgongs pa rab gsal* (Illumination of the Middle Way). P6143, vol. 154.

————*Lam rim chen mo/skyes bu gsum gyi rnyams su blang ba'i rim pa thams cad tshang bar ston pa'i byang chub lam gyi rim pa* (Great exposition of the stages of the Path). P6001, vol. 152.

————*The Collected Works of Rje Tson-kha-pa Blo-bzan-grags-pa.* New Delhi: Ngawang Gelek Demo, 1975–.

Tweed, Thomas Anthony. "The American Encounter with Buddhism, 1844–1912: Responses to Buddhism, Dissent and Consent, and Victorian Religious Culture." Ph.D. dissertation, University of Michigan, 1989.

Vasubandhu. *Abhidharmakośabhāṣya/Chos mngon pa'i mdzod kyi bshad pa*. P5591. Translated by Louis de la Vallée Poussin as *L'Abhidharmakośa de Vasubandhu* (Paris: Geuthner, 1923–31).

Wallace, Kathleen. "Reconstructing Judgment: Emotional and Moral Judgment." *Hypatia* 8, no. 3 (Summer 1993).

Wangyal, Tenzin. *The Wonders of the Natural Mind*. Barrytown, N.Y.: Station Hill Press, 1993.

Warhol, Robyn R., and Diane Price Herndl, eds. *Feminisms: An Anthology of Literary Theory and Criticism*. New Jersey: Rutgers University Press, 1991.

Weedon, Chris. *Feminist Practice and Poststructuralist Theory*. Oxford: Basil Blackwell, 1987.

Whitford, Margaret. *Luce Irigaray: Philosophy in the Feminine*. London: Routledge, 1991.

Whitney, William Dwight. *Sanskrit Grammar*. Cambridge: Harvard University Press; London: Oxford University Press, 1967.

Williams, Raymond. *Keywords: A Vocabulary of Culture and Society*. 1976. London: Fontana, Flamingo Edition, 1983.

Willis, Janice D., ed. *Feminine Ground: Essays on Women in Tibet*. Ithaca: Snow Lion, 1989.

Winnington, Alan. *Tibet: Record of a Journey*. London: Lawrence and Wishart, 1957.

Yalom, Irvin D. *Existential Psychotherapy*. New York: Basic Books, 1980.

Young, Robert. *White Mythologies: Writing History and the West*. London: Routledge, 1990.

Zerilli, Linda M. G. "A Process without a Subject: Simone de Beauvoir and Julia Kristeva on Maternity." *Signs* 18, no. 1 (Autumn 1992): 111–35.

INDEX